STUDENT WORKBOOK AND STUDY GUIDE

TO ACCOMPANY

INTRODUCTION TO COMPUTERS AND DATA PROCESSING

Gary B. Shelly
Educational Consultant
Fullerton, California

&

Thomas J. Cashman, CDP, B.A., M.A.
Long Beach City College
Long Beach, California

ANAHEIM PUBLISHING COMPANY
1120 E. Ash, Fullerton, CA 92631
(714) 879-7922

ISBN 0-88236-116-3

Printed in the United States of America

© Copyright 1980 Anaheim Publishing Company

All Rights Reserved. No part of this publication may be reproduced, stored in a retrieval system, or transmitted, in any form or by any means, electronic, mechanical, photocopying, recording, or otherwise, without prior written permission of the publisher.

PREFACE
to the
INSTRUCTOR

This Student Workbook and Study Guide is designed to be used in conjunction with the textbook, Introduction to Computers and Data Processing, by Gary B. Shelly and Thomas J. Cashman. The purpose is to provide a series of learning activities that will be of value to the student in mastering the material contained within the text and also encourage the student to develop a spirit of inquiry through the use of research in the field of computers and data processing. In addition, a series of laboratory projects is included in the first eight chapters which are designed to acquaint the introductory student of data processing with some of the uses of computers and computer terminals that they are likely to encounter in their daily lives.

Organization of the Workbook and Study Guide

The projects contained in this Student Workbook and Study Guide correspond, on a chapter by chapter basis, to the material contained within the textbook. Although some chapters may vary slightly in content, most chapters include the following:

- **Chapter Objectives** — The chapter objectives state the major concepts which the student should understand upon completion of the study of the material contained within the textbook and workbook.

- **Chapter Overview** — The chapter overview provides a summary of the important concepts contained within each chapter and provides a convenient and rapid review of important subject matter.

- **Key Terms** — The key terms are taken from the glossary and represent terms which were introduced or explained in the chapter. These key terms are presented in each chapter where a reference is made to them. The student should study and understand each of the terms in this section.

- **Chapter Projects** — The several projects in each chapter consist of a series of interesting activities which are designed to improve the student's understanding of many of the illustrations and diagrams within the textbook. These projects also enhance the student's understanding of the concepts expressed by the written text material.

- **Testing Your Knowledge - Key Terms** — These projects are designed to assist the student in mastering the vocabulary of computers and data processing through the use of a matching type of quiz.

- **Testing Your Knowledge - Definitions** — These activities require students to define selected terms used within the chapter and serve as a self-test of the terminology contained within the chapter.

- **Testing Your Knowledge - True/False Questions** — A self-study test consisting of 35 true/false questions is contained in this project. After completing these questions, the answers should be checked. The answers are presented at the end of the chapter in the workbook.

- **Testing Your Knowledge - Multiple-Choice Questions** — A self-study test of 15 multiple-choice questions is contained in this project. After completing the questions, the answers should be checked. The answers are presented at the end of the chapter.

- **Computer Laboratory Project** — These computer laboratory projects consist of a series of activities designed to illustrate common applications of computers and computer terminals and acquaint the student with the use of the computer terminal as it is used in many businesses today. The use of this project is dependent upon the availability of computing power at the school.

- **Developing Communications Skills** — These projects contain a series of suggested activities designed to encourage the development of oral and written communications skills and to encourage original research in the field of computers and data processing.

- **Answers to Selected Projects** — This section contains the answers to the self-study projects for key terms, true/false questions, and multiple-choice questions.

In addition to these activities, Chapter 10 contains a project designed to acquaint the student with the process of designing a computerized system; Chapter 11 contains a number of projects which provide the opportunity to develop the logic used in solving common types of programming problems; and Appendix A contains a number of programming assignments which are to be written using the BASIC language.

Use of the Student Workbook and Study Guide

There are several approaches when using this Workbook and Study Guide in the classroom. With the first approach, the workbook is used on an individual study basis; that is, the teacher merely suggests to the student that all key terms be studied and all projects, true/false questions, and multiple-choice questions be completed by a given time — normally prior to testing. As the answers to many of the activities are contained in the Student Workbook and Study Guide, this approach provides a formalized method of review for interested students.

The second approach uses the Study Guide and Workbook as an integral part of class activity; that is, during a lecture, one of the activity projects illustrating a particular concept could be assigned, completed, and discussed to assure student understanding of the concepts presented. After the chapter is completed, activities involving the key terms, true/false questions, and multiple-choice questions could be assigned as homework and then reviewed the next meeting as a part of the class activity.

The approach taken by the teacher will usually be dependent upon the number of hours the class meets, the capabilities of the class, and the teaching philosophy of the instructor.

Computer Laboratory Projects

Often in the introduction to data processing classes, the only contact a student has with the computer comes after many weeks of instruction, and then in the form of programming using one of the programming languages.

It became evident in developing the instructional materials for the beginning student of data processing and in analyzing the use of computers in our society that the computer and computer terminals are an important part of daily human activity. Students, therefore, should be acquainted with some of the uses of computers and computer terminals in a variety of application areas. To accomplish this objective, a series of computer laboratory projects is included for each of the first eight chapters. Projects include such activities as computer assisted instruction, word processing, data entry, inquiry, and airline reservations. Detailed instructions for the use of each of these projects are contained in this Workbook and Study Guide. The computer programs to implement these projects are contained in the Instructor's Guide for the Workbook and Study Guide (which is available through the Marketing Department of Anaheim Publishing Company). It is strongly suggested that these projects be assigned to all students, as the interaction for the student with the computer after completing the very first chapter in the textbook is certain to be an interesting and exciting educational experience for the beginning student. Similarly, the remaining projects which are to be completed after each of the first eight chapters are designed to directly involve the student with the use of the computer throughout the entire school term.

Developing Oral and Written Communication Skills

    Another unique feature of this Workbook and Study Guide is the inclusion, at the end of each chapter, of a series of oral and/or written projects which are designed to provide the opportunity for the student to do original research in data processing; and to also develop the student's ability to communicate the results of this research to the class or to the teacher. Most studies indicate that the leaders in our society have strong oral and written communication skills, and most educators agree that the development of these skills is an important function of education. It is, therefore, strongly recommended that the instructor assign one or more of these projects to students throughout the school term.

    The computer industry is the most exciting and dynamic industry in the world. Through the extensive use of color photographs in the textbook and the supplementary material contained in the Workbook and Study Guide, the authors have hopefully provided an exciting educational experience for the student.

Gary B. Shelly

Thomas J. Cashman

TO THE STUDENT

One of the important purposes of the study of any subject area is the mastery of the content of the course so that one may better understand and appreciate the world in which we live. To assist you in understanding the world of computers and data processing, the textbook, Introduction to Computers and Data Processing and the Student Workbook and Study Guide which accompanies the textbook are provided as source material.

The textbook has been profusely illustrated with diagrams and photographs of the latest computer technology. It is important to read the material in the textbook very carefully, including the "Picture Stories" at the end of each chapter. These "Picture Stories" illustrate the use of computers in a variety of application areas and contain a great deal of significant instructional material. A unique feature of the textbook is that the illustrations used throughout the textbook are not merely designed to supplement the text material but are designed to teach important concepts. It should be noted that each of the illustrations is annotated with a caption explaining the photograph or diagram. These captions provide an important part of the text material.

After reading the assigned chapter within the textbook, the Workbook and Study Guide can be used as a study aid. The first portion of the study guide provides a statement of the objectives for each chapter and gives a brief chapter overview. The chapter overview highlights significant concepts presented in the chapters, but must not be used in place of reading the assigned chapter in the textbook if a full understanding of all material is desired. The overview is designed merely to refresh one's memory as to the overall structure of the chapter being studied.

The key terms represent terms introduced or reviewed within each chapter. These terms should be carefully studied as they provide the basis for understanding many of the concepts presented. The next several projects are designed to test your understanding of many of the diagrams contained within the textbook. If any of the diagrams is not fully understood, the text material relating to these diagrams should be reviewed.

A variety of self-testing projects are also included in the workbook to assist in testing your mastery of the subject matter prior to formal testing in the classroom. These self-test projects include key terms, true/false questions, and multiple-choice questions. The answers to each of the questions in these sections are included at the end of each chapter in the workbook. Any questions missed upon completing these projects should be reviewed and the appropriate area of the textbook examined to clarify the concepts presented.

Depending upon the availability of computer terminals at your school, laboratory projects may be assigned by the instructor. These projects are designed to introduce you to the power of the computer, clarify some of the material presented in each chapter, and introduce you to some realistic uses of the computer in industry today.

The final segment of the workbook contains a series of projects to improve oral and written communications skills. These projects may be assigned at the option of the instructor and may involve original research to further acquaint you with the world of data processing.

It is the hope of the authors that the textbook and accompanying workbook and study guide will provide the basis for an interesting and exciting introduction to computers and data processing.

Gary B. Shelly

Thomas J. Cashman

Chapter 1
Introduction to the Computer

Chapter Objectives

- Familiarization with the basic data processing cycle — input, process, and output
- Familiarization with the function of a computer
- Familiarization with the types of equipment found in typical computer centers
- Familiarization with the roles played by computer operators, data entry operators, tape librarians, programmers, and systems analysts in typical computer centers
- Familiarization with different sizes and types of computers

Chapter Overview

The purpose of this chapter is to provide an introduction to the structure, purpose, and basic operational characteristics of a computer. In addition, it is intended to provide an insight into the environment of a computer center and related job duties of individuals working within the computer center. The chapter concludes with a number of illustrations of various computer systems to develop an awareness of the size and cost of modern computer systems.

The chapter begins with a definition and illustration of a computer. Figure 1-1 illustrates a computer on a chip; that is, the electronic circuitry that forms the basis of modern computer systems. Figure 1-2 contains a picture of the world's most powerful computer system. It is important to understand that all computers, regardless of size, perform three basic operations: 1) Input/output operations; 2) Arithmetic operations; 3) Logical operations. These basic operations are carried out by the electronic circuitry found on the small chip.

The purpose of a computer is to process data. This processing of data is accomplished by a computer system of some type, all of which contain: 1) Input units which can read or accept the data and transfer the data to a processor unit for processing; 2) A processor unit which contains the central processing unit (CPU) and main computer storage; 3) Output units which display or otherwise make available to people the results of the processing of the data.

It is important to understand that with a computer system, processing is controlled by a set of instructions called a program, which is placed in main computer storage. These instructions are written by an individual called a computer programmer.

Figure 1-5 illustrates the basic data processing cycle of input/process/output. It is important to carefully review the diagram to understand this cycle of events.

Although there are many forms of input to a computer system, punched cards and floppy disks are widely used. Data to be processed is stored on these forms of input and transferred into main computer storage within the processor unit by card readers and floppy disk readers.

Although there are many forms of output, the printer is one of the most widely used forms. Data which has been processed is printed out for review by users of computer systems.

In many cases, data which has been processed must be stored for subsequent use. For example, in a computerized system, the balance due on customer charge accounts must be saved along with identifying information, for processing at a later date. To provide for storage of this type of data, auxiliary storage devices are used. Common forms of auxiliary storage include magnetic tape and magnetic disk.

Data stored on auxiliary storage can be read into the main storage of the processor unit for processing.

Within the computer center, there are a variety of job duties that must be performed. For the storing of magnetic disk and magnetic tape, tape and disk libraries exist. These libraries often contain many hundreds and even thousands of reels of tape and/or disks. To keep track of these forms of auxiliary storage, a tape librarian is employed.

To prepare data for processing, that is, to record data from original source documents to punched cards or floppy disks, data entry operators are required. These data entry operators commonly work in a data entry department within the computer center.

Computer operators are employed to operate the computer, feed cards or disks into readers for reading the data, monitoring the computer console, and mounting tape and disk units as required.

After the output has been generated, individuals must be utilized to operate bursting and decollating machines to separate and otherwise process and assemble the output.

Two of the most important and highly paid employees within a computer center are the systems analyst and the computer programmer. The systems analyst designs computerized systems, for example, to determine how to convert a manual payroll system to one that can process data and prepare the paychecks and related reports on a computer. The computer programmer takes the detailed specifications from the systems analyst and writes the instructions for the computer that will cause the actual processing to occur.

In most organizations, all of the employees in a computer center are under control of a data processing manager. This individual is responsible for the successful operation of the computer center and the information produced.

It is important to realize that computers only exist to provide information to users. Users of computer systems consist of many types of individuals including engineers, factory workers, office workers, and management personnel.

Computer systems are no longer tremendously expensive devices affordable by only a few giant corporations. Microcomputers are now available for less than $1,000.00 that can be useful in the home, in small businesses, in education, and in the laboratory. Small desk top computers now populate the office in many companies. There are many such systems available for $5,000.00 to $20,000.00.

Minicomputers introduced in the mid-1960's were initially placed in engineering and scientific installations because there was very little software; that is, programs written by the computer manufacturer to aid in programming the computer system. Today, however, minicomputers are used in many application areas and such systems have a wide range of sizes and costs.

Very large computer systems are called mainframes and are characterized by very rapid internal processing and large main storage. Such systems are supported by a variety of auxiliary storage devices and often have the capability of allowing other computers to communicate with them.

Chapter 1

Key Terms

Auxiliary Storage Devices Devices, generally magnetic tape and magnetic disk, on which data can be stored for use by computer programs; also known as secondary storage.

Bursting The process of separating each page of continuous forms.

Card Reader A device capable of reading the data stored in a punched card and transmitting it to main computer storage.

Central Processing Unit Electronic components which cause processing on a computer to occur by interpreting instructions, performing calculations, moving data in main computer storage, and controlling the input/output operations. It consists of the arithmetic/logic unit and the control unit.

Computer A device which can perform computations, including arithmetic and logic operations, without intervention by a human being.

Computer Center The area in a company that is used to house the computer system and the people who program and operate the computer system.

Computer Operator An individual who operates the computer system.

Computer Program A series of instructions which directs the computer to perform a sequence of tasks that produce a desired output.

Computer Programmers People who design, write, test, and implement the programs which process data on a computer system.

Computer System The actual computer hardware, which consists of the processor unit, operator console, input devices, output devices, and auxiliary storage devices.

Console Terminal A device through which the computer operator communicates with the processor unit.

Data A representation of facts, concepts, or instructions in a formalized manner suitable for communication, interpretation, and processing by humans or machines.

Data Entry The process of preparing data in some machine-processable form or entering data directly into a computer system.

Data Entry Department The department where data is prepared for processing on a computer system.

Data Processing Manager The individual who is in charge of and manages a data processing department.

Desk Top Computers Computer Systems which are small enough to be placed on the top of a desk for use.

Dinosaur A term given to large computer systems by minicomputer and microcomputer supporters.

Disk Drive A device consisting of a spindle on which a disk pack can be mounted for electronically storing data.

Disk Pack A unit which consists of multiple metal platters connected to a common hub. Each platter is coated with a metal oxide on which data can be electronically stored.

Floppy Disk An oxide-coated plastic disk about 8" in diameter enclosed in a protective covering that can be used for magnetically storing data.

Floppy Disk Reader A device which can read data stored on a floppy disk.

General Purpose Computers Computers which can perform any task by changing the application program in main computer storage.

Input/Processing/Output The sequence of events that occurs when data is processed on a computer system.

Input Units Units that are a part of a computer system which present data to the processor unit for processing.

Magnetic Disk A form of auxiliary storage in which data is stored on rotating disk.

Mainframes Large computers which are capable of processing large amounts of data at very fast speeds with access to billions of characters of data.

Key Terms

Microcomputer A computer system commonly consisting of a CRT, keyboard, and limited storage based upon a microprocessor and costing less than $10,000.00.

Minicomputers A computer system which has smaller computer storage, slower processing speeds, and lower cost than large computer systems.

Operations Department The department that is responsible for carrying out the day-to-day processing on a computer once a system is operational.

Output Information that is produced as a result of processing input data.

Output Units Units which are a part of a computer system that can display, print, or otherwise make available to people the results of processing data.

Printed Reports Reports which are printed by printers attached to the computer system.

Printers Devices which are connected to the computer system and which can prepare printed reports under the control of a computer program.

Processor Unit The unit which stores the data and contains the electronic circuitry necessary to carry out the processing of the stored data. It consists of the central processing unit and main computer storage.

Programming Manager The person in charge of the programming group in a data processing department.

Punched Cards A piece of lightweight cardboard capable of storing data in the form of punched holes recorded in predefined locations.

Software, Application Computer programs written for computer systems to solve a particular type of business or mathematical problem.

Special Purpose Computers Computers which are developed to perform specific tasks.

Storage, Main Computer Electronic components which can electronically store letters of the alphabet, numbers, and special characters.

Systems Analysts People who design and develop systems which will be implemented on a computer system.

Systems Manager The person who is in charge of the systems analysis and design group within a data processing department.

Tape, Magnetic A 1/2" wide piece of mylar on which data can be stored electronically. Typical lengths for tape are 600 feet, 1200 feet, and 2400 feet.

Tape Library An area in a data processing department where tape reels are stored when not being used on the computer system.

Tape Reels A plastic container on which magnetic tape is stored for processing on a computer system.

TRS-80 A microcomputer system made by Radio Shack.

NAME_____ DATE_____

Chapter 1

Project 1
Identifying the components of a computer system

Instructions: Analyze the diagram of the computer system illustrated below and label the numbered parts.

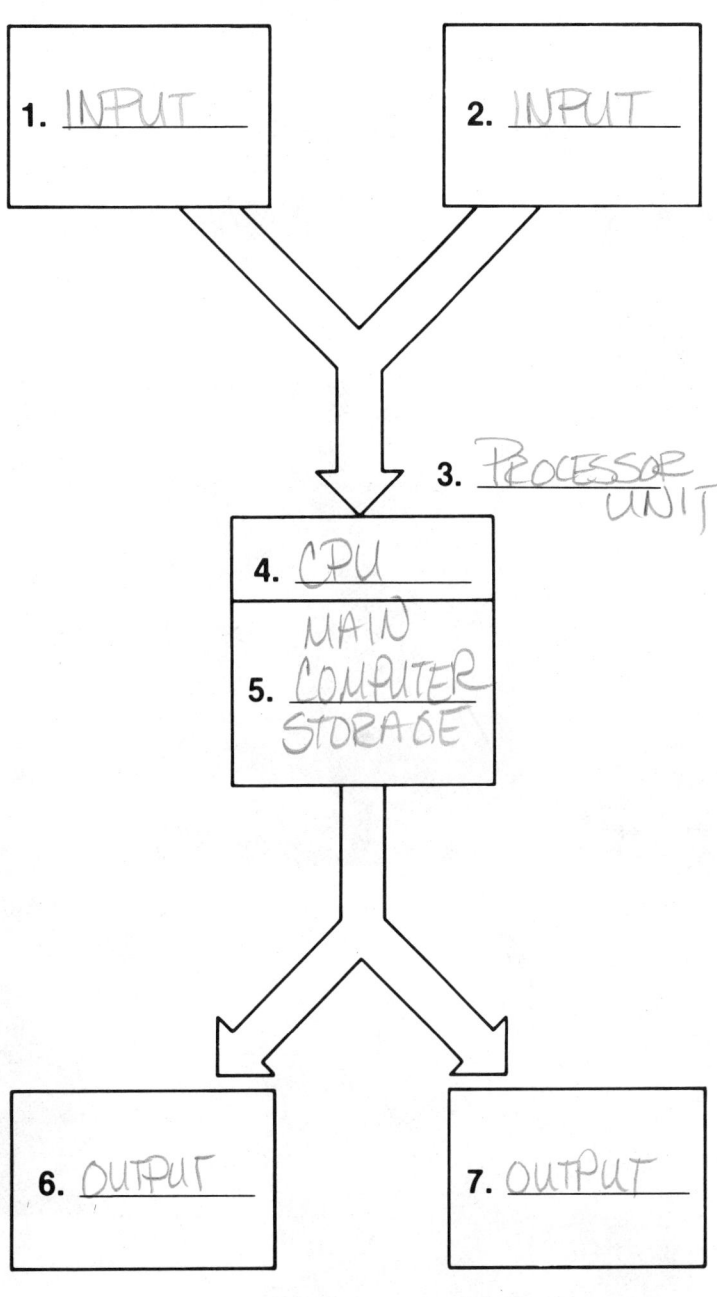

1. INPUT
2. INPUT
3. PROCESSOR UNIT
4. CPU
5. MAIN COMPUTER STORAGE
6. OUTPUT
7. OUTPUT

Chapter 1
Project 2
Identifying input/output and auxiliary storage units

Instructions: Label each of the components of the computer system illustrated below in the space provided.

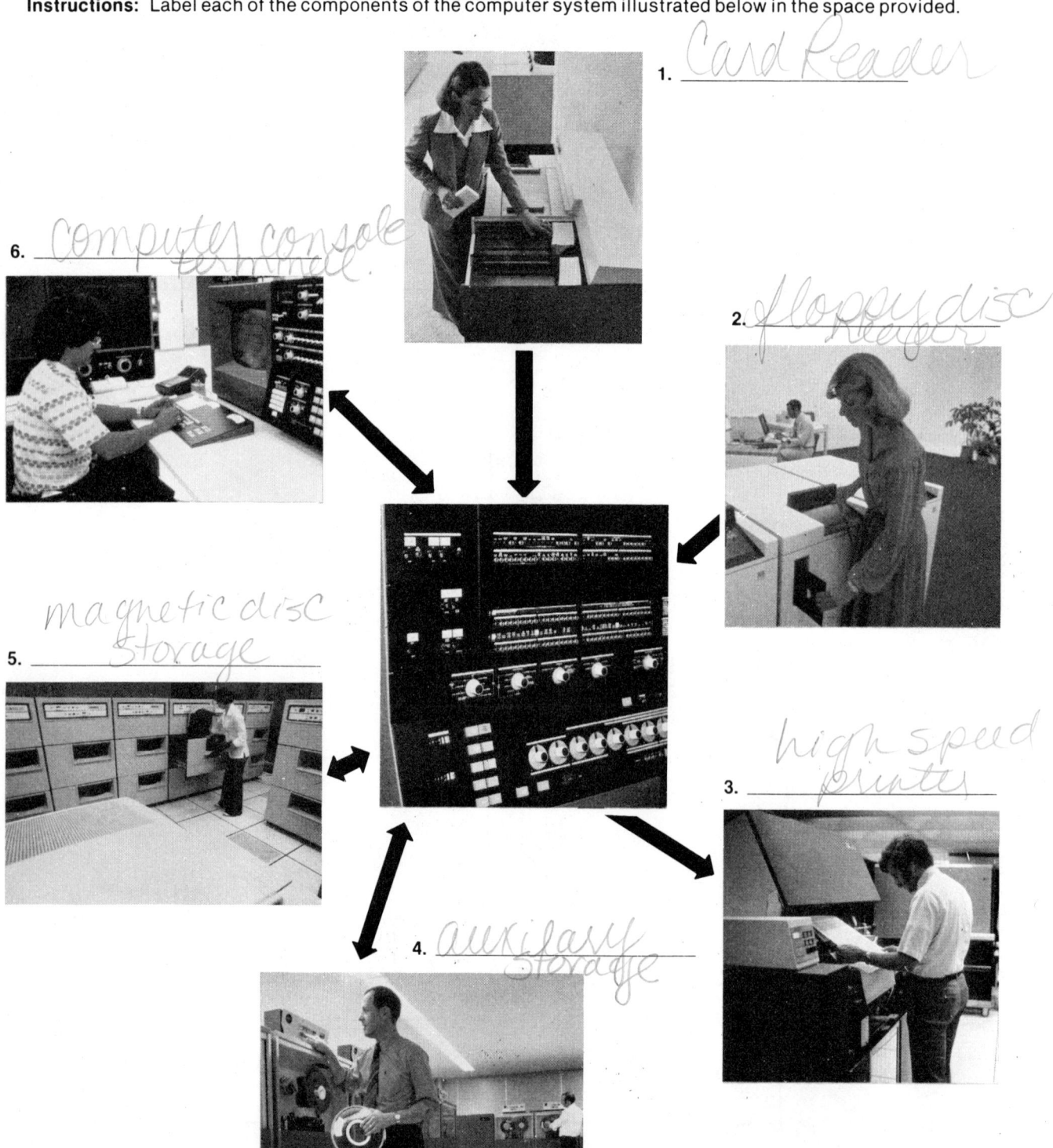

1. Card Reader
2. floppy disc reader
3. high speed printer
4. auxiliary storage
5. magnetic disc storage
6. computer console terminal

NAME _____ DATE _____

Chapter 1
Project 3
Testing your knowledge — Key Terms

Instructions: Fill in the blanks with the appropriate term from the list of terms on the right side of the page.

1. Magnetic tape and magnetic disk are _____ B _____.

2. That portion of the processor unit which contains the electronic components which causes processing to occur by interpreting instructions, performing calculations, moving data in main storage, and controlling input/output operations is called the _____ C _____.

3. A series of instructions which directs the computer to perform a sequence of tasks is called a _____ E _____.

4. Large computers which are capable of processing large amounts of data at very fast speeds are called _____ L _____.

5. A _____ M _____ system commonly consists of a CRT, keyboard, limited storage, and can cost less than $1,000.00.

6. The _____ P _____ of a computer system consists of the central processing unit and main computer storage.

7. Computer programs written for computer systems to solve a particular type of business or mathematical problem are also called _____ A _____.

8. _____ K _____ consists of electronic components which can electronically store letters of the alphabet, numbers, and special characters.

9. People who design and develop systems which will be implemented on a computer system are called _____ S _____.

10. An area in a data processing department where tape reels are stored when not being used is called the _____ T _____.

11. People who design, write, test, and implement programs to process data on a computer are called _____ F _____.

12. Data is prepared for processing on a computer in the _____ G _____.

13. The individual who mounts tape on magnetic tape units, checks the printer, and monitors the computer is called the _____ D _____.

14. Two common forms of input are _____ Q _____ and _____ H _____.

15. One of the most common forms of output is the _____ O _____.

A. Application software
B. Auxiliary storage devices
C. Central processing unit
D. Computer operator
E. Computer program
F. Computer programmers
G. Data entry department
H. Floppy disk
I. Magnetic disk
J. Magnetic tape
K. Main computer storage
L. Mainframes
M. Microcomputer
N. Minicomputer
O. Printed report
P. Processor unit
Q. Punched cards
R. Special purpose computers
S. Systems analysts
T. Tape library

NAME_____ DATE_____

Chapter 1
Project 4
Testing your knowledge — Definitions

Instructions: Briefly define or explain each of the following terms:

1. Auxiliary storage

2. Computer program

3. Main computer storage

4. Mainframe

5. Microcomputer

6. Minicomputer

7. Processor unit

1.8

NAME_____ DATE_____

Chapter 1

Project 5
Testing your knowledge — True/False Questions

Instructions: Circle T if the question is true and F if the question is false for each of the true/false questions below and on the following page.

(T) F 1. A computer is a device which can perform computations, including arithmetic and logic operations, without intervention by a human being.

T **(F)** 2. A computer can perform only two basic operations: input/output operations and arithmetic operations. *Logic*

T **(F)** 3. The Cray computer, which is one of the world's fastest computers, can process a maximum of 800,000 instructions per second.

(T) F 4. The basic purpose of any computer system is to process data of some type.

(T) F 5. A computer system consists of input units, the processor unit, and output units.

T **(F)** 6. The processor unit consists of the central processing unit and auxiliary storage.

T **(F)** 7. The central processing unit (CPU) contains the electronic components that make up the main computer storage.

T **(F)** 8. Main computer storage is used to permanently store data.

T **(F)** 9. Main computer storage is composed of electronic components which are used to interpret computer instructions.

(T) F 10. A computer program is a series of instructions that is stored in main computer storage.

T **(F)** 11. Computer programs are normally written by the engineers who design the computer.

T **(F)** 12. The dials, switches, and lights on the computer console are the primary means by which the computer operator communicates with True processor unit.

(T) F 13. The computer console consists of the card reader and other input devices.

(T) F 14. A computer operator is responsible for mounting magnetic tapes as required by the computer system.

(T) F 15. Card readers and floppy disk readers are two of the more commonly found input devices.

T **(F)** 16. The computer console terminal is the most widely used output printing device.

T **(F)** 17. Computer printers found in a computer center commonly operate at speeds ranging from 1,000 to 2,000 characters per minute.

T **(F)** 18. Auxiliary storage is used to temporarily store data until the processor unit can accept information.

1.9

Testing your knowledge—True/False Questions

(T) F 19. Magnetic tape and magnetic disk are two commonly used forms of auxiliary storage.

T (F) 20. All auxiliary storage disk packs are permanently mounted and cannot be removed from disk drives the same as reels of magnetic tape can be from tape drives.

T (F) 21. The tape library is used to house historical records of a company stored on magnetic tape that will not be processed unless operating records are destroyed.

(T) F 22. In most computer centers, bursting and decollating are common activities.

T (F) 23. The data entry department is only concerned with the recording of data on punched cards for processing by the computer.

T (F) 24. Computer programmers normally design, write, and test programs and operate the computer once the program becomes operational.

(T) F 25. Systems analysts design the systems which are required to process the data and serve as a contact between the users and the data processing department.

(T) F 26. Large computer systems may have main computer storage capacities of 1 to 2 million characters.

(T) F 27. Auxiliary storage capacities of 2 billion characters or more are possible with some computer systems.

T (F) 28. A computer system can have more than one type of auxiliary storage but can have only a single output printer.

T (F) 29. Office personnel are the primary users of computer systems.

T (F) 30. Very small computers, called microcomputers, have found limited use in business.

T (F) 31. Microcomputers cost approximately $5,000.00 for the least expensive system.

(T) F 32. Many offices now use desk top computers for word processing, accounting functions, and other typical business applications.

T (F) 33. Minicomputers are used primarily in scientific applications.

(T) F 34. The term "mainframe" is often used to describe a large scale computer system.

T (F) 35. Special purpose computers are seldom necessary anymore because general purpose computers can be used for both business and scientific purposes.

NAME_____   DATE_____

Chapter 1

Project 6

Testing your knowledge — Multiple-Choice Questions

Instructions: Circle the correct response to the multiple choice questions below and on the following page.

1. Basic operations which can be performed by any computer system include:

    A. Logical operations and addition operations.
    B. Input/output operations and addition operations.
    C. Input/output operations, arithmetic operations, and logical operations.
    D. Input/output operations and logical operations.

2. The three primary units of a computer system are:

    A. Input units, auxiliary storage units, and output units.
    B. Input units, programs, and output units.
    C. Card reader, magnetic tape units, and magnetic disk units.
    D. Input units, processor unit, and output units.

3. The basic components of the processor unit are:

    A. Central processing unit and main computer storage.
    B. Central processing unit and auxiliary storage.
    C. Auxiliary storage and main computer storage.
    D. Central processing unit and the computer console.

4. A computer program refers to:

    A. The data entered from the console terminal by the computer operator.
    B. The data recorded on auxiliary storage devices.
    C. A series of instructions which are stored in main computer storage and specify the operations which are to occur.
    D. The data recorded on punched cards for processing in main computer storage.

5. Two of the most common forms of input to a computer system are:

    A. Punched cards and floppy disks.
    B. Typewriters and computer terminals.
    C. Switch settings on the console and punched cards.
    D. Magnetic disk and direct console data entry.

6. Two of the most common forms of auxiliary storage include:

    A. Punched cards and floppy disks.
    B. Magnetic tape and magnetic disks.
    C. Magnetic disk and main computer storage.
    D. Magnetic tape and main computer storage.

7. A computer system commonly consists of:

    A. Card readers, floppy disk readers, printers, and auxiliary storage devices.
    B. Card readers, floppy disk readers, printers.
    C. Processor unit, the operator console, the input/output devices, and auxiliary storage.
    D. Processing unit and input/output units with auxiliary storage units in a separate department.

Testing your knowledge — Multiple-Choice Questions

8. Auxiliary storage is used to:

    A. Permanently store all data printed on the high-speed printer for historical purposes.
    B. Permanently store data recorded on punched cards for historical purposes.
    C. Store data no longer used in a company.
    D. Store data so that it can be used at a later time.

9. The job duties of the computer operator include:

    A. Bursting and decollating reports, operating the computer console, and writing instructions for the computer.
    B. Maintaining the tape library, operating the computer console, and writing instructions for the computer.
    C. Recording data on punched cards and floppy disks for processing on the computer.
    D. Mounting tapes and disks as required, communicating with the processor unit through the console, and keeping the computer "running".

10. The job duties of the computer programmer include:

    A. Designing systems that will utilize the computer to process data.
    B. Operating the system; that is, processing the data as it is received.
    C. Writing, testing, and implementing computer instructions to process data on the computer.
    D. Preparing input data that is to be processed on the computer.

11. The job duties of the systems analyst include:

    A. Designing systems that will utilize the computer to process data.
    B. Operating the system to process the data as it is received.
    C. Writing, testing, and implementing computer instructions to process data on the computer.
    D. Preparing input data that is to be processed on the computer.

12. Microcomputers are used:

    A. As home and personal computers.
    B. In education.
    C. In business.
    D. All of the above.

13. Minicomputers have found:

    A. Limited use in scientific applications because of their relatively slow processing speed.
    B. Limited use in business applications because of a lack of input/output devices.
    C. Limited use in all areas because of a lack of software.
    D. Widespread use in business, scientific, and engineering applications.

14. Large computers may be found with main computer storage of:

    A. 1 to 2 thousand characters.
    B. 1 to 2 million characters.
    C. 100 to 200 million characters.
    D. 1 to 2 billion characters.

15. The term mainframe is used to describe:

    A. Large computer systems.
    B. Large auxiliary storage devices.
    C. Minicomputer processor units.
    D. Any central processing unit.

NAME_____ DATE_____

Chapter 1

Project 7
Computer Laboratory Project — Calculating the Effects of Inflation

---

Description: This project is designed to acquaint individuals with the basic operating characteristics of a computer and a computer terminal; and to demonstrate the calculating power of a computer through the use of a program that calculates the effects of inflation on the price of goods and services until the year 2000.

The program for this project must be loaded into main computer storage for execution. The method for accomplishing this will vary between different computer systems. After the program is placed in main computer storage, it must be executed. The method for initiating the execution of the program is also dependent upon the type of machine being used. Directions for loading and executing the program must be determined from an instructor or from the computer center.

After the program is loaded into storage and is executed, the display below and on the left will appear on the terminal screen, one line at a time. The operator must enter the current year, the value of some product or service (from one dollar to one million dollars), and an estimated rate of inflation (from zero to 25 percent). A sample of the output that will be produced with a year of 1980, an amount of 1000, and a rate of inflation of 8.25 percent is illustrated on the right below. The output lists the cost of the product or service from the year specified to the year 2000, taking into account the inflation rate specified.

```
INTRODUCTION TO COMPUTERS AND
   DATA PROCESSING
SHELLY/CASHMAN...ANAHEIM PUBLISHING CO.
CHAPTER 1 - PROJECT 7
CALCULATING EFFECTS OF INFLATION

ENTER YEAR ? 1980
ENTER VALUE ? 1000
ENTER INFLATION RATE ? 8.25
```

YEAR	VALUE	YEAR	VALUE
1980	1,000.00	1991	2,391.70
1981	1,082.50	1992	2,589.02
1982	1,171.81	1993	2,802.61
1983	1,268.48	1994	3,033.83
1984	1,373.13	1995	3,284.12
1985	1,486.41	1996	3,555.06
1986	1,609.04	1997	3,848.35
1987	1,741.79	1998	4,165.84
1988	1,885.49	1999	4,509.52
1989	2,041.04	2000	4,881.55
1990	2,239.42		

```
MORE VALUES TO ENTER?
  Y (YES) OR N (NO) ?
```

Computer Laboratory Project — Calculating the Effects of Inflation

Assignment 1: The average cost of an automobile in 1980 was $5995. What will be the cost of the automobile for each of the years from 1980 through the year 2000, assuming a constant rate of inflation of 12.5 percent?
(NOTE: Steps 1 through 5 below provide detailed instructions for the completion of this assignment).

Step 1: Load and execute the program for this project. When the words ENTER YEAR ? are displayed on the screen, the year 1980 should be entered on the keyboard. The question mark indicates the computer is ready to accept data from the keyboard. After the year 1980 is entered, the appropriate key should be depressed to continue (the ENTER or RETURN key on most terminals).

Step 2: When the words ENTER VALUE ? are displayed on the screen, the value 5995 should be entered on the keyboard. The dollar sign ($) and the comma (,) should <u>not</u> be included in the value. The appropriate key should then be depressed to continue (the ENTER or RETURN key on most terminals).

Step 3: When the words ENTER INFLATION RATE ? are displayed on the screen, the rate 12.5 should be entered. The appropriate key should then be depressed to continue (the ENTER or RETURN key on most terminals).

Step 4: After the inflation rate is entered and the appropriate key is depressed to continue, a table listing the value of the product from the year 1980 through the year 2000 will be displayed. After the table is displayed, answer the following questions.

Questions:

1. What would be the cost of the automobile in 1985?   Answer _____

2. What would be the cost of the automobile in 1990?   Answer _____

3. What would be the cost of the automobile in 1995?   Answer _____

4. What would be the cost of the automobile in 2000?   Answer _____

Step 5: The last two lines of the output state MORE VALUES TO ENTER? Y (YES) OR N (NO) ? To repeat the operation, the value Y should be entered on the keyboard and the appropriate key depressed to continue operation. To terminate the project, an N should be entered and the appropriate key depressed.

Assignment 2: Enter the same values as in assignment 1; however, change the rate of inflation to 20% and answer the question below.

Question:

1. What would be the cost of the automobile in 2000?   Answer _____

Computer Laboratory Project — Calculating the Effects of Inflation

Assignment 3: The average wage of a beginning programmer in 1980 was $15,555.00. Assuming a 15% pay increase each year, determine the yearly pay of the programmer until the year 2000. Answer the questions below.

Questions:

1. What will be the pay of a beginning programmer in 1990?   Answer _____

2. What will be the pay of a beginning programmer in 2000?   Answer _____

Assignment 4: Utilize the computer to enter other values of interest to you to determine their cost in the year 2000 (cost of a hamburger and soft drink, cost of a movie ticket, cost of housing, etc.).

Program Messages

The following table contains error messages that may appear when incorrect entries are keyed into the terminal and the corrective action which should be taken.

ERROR MESSAGE	CAUSE	CORRECTIVE ACTION
INVALID YEAR-REENTER ?	No entry was made for YEAR or an entry was made that was not between 1980 and 2000	Enter a YEAR from 1980 to 2000
INVALID VALUE-REENTER ?	No entry was made for VALUE or a value less than one or greater than one million was entered	Enter a VALUE from one to one million
INVALID RATE-REENTER ?	No entry was made for INFLATION RATE or a value of less than zero or greater than 25 was entered	Enter an INFLATION RATE of 0 to 25
INVALID ENTRY-REENTER ?	No entry was made or an entry other than Y or N was made when asked MORE VALUES TO ENTER	Enter a Y or N
? REDO *	An alphabetic character was entered where numeric data is required	Enter a valid numeric value
OV ERROR IN _____ *	An excessive number of characters was entered	Begin project again. Reexecute the program and enter the proper values
?EXTRA IGNORED*	A comma was entered as a part of a numeric field. Only the data to the left of the comma will be used and incorrect output will result	Ignore output and redo problem entering the correct numeric values

* These error messages are generated by the system and may vary on different computer systems.

NAME_____ DATE_____

Chapter 1

Project 8
Developing Communication Skills

Instructions: Prepare an oral or written report on one or more of the following subjects.

1. A variety of positions, such as computer operator and computer programmer, are found in a computer center. Each of these positions requires certain skills. Determine the entry-level skills and knowledge required for: a) Computer operators; b) Computer programmers; c) Systems analysts.

2. The various positions found in computer centers command different salaries. Research the salaries of computer operators, computer programmers, systems analysts, and data processing department managers both in your local area and nationwide.

3. Users of computer systems vary in their satisfaction with the results of their interaction with computer systems. Interview a user of computer systems at your school or at one of the local companies to determine their view of computers and their satisfaction with the way computers are used to help in their jobs.

4. Tape librarians have a large responsibility to safeguard the media on which data is stored. Visit a local installation to interview the tape librarian. Determine the background required for the position, the specific job tasks, and the good and bad parts of being a tape librarian.

5. Microprocessors are used in many different applications for many different reasons. Contact manufacturers of microprocessors to determine the different applications which are using these small devices.

6. Data processing managers usually have many years' experience in the data processing industry before attaining their position. Interview a data processing manager in your locale to determine the background needed to be successful in this responsible job.

7. Minicomputers have become extremely important in the recent years, performing many different tasks within the scientific and business applications area. Perform a survey in your area of the country to determine what use is being made of minicomputers.

8. Contact a local installation and arrange a tour of their computer center. Report the types of computers being used, the types of applications being processed on a computer, and the working conditions found in a computer center.

9. Many data processing installations are proud to explain their computer operations. Write a letter inviting a data processing manager in your area to your class to inform the members of your class about his or her installation.

Chapter 1
Answers to selected projects

Chapter 1, Project 3, Testing your knowledge — Key Terms

1. B	4. L	7. A	10. T	13. D
2. C	5. M	8. K	11. F	14. H, Q
3. E	6. P	9. S	12. G	15. O

Chapter 1, Project 5, Testing your knowledge — True/False Questions

1. T	8. F	15. T	22. T	29. F
2. F	9. F	16. F	23. F	30. F
3. F	10. T	17. F	24. F	31. F
4. T	11. F	18. F	25. T	32. T
5. T	12. F	19. T	26. T	33. F
6. F	13. F	20. F	27. T	34. T
7. F	14. T	21. F	28. F	35. F

Chapter 1, Project 6, Testing your knowledge — Multiple Choice Questions

1. C	4. C	7. C	10. C	13. D
2. D	5. A	8. D	11. A	14. B
3. A	6. B	9. D	12. D	15. A

Chapter 2
The Evolution of the Electronic Computer Industry

> **Chapter Objectives**
>
> - An understanding of the development of computer hardware which has led to modern computing devices
> - An understanding of the role played by computer software in the history of the computing industry
> - An understanding of the important contributions from people in the evolution of the electronic computer industry
> - An appreciation of the major companies in the computer industry and the contributions they have made
> - An appreciation of the excitement and vitality of the data processing industry

Chapter Overview

Chapter 2 is intended to provide a review of the historical events which have led to the development of the data processing industry. Throughout the chapter, emphasis is placed not only on the dates of significant events, but more importantly, on how the introduction of new computer hardware and software has led to the development of the data processing industry as it now exists.

For many years, the contributions of Dr. John V. Atanasoff and Clifford Berry were overlooked; however, it is now recognized that the ABC computer which they developed in the late 1930's formed the foundation for the concept of the electronic digital computer which was further developed by others in later years.

The first large scale electronic digital computer, called ENIAC, was developed by J. Presper Eckert and John W. Mauchly at the University of Pennsylvania in 1946. ENIAC was programmed by connecting external wires and setting switches. Several years later, Dr. John von Neuman was credited with developing the concept of storing instructions in the main storage unit of the computer. This stored program concept was first implemented on the EDSAC computer completed in May of 1949.

Early computers were used primarily in engineering and scientific applications. The first commercially available computer dedicated to data processing applications was the Univac I, delivered in 1951. This computer was sold by a company called Remington-Rand, one of the early leaders in the computer industry. The Univac I was developed by Mauchly and Eckert.

In the early 1940's, IBM developed a calculating device called the Mark I. The Mark I was significant because it was the first calculating device to follow a sequence of instructions stored on punched paper tape.

IBM and Remington-Rand emerged as the two leading computer companies in the early 1950's. By the end of 1956 IBM had, however, announced a number of new products which allowed the company to take a lead in the industry which it has not yet relinquished.

The first stored program computers were programmed in machine language. Machine language instructions consist of a series of numbers, letters of the alphabet, or special characters which could be interpreted by the computer's electronic circuitry. Programming in machine language was very difficult and time consuming. To assist the programming process, automatic programming languages evolved which allowed instructions to the computer to be expressed in symbolic notation. A compiler or translator was required, however, to convert this symbolic notation into machine language instructions which the computer could understand. High-level languages (languages that were far removed from the internal characteristics of the machine) then began to appear. FORTRAN, a scientific and mathematical language, was developed by IBM and released in 1957. COBOL, a business language, was developed by a group of diverse computer users and released in 1960.

In 1958, the second generation of computer systems was announced. These computers were faster, smaller in size, and less costly than previous computer systems, and were characterized by the use of transistors in their internal electronic circuitry. This development lead to great growth in the use of computers in business as well as science and numerous manufacturers of computer systems emerged following the development of second generation technology.

The IBM System/360 computers, announced in 1964, were considered to be the first of the third generation of computer systems. These computers utilized new electronic technology in which circuits were stored on small chips rather than being composed of discrete components. Third generation computers consisted of a family of computer systems ranging from small to large systems useful for both business and scientific applications. The period following the announcement of the third generation of computers was one of explosive growth with numerous computers being installed, a great need for personnel, the birth of the software industry, and the widespread use of operating systems.

The early 1970's saw evolutionary growth in computer systems. New data entry devices which stored data on magnetic tape and magnetic disk gained increased acceptance. The use of computer terminals and transaction-oriented processing systems were starting to be more widely used. Social issues became a concern, and computer crime, computer fraud, and privacy were important topics of discussion.

The mid-1970's saw revolutionary technological developments with the development of microelectronics in which thousands of circuits could be created and stored on a very small electronic chip less than ¼ inch square. This led to the development of the microprocessors and the microcomputers.

Today, computers can be found in the office, in education, in banking, in retailing, in transportation, and in manufacturing; and influence nearly every aspect of our lives.

Chapter 2

Key Terms

ABC Computer The first electronic digital computer, designed by Dr. John Atanasoff and Clifford Berry.
ACM Association for Computing Machinery: an association of computer specialists.
Atanasoff, Dr. John V. Designed the first electronic digital computer with Clifford Berry.
Banking, Computers in Computers are widely used in banks for processing checks and updating and maintaining financial records of all types.
Batch Processing The accumulation and processing of data as a group.
Berry, Clifford Designed the first electronic digital computer with Dr. John Atanasoff.
Certificate in Data Processing (CDP) A professional certificate awarded by the ICCP to individuals who have passed a comprehensive examination.
COBOL Common Business Oriented Language: one of the most widely used business programming languages.
Compiler A program that interprets computer statements written in a symbolic form and converts the statements to machine language instructions.
Crime, Computer The use of a computer system to steal, embezzle, or maliciously access or destroy data or files used with computer systems.
Data Communications The transmission of data from one location to another using communications channels such as telephone lines, coaxial cables, microwaves, or other means.
DPMA Data Processing Management Association: a professional association of data processing managers, programmers and systems analysts.
Dump, Core A printout of the contents of main storage.
Eckert, J. Presper Working with Dr. John W. Mauchly, designed the ENIAC computer.
EDSAC The first computer which was operational using the stored program concept.
EDVAC An early computer developed by John von Neumann that utilized the stored program concept.
FORTRAN A high-level language designed for scientists, mathematicians, and engineers.
Hexadecimal Number System A number system with a base 16 that uses 16 individual symbols to represent values.
High-level programming language A programming language far removed from the internal characteristics of the machine.
Hoff, Dr. Ted One of the first electronic engineers to design an entire central processing unit on a single silicon chip.
Instructions, Computer The unique numbers, letters of the alphabet, or special characters that, when interpreted by the computer's circuitry, cause a particular operation to be performed.
Intelligent Computer Terminal A terminal with the ability to process data using the electronic components within the terminal without the need to access the power of a large computer.
Large Scale Integration (LSI) Method of constructing electronic circuits in which many thousands of circuits can be stored on a single chip of silicon.
Machine Language Instructions A series of numbers, letters, and other bit configurations which can be interpreted by the electronic circuitry of a computer, causing operations to be executed.
Manufacturing, Computers in In manufacturing, computers are used in product design and control of the manufacturing process itself.
Mark I A calculator built by IBM which was one of the first machines to follow a sequence of instructions on paper tape.
Mauchly, Dr. John Working with J. Presper Eckert, he designed the ENIAC computer.
Microelectronics The science of creating very small electronic circuits on a thin wafer of germanium or silicon.

Key Terms

Microprocessor The electronic components of an entire central processor unit created on a very small single silicon chip.

Office, Computers in the Computers are widely used in word processing activities for inquiry and updating files. Computer terminals are replacing the typewriter as an office tool in many companies.

Privacy Act of 1974 A law enacted in 1974 to protect rights of citizens from invasion of privacy.

Programming The process of writing instructions for a computer.

Programming, Automatic An early term used to describe writing a computer program in a notation other than machine language.

Programming Languages The software supplied as a part of the computer system that provides a means of instructing the computer to perform operations.

Programming, Machine-Language The writing of instructions for a computer by means of numbers, letters of the alphabet, and special characters that can be understood by the electronic circuitry.

Programming, Symbolic Programming using simple words or abbreviations to express the operations to be performed.

Programs, Unreliable Programs that do not always produce consistent results.

Retailing, Computers in Computers are widely used in retailing for keeping track of sales, inventories, central credit, and check verification.

Second Generation Computers introduced in 1959 that were transistorized.

Social Issues Those issues relative to the use of computers and its impact upon how people live.

Software Programs written for computer systems.

Software, Application Computer programs written for computer systems to solve a particular type of business or mathematical problem.

Software, System Programs written to aid in the operation of a computer system.

Software Industry The group of companies that specialize in writing system or application software.

Stibitz, Dr. George One of the early leaders in the development of modern computing devices.

Storage, Main Computer Electronic components which can electronically store letters of the alphabet, numbers, and special characters.

Storage, Vacuum Tubes One of the first methods used to store data electronically in main storage.

Stored Program Concept The concept in which instructions are stored internally in the main storage unit of the computer.

TRADIC The first transistorized computer.

Transaction-Oriented Processing System That type of system in which data is entered into the computer at the time the transaction occurs.

Transportation, Computers in Computers are widely used in airline and hotel reservation systems, as well as in the guidance systems of aircraft, training systems, and other support areas.

Unbundling The separate pricing of hardware, software, and related services.

UNIVAC I The first electronic computer dedicated to data processing applications.

von Neumann, Dr. John Prepared the first written documentation of the "stored program" concept: a pioneer in the use of program flowcharts.

Watson, Thomas J., Jr. Led IBM in the 1950's and 1960's during the time it became the world leader in electronic computers.

Watson, Thomas J., Sr. Chairman of the Board of IBM for 40 years and a guiding force in its early years of growth.

Wilkes, Maurice V. A student of John von Neumann who designed the EDSAC computer.

NAME_____   DATE_____

Chapter 2
Project 1
Computer systems — A historical review

Instructions: Write a brief paragraph explaining the historical significance of the computer system illustrated below.

Explanation:_____

_____

_____

_____

NAME_____ DATE_____

Chapter 2

Project 2
Historical chronology of computers

Instructions: Briefly explain the significant events that occurred in the development of computer systems in the years specified below.

1946–1950

1950–1958

1958–1964

1964–1970

1970–1980

NAME_____ DATE_____

Chapter 2

Project 3
Testing your knowledge — Key Terms

Instructions: Fill in the blanks with the appropriate term from the list of terms on the right side of the page.

A 1. The first electronic digital computer ever designed was called the ___ __ABC Computer__ .

H 2. The first large scale electronic digital computer, called __ENIAC__, was developed at the University of Pennsylvania by Eckert and Mauchly.

S 3. __Vacuum tubes__ were the first components used to store data electronically in main storage.

N 4. The technique of placing computer instructions in main computer storage for execution is called the __Stored program concept__.

T 5. __J. von Neumann__ prepared the documentation for the first stored program concept.

K 6. The calculator built by IBM which was designed to follow a sequence of instructions on paper tape was the __Mark I__

J 7. __Machine lang. instruc__ consist of a series of numbers, letters of the alphabet or other characters which can be interpreted by the electronic circuitry of a computer causing operations to be performed.

I 8. __FORTRAN__ is a high-level programming language designed for scientists, mathematicians, and engineers.

D 9. One of the most widely used business oriented programming languages is __COBOL__ .

E 10. A __Compiler__ is a program that interprets a statement written in a symbolic form and converts the statement to a machine language instruction.

F 11. The transmission of data from one location to another over telephone lines and other methods is called __Data communications__

C 12. The accumulating and processing of data as a group is called __Batch processing__.

P 13. A __transaction-oriented processing system__ is one in which transactions are entered into a computer as the transaction occurs.

O 14. Programs written to aid in the operation of a computer system are called __system software__.

M 15. A __Microprocessor__ contains the electronic components of an entire central processing unit on a very small silicon chip.

A. ABC computer
B. Application software
C. Batch processing
D. COBOL
E. Compiler
F. Data communications
G. EDSAC
H. ENIAC
I. FORTRAN
J. Machine language instructions
K. Mark I
L. Mauchly, John W.
M. Microprocessor
N. Stored program concept
O. System software
P. Transaction-oriented processing system
Q. Transistors
R. Univac I
S. Vacuum tubes
T. Von Neumann, John
U. Watson, Thomas Jr.

2.7

NAME _____ DATE _____

Chapter 2
Project 4
Testing your knowledge — Definitions

Instructions: Briefly define or explain each of the following terms:

1. ENIAC

2. Stored program concept

3. Compiler

4. Machine language

5. COBOL

6. FORTRAN

7. Batch processing

8. Transaction-oriented processing

9. Microprocessor

NAME_____   DATE_____

Chapter 2

Project 5
Testing your knowledge — True/False Questions

Instructions: Circle the T if the question is true and F if the question is false for each of the true/false questions below and on the following page.

(T) F   1. The design of the ABC computer by John V. Atanasoff and Clifford Berry in the late 1930's provided the foundation for the development of electronic digital computers.

T (F)   2. ENIAC was the first large scale electronic digital computer to utilize the stored program concept.

(T) F   3. ENIAC's internal electronic circuitry was composed of approximately 18,000 vacuum tubes.

T (F)   4. ENIAC became operational in 1946 but had little practical value as a computing device.

T (F)   5. EDSAC was the first of the second generation computers to use the stored program concept.

(T) F   6. Dr. John von Neumann is credited with developing the concept of the stored program.

(T) F   7. John W. Mauchly and J. Presper Eckert designed both the ENIAC and the Univac I computers.

(T) F   8. Univac I, delivered in 1951, was the first computer utilized for a data processing type application.

T (F)   9. Univac I was developed by International Business Machines (IBM).

(T) F   10. The Mark I calculating device was developed by IBM and is significant because it was the first device to be able to follow a sequence of instructions stored on punched paper tape.

T (F)   11. Thomas Watson Sr. of IBM was a strong supporter of the use of the computer for business, and is largely responsible for the success of IBM in the computer field.

(T) F   12. The IBM 650 computer developed in the 1950's was a very successful medium sized computer useful for business applications.

(T) F   13. ACM stands for the Association of Computing Machinery and is an association of computer professionals.

T (F)   14. With machine language programming, the programmer is required to enter instructions into main computer storage by means of switches and dial settings on the computer console.

T (F)   15. Machine language programming is normally very easy because it is closely related to the internal characteristics of the computer.

T (F)   16. FORTRAN was developed in 1957 as a business programming language but has gained widespread use in the scientific community.

T (F)   17. A compiler is a program that converts machine language instructions into high-level programming statements.

2.9

Testing your knowledge — True/False Questions

(T) F 18. COBOL is a widely used business programming language.

(T) F 19. FORTRAN is considered to be a high-level programming language because the notation used is far removed from the internal characteristics of the computer.

T **(F)** 20. By the end of 1950, only two programming languages were in existence — FORTRAN and COBOL.

(T) F 21. In the early 1960's, most manufacturers had developed two types of computers— computers for scientific use and computers for business use.

(T) F 22. The second generation of computers is characterized by the use of transistorized circuitry.

T **(F)** 23. In the 1960's only two companies were significant forces in the industry — IBM and Remington-Rand.

(T) F 24. The third generation of computers was characterized by the design of a single computer for both business and scientific applications and the use of solid logic technology.

(T) F 25. The IBM/360 computer was one of the first of the third generation of computers.

T **(F)** 26. A significant advantage of third generation computers was that the internal architecture was similar to previous generations, only much faster.

(T) F 27. Application software refers to programs written for specific applications of a company.

(T) F 28. System software refers to programs written to aid in the operation of the computer system.

T **(F)** 29. The operating systems provided with third generation computer systems were extremely complex but virtually error-free.

T **(F)** 30. The first minicomputer was introduced in about 1975.

T **(F)** 31. Minicomputers, when initially announced, were characterized by a variety of software products to assist the small business system user.

T **(F)** 32. In the late 1960's, there was unanimous agreement that the value of computers in business far exceeded the benefits anticipated by most companies.

T **(F)** 33. Transaction-oriented processing systems use punched cards as the main method of input.

T **(F)** 34. Because of the complexity of operations, computerized systems are virtually fool-proof against fraud and unauthorized tampering of data.

(T) F 35. The central processing unit of a computer developed on a very small chip of silicon is called a microprocessor.

NAME_____   DATE_____

Chapter 2

Project 6
Testing your knowledge — Multiple-Choice Questions

Instructions: Circle the correct response to the multiple choice questions below and on the following page.

1. The first large scale electronic computer was:

    A. The ABC computer which became operational in 1946.
    B. The ENIAC which became operational in 1946. *(circled)*
    C. The Univac I which became operational in 1946.
    D. The ENIAC which became operational in 1956.

2. The individual credited with developing the concept of the stored program was:

    A. John V. Atanasoff.
    B. J. Presper Eckert.
    C. John W. Mauchly.
    D. John von Neuman. *(circled)*

3. The first computer system to be used for business data processing applications was:

    A. The ABC computer which became operational in 1939.
    B. The ENIAC computer which became operational in 1946.
    C. The Univac I computer which became operational in 1951. *(circled)*
    D. The IBM 650 which became operational in 1953.

4. The early leader in the development of computer systems was:

    A. IBM.
    B. Remington-Rand. *(circled)*
    C. R.C.A.
    D. General Electric.

5. The first electronic computer was controlled by:

    A. Machine language instructions.
    B. External wires and switches. *(circled)*
    C. Automatic programming languages.
    D. High-level programming languages.

6. The FORTRAN programming language was developed as:

    A. A type of simplified machine language.
    B. A low-level language.
    C. A scientific and mathematical language. *(circled)*
    D. A business-oriented language.

7. To translate programs written in a symbolic programming language into machine language requires:

    A. An emulator.
    B. Application software.
    C. A very large computer.
    D. A compiler. *(circled)*

2.11

Testing your knowledge — Multiple-Choice Questions

8. COBOL was developed as:

    A. A business programming language. *(circled)*
    B. A scientific programming language.
    C. A mathematical programming language.
    D. A low-level programming language.

9. The second generation of computer systems were announced in:

    A. The late 1940's and were transistorized.
    B. The late 1950's and were transistorized. *(circled)*
    C. The late 1960's and used microprocessors.
    D. The late 1970's and used microprocessors.

10. The computer industry for the period 1965-1970 was characterized by:

    A. Extremely efficient and reliable operating systems and software.
    B. Problems concerning the reliability of operating systems and software. *(circled)*
    C. Problems concerning the reliability of computer hardware.
    D. A surplus of trained personnel including programmers, systems analysts, and operators.

11. Third generation computers were characterized by:

    A. Solid logic technology.
    B. A single family of computers useful for both business and scientific applications.
    C. The use of operating systems.
    D. All of the above. *(circled)*

12. Transaction-oriented processing systems require:

    A. Computer terminals, large amounts of auxiliary storage, and data communications. *(circled)*
    B. Minicomputers.
    C. Punched card readers, large main storage, and high speed printers.
    D. Computer terminals with microprocessors.

13. In a batch processing system:

    A. The data to be processed is gathered together as a group and processed as a group. *(circled)*
    B. The data to be processed is entered from a computer terminal as the transaction takes place.
    C. The data to be processed is transmitted over data communications lines as it is entered by an operator as the transaction occurs.
    D. Punched cards are not used; instead data is recorded and processed in groups stored on magnetic disk and magnetic tape.

14. When using computer systems:

    A. Computer fraud is virtually impossible because of the complexity of internal operations of the computer system.
    B. The privacy of an individual is protected because data on disk or tape cannot be visually read.
    C. Computer fraud and privacy are important social issues of concern. *(circled)*
    D. Answers A and C.

15. An entire central processor unit stored on a very small silicon chip is called:

    A. A microprocessor. *(circled)*
    B. A minicomputer.
    C. An intelligent terminal.
    D. A third generation computer.

NAME_____ DATE_____

Chapter 2

Project 7
Computer Laboratory Project — Computer Assisted Instruction

Description: This project is designed to acquaint individuals with the use of computer assisted instruction, CAI, as a learning methodology. The project consists of answering a series of multiple-choice questions concerning the subject matter contained in Chapter 2. The questions will be displayed on a computer terminal.

The program for this project must be loaded into main computer storage for execution. The method for accomplishing this will vary between different computer systems. After the program is placed in main computer storage, it must be executed. The method for initiating the execution of the program is also dependent upon the type of machine being used. Directions for loading and executing the program must be determined from an instructor or from the computer center.

Load the program for this project into storage. After the program is loaded into storage and executed, a series of multiple-choice questions will be displayed on the terminal. The first question is illustrated below.

```
INTRODUCTION TO COMPUTERS AND DATA PROCESSING
SHELLY/CASHMAN...ANAHEIM PUBLISHING COMPANY
CHAPTER 2 - PROJECT 7
COMPUTER ASSISTED INSTRUCTION (CAI)

1. THE FIRST LARGE ELECTRONIC DIGITAL
   COMPUTER WAS THE:
   A. UNIVAC I
   B. SYSTEM/360
   C. ABC
   D. ENIAC

ENTER ANSWER: ?D
ABSOLUTELY RIGHT!

WHEN FINISHED VIEWING, DEPRESS
   THE APPROPRIATE KEY TO
   DISPLAY THE NEXT QUESTION
```

Assignment 1: The following steps should be followed in answering the questions using a computer terminal:

Step 1: Load and execute the program for this project. Review the question and select the correct response by entering the appropriate letter of the alphabet A, B, C, D. Do not use the shift key on the terminal. After the response has been entered, depress the appropriate key to continue (the ENTER or RETURN key on most terminals).

Computer Laboratory Project — Computer Assisted Instruction

Step 2: If the correct response was given, a message indicating a correct answer will be displayed. The next question can then be displayed by depressing the appropriate key to continue.

Step 2a: If an incorrect response is given, a message indicating an incorrect response will be displayed, together with the correct answer. By depressing the appropriate key to continue, another question covering the same subject matter will be presented. If this question is answered incorrectly, a reference to a page number in the text will be given to provide for additional study and review. By depressing the appropriate key, a new question will appear.

If a character other than an A, B, C, or D is entered as a response, the following message will appear:

INVALID ANSWER–REENTER
ENTER ANSWER

One of the valid responses (A, B, C, or D) should then be entered.

After the review has been completed (a minimum of 10 questions and a maximum of 20 questions, depending upon the number of questions missed), the following display will appear. In the example below, all 10 questions were answered correctly the first time.

```
QUESTIONS ASKED:    10
CORRECT ANSWERS:    10
PERCENT CORRECT:   100 %

END OF CAI ASSIGNMENT
```

Assignment 2: After completing Assignment 1, answer the questions below and write a brief statement regarding your reaction to computer assisted instruction as a method of learning. Include in your comments statements as to whether, in your opinion, CAI is a good method for review; Did you enjoy the assignment? Would you use CAI in this class and other classes if available? What place should CAI play in the school of the future?

QUESTIONS ASKED: _____
CORRECT ANSWERS: _____
PERCENT CORRECT: _____

My opinion of Computer Assisted Instruction:

_____

_____

Chapter 2
Project 8
Developing Communication Skills

Instructions: Prepare an oral or written report on one or more of the following subjects.

1. Contact the school librarian and obtain a list of the data processing periodicals published in the data processing industry. Distribute the list to your class.

2. Contact the data processing manager in a local computer installation and determine the data processing periodicals recommended by that company.

3. Contact the school library and obtain a list of data processing periodicals that are available in the library for research. Based upon the findings of project 1 and 2 above, submit your recommendations to the school librarian to improve the data processing periodicals available.

4. Write a letter to the Association for Computing Machinery to determine the purpose of the association and the requirements for membership.

5. Locate the nearest chapter of the Association of Computing Machinery in your community. Attend a meeting and report to class concerning the program presented.

6. Write a letter to the Data Processing Management Association to determine the purpose of this association and their requirements for membership. Report your findings to the class.

7. Locate the nearest chapter of the Data Processing Management Association. Attend a local meeting and report to class concerning the program presented.

8. Contact either ACM or DPMA and determine if they have student chapters and what services they provide. Ask a representative to appear at your school as a guest speaker explaining their service.

9. Write a letter to the Institute for the Certification of Computer Professionals (ICCP) and obtain information on the Registered Business Programmer examination and the Certificate in Data Processing examination. Report your findings to the class.

10. Contact 10 people at random by telephone or in person and ask if they have ever experienced "problems" with a computer, such as incorrect billing, etc. Summarize your findings in a report.

11. Many personnel agencies specialize in the placement of data processing employees. Contact one of these agencies and ask if a staff member can appear as a guest speaker to discuss data processing opportunities in your community.

Chapter 2
Answers to selected projects

Chapter 2, Project 3, Testing your knowledge — Key Terms

1. A	4. N	7. J	10. E	13. P
2. H	5. T	8. I	11. F	14. O
3. S	6. K	9. D	12. C	15. M

Chapter 2, Project 5, Testing your knowledge — True/False Questions

1. T	8. T	15. F	22. T	29. F
2. F	9. F	16. F	23. F	30. F
3. T	10. T	17. F	24. T	31. F
4. F	11. F	18. T	25. T	32. F
5. F	12. T	19. T	26. F	33. F
6. T	13. T	20. F	27. T	34. F
7. T	14. F	21. T	28. T	35. T

Chapter 2, Project 6, Testing your knowledge — Multiple Choice Questions

1. B	4. B	7. D	10. B	13. A
2. D	5. B	8. A	11. D	14. C
3. C	6. C	9. B	12. A	15. A

Chapter 3
Processing Data On a Computer

Chapter Objectives

- A detailed understanding of the input/process/output basic processing cycle
- An understanding of the operational capabilities of a computer system — input/output, arithmetic, and logical operations
- An understanding of the capability of a computer system to store data on auxiliary storage for access at a later time by the same or a different program
- An appreciation and understanding of data storage and retrieval, inquiry processing, update processing, and sorting
- An understanding of control break processing; classifying, selecting, and summarizing data; and the manipulation of data in a computer system for the production of useful information

Chapter Overview

Chapter 3 is designed to provide an overview of the basic processing cycle of input, process, and output; and to develop an understanding of common applications which involve storing data on auxiliary storage devices, inquiry and updating of files, sorting, selecting, classifying and summarizing data.

When data is processed on a computer system, it is normally organized into logical entities called fields, records, and files. A field is defined as one unit of data. Fields are commonly grouped together to form a record. A record is defined as a collection of fields related to a specific unit of information. Records are usually grouped together to form a file. A file is a collection of records.

The data organized in fields, records, and files is commonly stored on an external medium in a machine-readable format prior to being read into main computer storage. Widely used input media include punched cards, magnetic tape, and magnetic disk. Computer terminals are also used to enter data directly into a computer system.

Once data is in main computer storage, it is processed under control of a computer program which is also stored in main computer storage. Operations are accomplished by means of the electronic circuitry in the central processing unit (CPU).

Two of the more popular forms of output are the printed report and output displayed on a cathode ray tube terminal (CRT).

Within the input/process/output processing cycle, computers are capable of performing three basic operations: 1) Input/output operations; 2) Arithmetic operations; and 3) Logical operations.

The basic processing that occurs in input/output operations involves the following steps: 1) Data from source documents is recorded onto an input medium; 2) The data on the input medium is read into main computer storage; 3) The data in main computer storage is processed; 4) The data which has been processed in main computer storage is printed.

In a computer system, the electronic circuitry is designed so that once data has been placed in main computer storage, it can be used in addition, subtraction, multiplication, division, and other arithmetic operations. The resultant answers can be stored in main computer storage for further processing.

An important capability of a computer system is derived from its ability to compare numbers, letters of the alphabet, or special characters, and perform alternative operations based upon the results of the comparison. Three types of comparing operations are commonly performed: 1) Comparing to determine if the values in two fields are equal; 2) Comparing to determine if the value in one field is less than the value in another field; 3) Comparing to determine if the value in one field is greater than the value in another field.

In the basic processing cycle, it is many times necessary to store data for subsequent use. Auxiliary storage is used for this purpose. Magnetic tape and magnetic disk are the two primary media used for auxiliary storage.

Within the basic data processing cycle, many applications can be performed, including applications such as word processing, which requires the storage and retrieval of data from auxiliary storage; inquiry and updating of files; sorting; control break reporting; and the selecting, classifying, and summarizing of data.

Chapter 3

Key Terms

Arithmetic Operations The performing of calculations on data by the internal electronic circuitry in the central processing unit.

Auxiliary Storage Devices Devices, generally magnetic tape and magnetic disk, on which data can be stored for use by computer programs; also known as secondary storage.

Card Reader A device capable of reading the data stored in a punched card and transmitting it to main computer storage.

Cathode Ray Tube Terminal A device used as a computer terminal which contains a television-like screen for displaying data. Most CRT terminals also have a typewriter-like keyboard.

Central Processing Unit Electronic components which cause processing on a computer to occur by interpreting instructions, performing calculations, moving data in main computer storage, and controlling the input/output operations. It consists of the arithmetic/logic unit and the control unit.

Classify To separate data into different categories according to some specification.

Comparing, Logical Operations The ability of the computer to compare data and perform alternative actions based upon the results of the comparison.

Data, Storage and Retrieval The process of recording and extracting data from auxiliary storage devices using a computer.

Data Banks A collection of data which is stored on auxiliary storage devices.

Fields A unit of data within a record.

File A collection of one or more records.

Floppy disk An oxide-coated plastic disk about 8" in diameter enclosed in a protective covering that can be used for magnetically storing data.

Floppy Disk Reader A device which can read data stored on a floppy disk.

Input/Output Operations A basic data processing function that requires the reading of data and producing some output from the data read.

Input/Processing/Output The sequence of events that occurs when data is processed on a computer system.

Input Units Units that are a part of a computer system which present data to the processor unit for processing.

Inquiry A request from the terminal operator to a computer system for information.

Output Units Units which are a part of a computer system that can display, print or otherwise make available to people the results of processing data.

Processor Unit The unit which stores the data and contains the electronic circuitry necessary to carry out the processing of the stored data. It consists of the central processing unit and main computer storage.

Records A collection of fields related to a specific unit of information.

Selecting The process of extracting specific types of data from a group.

Sorting The process of arranging records in ascending or descending sequence.

Summarizing The process of accumulating and printing values contained in records.

Summary Report A report in which one line is printed for each group of records.

Tape, Magnetic A 1/2" wide piece of mylar on which data can be stored electronically. Typical lengths for tape are 600 feet, 1200 feet, and 2400 feet.

Updating The process in which files are changed, with additions, deletions, and changes, to reflect the latest information.

Word Processing The storage, manipulation, and processing of data as needed in the preparation of letters and reports using terminals and related devices.

NAME_____ DATE_____

Chapter 3
Project 1
Basic Input/Output Operations

Instructions: The following diagram illustrates basic input/output operations being performed on a computer. Analyze the diagram and briefly explain each of the steps in the procedure as identified by the numbers 1, 2, 3, and 4.

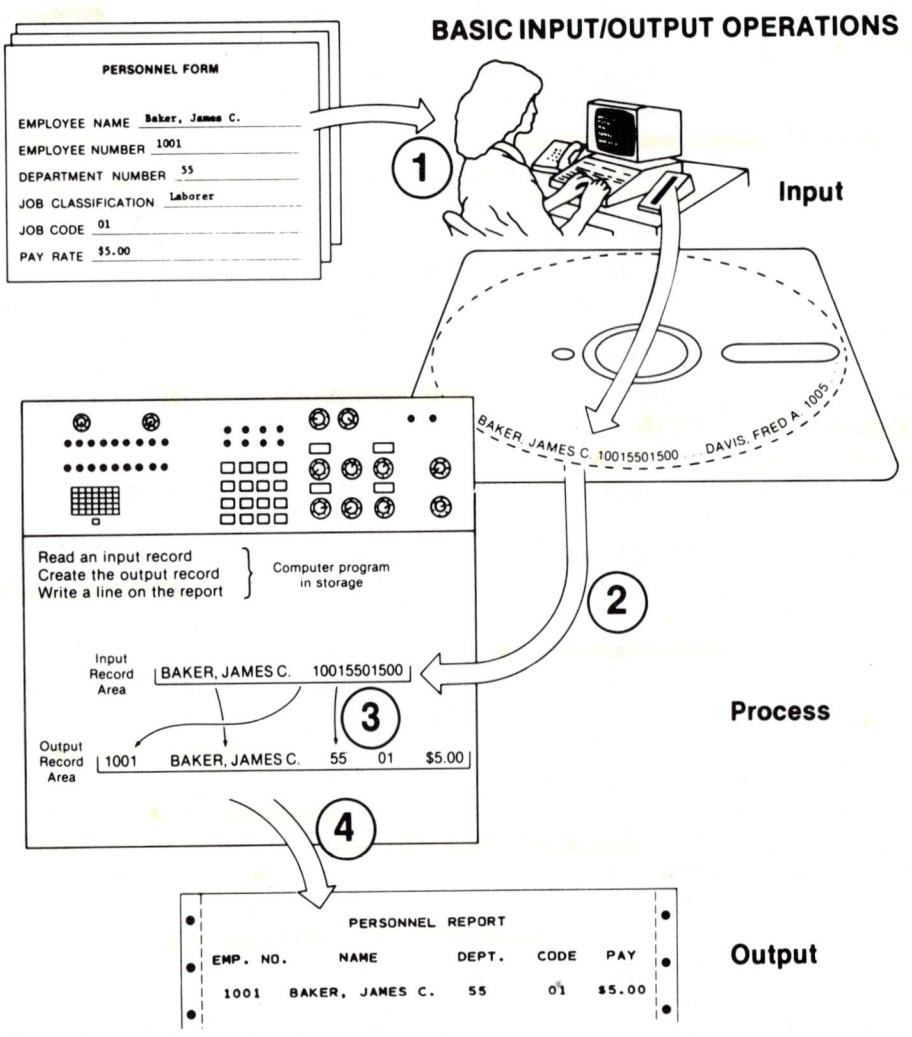

Step 1 ___Floppy disc_____

Step 2 ___Main storage_____

Step 3 ___processed_____

Step 4 ___output_____

3.4

NAME_____ DATE_____

Chapter 3
Project 2
Data Storage and Retrieval

Instructions: The following diagram illustrates the basic concepts of data storage and retrieval in a word processing application. Analyze the diagram and briefly explain each step in the procedure as identified by the numbers 1, 2, 3, 4, and 5.

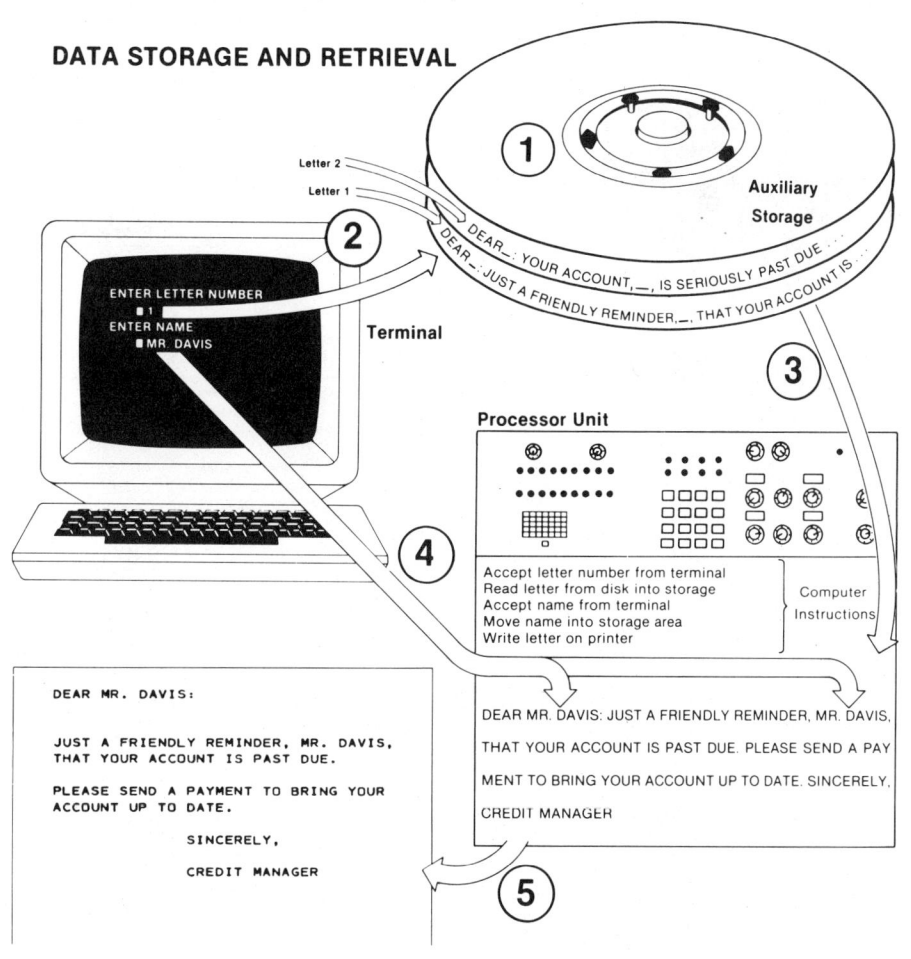

Step 1 _auxilary storage - form letters_

Step 2 _enter letter number_

Step 3 _letter retrieved → to main storage_

Step 4 _enter name of receiver_

Step 5 _printed_

3.5

NAME_____   DATE_____

Chapter 3
Project 3
Inquiry

Instructions: The following diagram illustrates the basic steps that occur in an inquiry application. Analyze the diagram and briefly explain each step in the procedure as identified by the numbers 1, 2, 3, and 4.

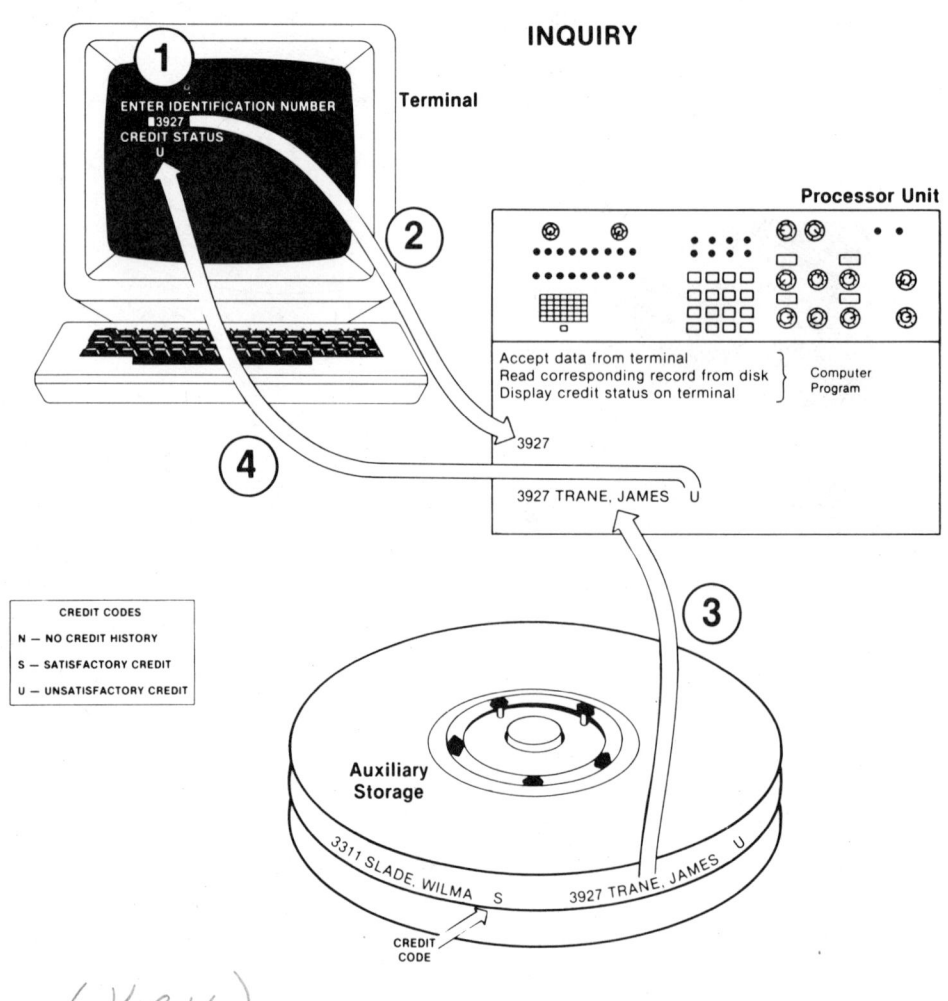

(Key)

Step 1 __I.D. # entered__

Step 2 __transmitted & stored in main storage__

Step 3 __corresponding record; auxil → main__

Step 4 __information to terminal__

3.6

NAME_____ DATE_____

Chapter 3
Project 4
Updating

Instructions: The diagram below illustrates the steps that occur in an updating application. Analyze the diagram and briefly explain each step in the procedure as identified by the numbers 1, 2, and 3.

UPDATING

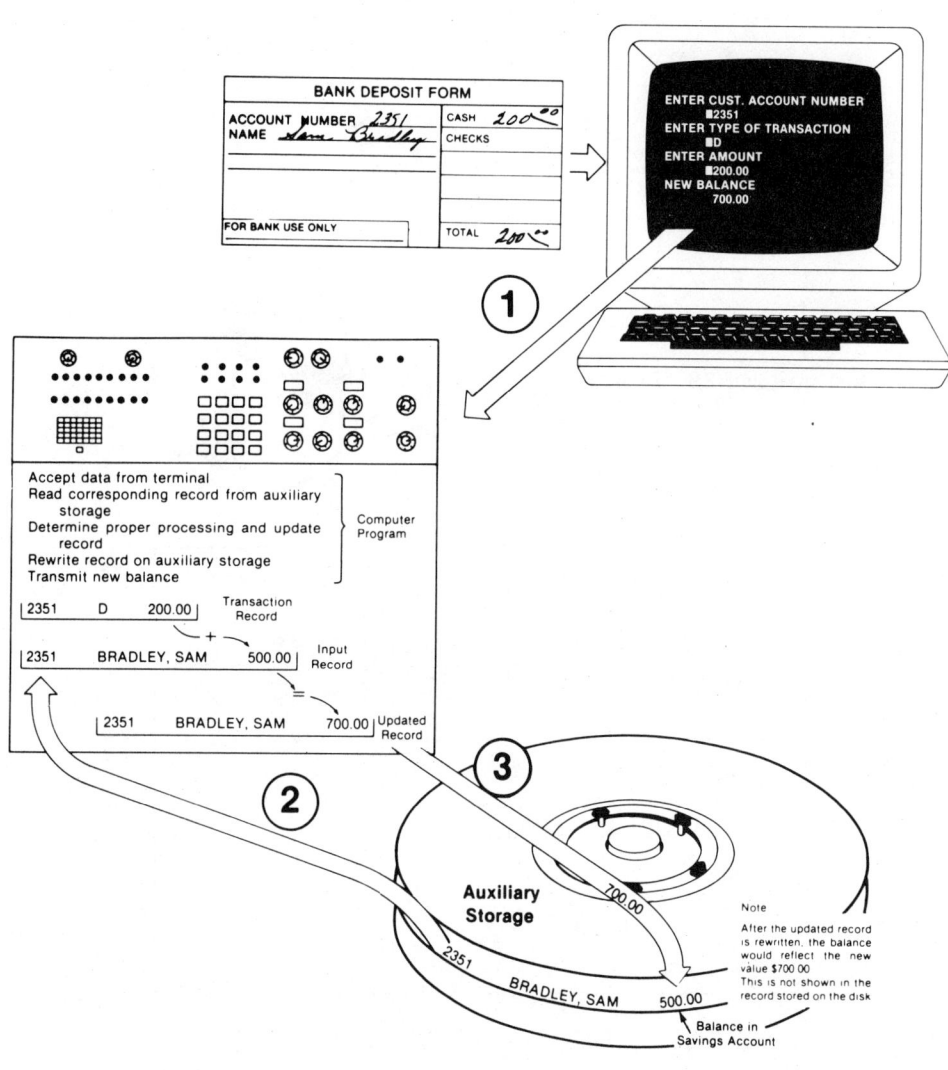

Step 1 _____

Step 2 _____

Step 3 _____

3.7

NAME_____   DATE_____

Chapter 3
Project 5
Sorting

Instructions: Analyze the diagram below. Illustrate what data would be contained on the reports after the data on the order sheet has been sorted in descending sequence by serial number, and after the data has been sorted in ascending sequence by buyer.

ORDER SHEET

Date 8/15

SERIAL NUMBER	QUANTITY	BUYER
7473	15	McJones
7474	30	Hale
7475	1	Hanes
7476	3	Norass
7477	5	Shims
7478	13	Dilbert

747315MCJONES   747430HALE . . .

747315MCJONES   747430HALE . . .

SALES BY SERIAL NUMBER
DATE 8/15

SERIAL NUMBER	QUANTITY	BUYER
____	____	____
____	____	____
____	____	____
____	____	____
____	____	____
____	____	____

SALES BY BUYER
DATE 8/15

SERIAL NUMBER	QUANTITY	BUYER
____	____	____
____	____	____
____	____	____
____	____	____
____	____	____
____	____	____

NAME_____   DATE_____

Chapter 3

Project 6
Testing your knowledge — Key Terms

Instructions: Fill in the blanks with the appropriate term from the list of terms on the right side of the page.

G 1. A _**field**_ is a unit of data within a record.

P 2. A collection of fields related to a specific unit of information is called a _**Record**_.

H 3. A _**File**_ is a collection of one or more records.

I 4. Units such as computer terminals, floppy disk readers, magnetic tape readers, and card readers which are used to present data to the processor unit are called _**input units**_.

O 5. The _**Processor unit**_ consists of the central processing unit and main computer storage.

N 6. The cathode ray tube (CRT) and printer are examples of _**output units**_.

J, A, L 7. Computers are capable of performing three basic operations: _**I/O Operation**_, _**Arith oper.**_, and _**Logical oper.**_

D 8. The ability of the computer to _**compare**_ and perform alternative operations is one of the greatest powers of a computer system.

B 9. _**Auxilary storage**_ is used to store data for subsequent use by computer programs.

K 10. A request from a terminal operator to a computer system for information is called an _**inquiry**_.

T 11. The process in which files are changed with additions, deletions, and changes to reflect the latest information is called _**updating**_.

R 12. _**Sorting**_ is the process of arranging records in ascending or descending sequence.

Q 13. The process of extracting specific types of data from a group is called _**selecting**_.

S 14. _**Summarizing**_ is the process of accumulating and printing values contained in records.

C 15. _**classifying**_ is the process of separating data into different categories according to some specification.

A. Arithmetic operations
B. Auxiliary storage
C. Classifying
D. Compare
E. Control break reporting
F. Data bank
G. Field
H. File
I. Input units
J. Input/output operations
K. Inquiry
L. Logical operations
M. Main computer storage
N. Output units
O. Processor unit
P. Record
Q. Selecting
R. Sorting
S. Summarizing
T. Updating
U. Word processing

NAME_____   DATE_____

Chapter 3
Project 7
Testing your knowledge — Definitions

Instructions: Briefly define or explain each of the following terms:

1. Field

2. Record

3. File

4. Updating

5. Sorting

6. Summarizing

7. Selecting

NAME_____   DATE_____

Chapter 3

Project 8
Testing your knowledge — True/False Questions

Instructions: Circle the T if the question is true and F if the question is false for each of the true/false questions below and on the following page.

(T) F   1. Data must be organized into logical entities called fields, records, and files for processing on a computer.

T (F)   2. A field can contain only alphabetic data.

T (F)   3. A file is made up of a number of identical fields in each record.

(T) F   4. A record is defined as a number of fields related to a specific unit of data.

T (F)   5. Files can only be stored on magnetic tape for processing on a computer system.

(T) F   6. Records may be entered into a computer system through the use of computer terminals.

(T) F   7. Input devices which provide for entering data into main computer storage include computer terminals, floppy disk readers, magnetic tape readers, and card readers.

T (F)   8. The computer program is first stored in the central processing unit and is then brought into main computer storage to process data.

(T) F   9. The computer program and data both reside in main computer storage at the same time.

(T) F 10. Data in main computer storage is processed under control of a computer program.

(T) F 11. Operations within the computer are accomplished by the electronic circuitry in the central processing unit under direction of the program.

T (F) 12. The CRT terminal can only be used as input.

(T) F 13. Within the input/process/output cycle, the basic operations that can be performed include input/output operations, arithmetic operations, and logical operations.

T (F) 14. A computer program is not required for basic input/output operations in which data is read into main storage and printed output is prepared since calculations are not performed.

(T) F 15. Looping is the process of repeating a sequence of instructions.

T (F) 16. To process 50 records, 50 sets of instructions (one set for each record) must be written and placed in main computer storage.

T (F) 17. Once data has been placed in main computer storage, the data cannot be moved; the data can be used only in calculations.

T (F) 18. Only numeric data may be recorded in main computer storage.

Testing your knowledge — True/False Questions

(T) F 19. Once numeric data has been recorded in main computer storage, it can be used in addition, subtraction, multiplication, division, and other arithmetic operations.

(T) F 20. Some modern computer systems can perform calculations in less than a millionth of a second.

(T) F 21. Basic types of comparing operations include comparing to determine if a field is equal to, less than, or greater than another field.

T **(F)** 22. Based upon the results of comparing operations, only one of two operations can be performed— the program can continue or the program can be terminated.

(T) F 23. Auxiliary storage is used to store data for subsequent use.

T **(F)** 24. Data on auxiliary storage can be printed without being temporarily stored in main computer storage.

T **(F)** 25. In word processing applications, information such as letters to be written could be stored on magnetic disk and placed in main computer storage as needed. Variable information, such as a person's name, would then be entered on a computer terminal each time that name was to appear within the letter.

(T) F 26. In a typical inquiry application, an identification code is entered on the terminal; this information is stored in main computer storage; the required data is retrieved from auxiliary storage and placed in main computer storage, and finally displayed on a terminal.

(T) F 27. Updating commonly occurs in the banking industry to reflect the current status of customers' savings accounts.

T **(F)** 28. In a banking application, a withdrawal of money from an account would not require updating of the file. Updating would occur only when deposits are made.

T **(F)** 29. Auxiliary storage is seldom required with modern computer systems because large main computer storage is sufficient for most applications.

T **(F)** 30. When using a computer, records can be arranged in ascending sequence but not descending sequence.

(T) F 31. It is the ability of the computer system to compare two values and determine if one is greater than the other that allows sorting to occur on a computer system.

T **(F)** 32. Control break reporting does not require that the input records be in any predetermined sequence before producing the desired output.

(T) F 33. Separating data into different groups according to some specification is called classifying.

(T) F 34. When summarizing, usually a single line of information is printed on a report from a group of records.

T **(F)** 35. When producing a report on a computer, each input record must be read and printed.

NAME_____ DATE_____

Chapter 3

Project 9

Testing your knowledge — Multiple-Choice Questions

Instructions: Circle the correct response to the multiple choice questions below and on the following page.

1. When data is to be processed on a computer system, it must be organized into logical entities called:

    A. Bits, bytes, and words.
    B. Letters, numbers, and words.
    C. Characters, fields, and records.
    D. Fields, records, and files. ⟵ circled

2. A reel of magnetic tape contains the names and addresses of the customers of a company. The name of a single customer is called a:

    A. Word.
    B. Field. ⟵ circled
    C. Record.
    D. File.

3. A reel of magnetic tape contains the names and addresses of the customers of a company. The name and address for one customer is called a:

    A. Word.
    B. Field.
    C. Record. ⟵ circled
    D. File.

4. A file is defined as:

    A. A group of fields.
    B. A group of records. ⟵ circled
    C. A single unit of information.
    D. A group of characters.

5. The processor unit of a computer system contains:

    A. The central processing unit, main computer storage, and auxiliary storage.
    B. The central processing unit and auxiliary storage.
    C. The central processing unit and main computer storage. ⟵ circled
    D. Main computer storage and auxiliary storage.

6. A computer terminal can be used:

    A. Only for input.
    B. Only for output.
    C. For input and output. ⟵ circled
    D. Only for communicating with the processor unit.

7. The computer program which controls the operation being performed is stored in:

    A. The central processing unit and then brought into main computer storage when needed.
    B. The central processing unit only.
    C. Main computer storage. ⟵ circled
    D. A special storage area supplementing main computer storage.

3.13

Testing your knowledge — Multiple-Choice Questions

8. When performing basic input/output operations on a computer, data is read from some input media:

   A. Into an input area, moved to an output area and is then printed.
   B. Into an input area and is then printed.
   C. Into an output area and is then printed.
   D. Into the central processing unit and is then printed.

9. The basic types of comparing operations which can be performed on a computer are:

   A. Comparing to determine if one value is equal to, less than, or greater than another value.
   B. Comparing to determine if one value is equal to or not equal to another value.
   C. Comparing to determine if one value is less than or greater than another value.
   D. Comparing to determine if one value is greater than or equal to another value.

10. Auxiliary storage is:

    A. Usually not required with modern computer systems.
    B. Used to store data for subsequent use.
    C. Used in place of main computer storage for storing and executing instructions.
    D. Part of the processor unit.

11. Inquiry into a file:

    A. Normally requires the use of auxiliary storage.
    B. Requires all records to be permanently stored in main computer storage.
    C. Does not require a processor unit because a terminal can directly access data on auxiliary storage.
    D. Does not require a computer program because inquiry is a basic function of all computer systems.

12. In many applications, sorting of data is required. Which of the following statements is true about sorting data which is to be processed on a computer?

    A. Data must be stored in some predetermined sequence on the input media prior to being sorted.
    B. Data read into main storage of a computer in an unsorted sequence can be sorted in either ascending or descending sequence.
    C. Sorting on a computer is possible because of the computer's ability to compare values and perform alternative operations based upon that comparison.
    D. Answers B and C.

13. With control break reporting:

    A. Records may be in any sequence.
    B. The input data must be sorted and grouped according to some control field prior to printing.
    C. Only selected fields are placed in main computer storage.
    D. Only selected records and totals are printed.

14. When producing a summary report:

    A. Each record is read and printed, and a final total accumulated.
    B. Only final totals are printed.
    C. Records are normally sorted according to some control field.
    D. Records are not normally sorted, but totals are printed for each group of records.

15. A report which contains all invoices with an amount of less than $20.00 is an example of:

    A. Control break reporting.
    B. Summarizing.
    C. Classifying.
    D. Selecting.

NAME_____   DATE_____

Chapter 3

Project 10

Computer Laboratory Assignment — Word Processing

Description: This project is designed to acquaint individuals with some of the basic concepts of word processing through the display of "personalized" letters to individuals interested in purchasing insurance. Three individual letters may be sent to customers. Letter 1 is a direct sales letter. Letter 2 is an answer to those responding to the direct sales letter, and letter 3 is a follow-up sales letter. The contents of the letters are illustrated below.

```
DEAR            :
    AS INFLATION INCREASES, IT IS
NECESSARY FROM TIME-TO-TIME TO EXAMINE
YOUR INSURANCE NEEDS. WE THINK,
            , THAT WE MAY HAVE
AN INSURANCE PROGRAM THAT EXACTLY FITS
THE NEEDS OF THE        FAMILY.
    I WILL BE HAPPY TO PRESENT THIS PLAN.
PLEASE RETURN THE ENCLOSED CARD. THANK
YOU,        , FOR YOUR TIME.

        SINCERELY,

        GENE COLDRUM
DEPRESS APPROPRIATE KEY TO CONTINUE?
```

LETTER 1

```
DEAR            :
    THANK YOU FOR YOUR INTEREST IN OUR
INSURANCE PLAN FOR THE
FAMILY. I WILL CONTACT YOU IN SEVERAL
DAYS,        , TO MAKE AN
APPOINTMENT.

        SINCERELY,

        GENE COLDRUM


DEPRESS APPROPRIATE KEY TO CONTINUE?
```

LETTER 2

```
DEAR            :
    I APPRECIATE VERY MUCH YOUR
HOSPITALITY DURING MY RECENT
PRESENTATION. I SINCERELY HOPE,
        , THAT THE PLAN
I SHOWED YOU WILL BE ACCEPTABLE.
    IF YOU HAVE FURTHER QUESTIONS,
PLEASE CONTACT ME.

        BEST REGARDS,

        GENE COLDRUM

DEPRESS APPROPRIATE KEY TO CONTINUE?
```

LETTER 3

Note that each letter contains from two to four blank areas to allow for the insertion of a name.

Computer Laboratory Project — Word Processing

To personalize each letter, provision is made for the program to insert the customer's name in a number of different locations within each letter. The following is an example of letter 1 that has been personalized. Note that the name Flanery has been inserted in the letter at certain predefined locations.

```
DEAR MR. FLANERY:

    AS INFLATION INCREASES, IT IS
NECESSARY FROM TIME-TO-TIME TO EXAMINE
YOUR INSURANCE NEEDS. WE THINK,
MR. FLANERY, THAT WE MAY HAVE
AN INSURANCE PROGRAM THAT EXACTLY FITS
THE NEEDS OF THE FLANERY FAMILY.
    I WILL BE HAPPY TO PRESENT THIS PLAN.
PLEASE RETURN THE ENCLOSED CARD. THANK
YOU, MR. FLANERY, FOR YOUR TIME.

            SINCERELY,

            GENE COLDRUM
DEPRESS APPROPRIATE KEY TO CONTINUE?
```

The program for this project must be loaded into main computer storage for execution. The method for accomplishing this will vary among different computer systems. After the program is placed in main computer storage, it must be executed. The method for initiating the execution of the program is also dependent upon the type of machine being used. Directions for loading and executing the program must be determined from an instructor or from the computer center. After the program is loaded into storage and is executed, the display below will appear on the terminal screen, one line at a time.

```
INTRODUCTION TO COMPUTERS AND
    DATA PROCESSING
SHELLY/CASHMAN...ANAHEIM PUBLISHING CO.
CHAPTER 3 - PROJECT 10

WORD PROCESSING

ENTER LETTER NUMBER: ?

ENTER TITLE (MR., MRS., OR MS.)
    AND LAST NAME: ?
```

The operator must then enter a letter number, an individual's title, and then the last name. Upon depressing the appropriate key, the letter will then be displayed with the name inserted in the required positions.

Computer Laboratory Project — Word Processing

Assignment 1: Letter 1 is to be sent to Mr. Roberts and Ms. Simms.
(NOTE: Steps 1 through 3 below provide detailed instructions for the completion of this assignment)

Step 1: Load and execute the program for this project. When the words ENTER LETTER NUMBER? are displayed, the number 1 should be keyed and the appropriate key to continue operation should then be depressed.

Step 2: The words ENTER TITLE (MR., MRS., OR MS.) AND LAST NAME will be displayed. The title and name, MR. ROBERTS, should be keyed, and the appropriate key depressed to continue. Letter 1 with the name MR. ROBERTS or ROBERTS will then be displayed.

Questions:

1. How many times was the name MR. ROBERTS or ROBERTS displayed within letter 1?
   Answer _____

2. Have you ever received such "personalized" letters at home in the past? Do you think this technique is a valuable sales tool for those who are not acquainted with computer generated letters?
   Comment: _____
   _____

Step 3: Repeat the operations above, generating a "personalized" letter for Ms. Simms.

Assignment 2: Generate letter 2 for Mr. Mann.

Assignment 3: Generate letter 3 for Mr. Rosinski.

Assignment 4: When the message ENTER LETTER NUMBER? appears, enter letter number 7.

Questions:

1. What message appeared on the screen? _____
   _____

2. What was the cause of the message? _____
   _____

3. What should be done to correct the error? _____
   _____

Computer Laboratory Project — Word Processing

Assignment 5: Enter letter number 1. When the words ENTER TITLE (MR., MRS., OR MS.) AND LAST NAME appear, enter the following: MISTER JAMES.

Questions:

1. What message appeared on the screen? _____

   _____

2. What should be done to correct the error? _____

   _____

Assignment 6: Enter letter number 1. When the words ENTER TITLE (MR., MRS., OR MS.) AND LAST NAME appear, enter the following: MS. JOLLINSKIUROPCKY.

Questions:

1. What message appeared on the screen? _____

   _____

2. Why did this message appear? _____

   _____

Assignment 7: Terminate the exercise by entering letter number 4.

Questions:

What value can you see in computer-generated letters for the office? Can this technique reduce office costs? Is it ethical to "fool" the consumer into thinking an individual letter has been typed for them? Write a brief paragraph answering these questions and summarizing your reaction to word processing.

Computer Laboratory Project — Word Processing

Program Messages

The following table contains error messages that may appear when incorrect entries are keyed into the terminal and the corrective action which should be taken.

ERROR MESSAGE	CAUSE	CORRECTIVE ACTION
Invalid letter number — Re-enter Enter letter number:?	A number other than 1 to 4 was entered for the letter number	Enter a valid letter number (1, 2, 3) or 4 to terminate the project
Invalid entry — Re-enter Enter title (MR., MRS., OR MS.) and LAST NAME:?	(1) The title MR., MRS., OR MS. was not entered correctly; or (2) No name was entered; or (3) The number of characters in the last name is greater than 15; or (4) More than one space was included after the title.	Enter the title and name in the correct format.
? REDO *	An alphabetic character was entered where numeric data is required	Enter a valid numeric value
OV ERROR IN _____ *	An excessive number of characters was entered	Begin project again. Reexecute the program and enter the proper values
?EXTRA IGNORED*	A comma was entered as a part of a numeric field. Only the data to the left of the comma will be used and incorrect output will result	Ignore output and redo problem entering the correct numeric values

* These error messages are generated by the system and may vary on different computer systems.

Chapter 3
Project 11
Developing Communication Skills

Instructions: Prepare an oral or written report on one or more of the following subjects.

1. Contact a manufacturer of word processing systems. Obtain technical literature which explains how the word processing systems operate. Give an oral report to class explaining the operation of the system.

2. Contact the local bank and inquire how they are using computer systems for updating checking or savings accounts. Report your findings to the class.

3. Contact the local police department to determine if they are using computers for making inquiries into files of any type. Report your findings to the class.

4. Visit your local department store and determine if they are using computer terminals for credit verification or approval. Write a brief report describing how the credit approval system operates.

5. Prepare a list of applications where an inquiry into a file through the use of a computer system might be valuable.

6. Visit a local installation and obtain a copy of a report illustrating one or more of the following: 1) Control breaks; 2) Summarizing; 3) Classifying; 4) Selecting. Present the report to the class and explain how the information is contained on the report.

7. Visit a local travel bureau that uses computer reservation systems. Determine the types of processing they perform using the computer and report back to the class.

8. Visit an airport and ask to view the manner in which inquiries and updates are made in order to make flight reservations and seating assignments. If possible, obtain some of the documents which are used for making the reservations and seat assignments. Present these documents to the class and explain how they are used.

9. Sorting is commonly performed for many different types of applications. Contact a local data processing installation and ask them to tell you how sorting is used in their applications. Report your findings to the class.

10. Storing data is required for most applications. Visit a local data processing installation and determine the types of data which are stored on auxiliary storage for a typical application. Make an oral report to the class on what you found.

Chapter 3
Answers to selected projects

Chapter 3, Project 5, Testing your knowledge — Key Terms

1. G
2. P
3. H
4. I
5. O
6. N
7. J, A, L
8. D
9. B
10. K
11. T
12. R
13. Q
14. S
15. C

Chapter 3, Project 7, Testing your knowledge — True/False Questions

1. T
2. F
3. F
4. T
5. F
6. T
7. T
8. F
9. T
10. T
11. T
12. F
13. T
14. F
15. T
16. F
17. F
18. F
19. T
20. T
21. T
22. F
23. T
24. F
25. F
26. T
27. T
28. F
29. F
30. F
31. T
32. F
33. T
34. T
35. F

Chapter 3, Project 8, Testing your knowledge — Multiple Choice Questions

1. D
2. B
3. C
4. B
5. C
6. C
7. C
8. A
9. A
10. B
11. A
12. D
13. B
14. C
15. D

Chapter 4
The Processor Unit

Chapter Objectives

- An understanding of how data is stored in main computer storage
- An understanding of the EBCDIC coding scheme
- An understanding of storing and referencing characters and fields stored in addressable main computer storage
- An understanding of the elements comprising a computer instruction and the method used by the central processing unit to execute an instruction
- An understanding of variable word length machines and fixed word length machines
- An understanding of the history, manufacture, and types of main computer storage

Chapter Overview

Chapter 4 is designed to provide an understanding of how data is stored and processed in main computer storage. It is important to understand that when data is read from an input device or from an auxiliary storage device, the data must be recorded in main computer storage of the processor unit before any processing can take place. Once data is in main computer storage, the computer system, under the control of a computer program, then processes the data to produce the required output.

The basic unit for storing data in main computer storage is the bit (binary digit). A bit, which consists of some type of electronic component, can assume one of two possible states; that is, the bit can be "on" or the bit can be "off." A combination of bits "on" and bits "off" can be used to electronically represent data in main computer storage.

One code for representing numbers, letters of the alphabet and special characters is the Extended Binary Coded Decimal Interchange Code (EBCDIC). In this coding scheme, data is represented through the use of 8 bits which together are called a byte. A byte is a storage location in which a number, letter of the alphabet, or special character can be stored.

Each byte is divided into two portions: a zone portion and a digit portion. Numeric values are represented in EBCDIC with all of the zone bits being "on," and the proper combination of bits in the digit portion of the byte being "on." It is important to understand that each byte stores only one digit; thus, a number such as decimal 10 would require two bytes to store the value.

Alphabetic data is stored in EBCDIC by a particular combination of bits in the zone and digit portions of the byte being "on."

Computers are found with as few as 4,096 bytes of storage to as many as 16 million bytes of storage. In main computer storage, each byte has a unique address associated with it; thus, data can be stored at unique locations and otherwise moved, referenced and manipulated.

Each character in an input record is stored at an adjacent, addressable location. Once a character has been stored in a location in main computer storage, it will remain there until another character is moved to the same location. When a program reads data into storage or moves data into a storage location, it will destroy what has previously been stored at that location.

A computer instruction is stored in main computer storage in exactly the same way that data is stored in main computer storage. A machine language instruction consists of: 1) An operation code; 2) Values indicating the number of characters to be processed; 3) The main storage addresses of the data to be used in the processing.

The central processing unit consists of the arithmetic/logic unit and the control unit. The arithmetic/logic unit performs the arithmetic and logic operations through its electronic circuitry, and the control unit directs and coordinates the entire computer system. When an instruction is executed in a computer system, the instruction in main computer storage is fetched by the control unit and placed in an instruction register; the data is fetched and placed in registers in the arithmetic/logic unit; the instruction is executed by the arithmetic/logic unit; and the answer is placed back in main computer storage by the control unit.

Machines where each number or letter of the alphabet is stored in main computer storage in a single addressable location are called variable word length machines. Some computer systems can store data in a fixed number of bits regardless of the size of the data. These are called fixed word length machines. Numeric values are stored in fixed word length machines as binary numbers.

Three generations of main computer storage have evolved over the last 40 years. The major types of electronic components which have been used for main computer storage are vacuum tubes, core memory, and semiconductor memory.

Random Access Memory (RAM) is used in computer systems for writing, reading, and then rewriting data in storage. Read Only Memory (ROM) has values stored in it when the memory is manufactured, and the values cannot be changed. Programmable Read Only Memory (PROM) allows the user to store data in memory prior to assembling a system. Once data is stored in PROM, it can be read — but its contents cannot be altered.

Chapter 4

Key Terms

Address That portion of a computer instruction that references the location of the data to be processed.
Addressable Storage The method used to reference data in storage by assigning a unique number to each storage location.
Arithmetic/Logic Unit (ALU) The electronic circuitry in the central processing unit that controls all arithmetic and logical operations.
Binary Digit A single bit.
Bit (Binary Digit) The smallest unit for storing data in main computer storage.
Byte A given number of bits considered as a unit to form a storage location.
Central Processing Unit Electronic components which cause processing on a computer to occur by interpreting instructions, performing calculations, moving data in main computer storage, and controlling the input/output operations. It consists of the arithmetic/logic unit and the control unit.
Control Unit That part of the central processing unit that directs and coordinates the entire computer system.
Executing Instructions The process of analyzing machine language instructions on a computer and carrying out the functions to be performed.
Extended Binary Coded Decimal Interchange Code (EBCDIC) A widely used coding system for representing data in computer storage and on auxiliary storage devices.
Fixed Word Length Computers Computers using a representation of data in main storage in which all values are stored in a fixed number of bits regardless of the size of the number.
Instruction Register An area of storage in the central processing unit where machine-language instructions are stored and analyzed prior to execution.
Instructions, Computer The unique numbers, letters of the alphabet, or special characters that, when interpreted by the computer's circuitry, cause a particular operation to be performed.
Large Scale Integration (LSI) A method of constructing electronic circuits in which many thousands of circuits can be stored on a single chip of silicon.
Memory, Programmable Read Only (PROM) A type of memory where its contents can be read but cannot be altered when used as a part of the computer system; it can be programmed by the user before being assembled as a part of the system.
Memory, Random Access (RAM) A type of storage in which data can be written into and read from the storage element.
Memory, Read Only (ROM) A type of memory in which data can be read from and used but cannot be altered.
Memory, Semiconductor A type of memory in which transistors etched on crystals of silicon are used as a storage device.
Microcomputer A computer system commonly consisting of a CRT, keyboard, and limited storage based upon a microprocessor and costing less than $10,000.00.
Microelectronics The science of creating very small electronic circuits on a thin wafer of germanium or silicon.
Microprocessor The electronic components of an entire central processing unit created on a very small single silicon chip.
Microsecond One millionth of a second.
MPU Microprocessor unit.
Nanosecond One billionth of a second.
Operand That portion of a computer instruction that commonly indicates the address of data to be processed.
Operation Code That portion of a computer instruction which indicates the operations to be performed.
Processor Unit The unit which stores the data and contains the electronic circuitry necessary to carry out the processing of the stored data. It consists of the central processing unit and main computer storage.

Key Terms

Programming, Machine-Language The writing of instructions for a computer by means of numbers, letters of the alphabet, and special characters that can be understood by the electronic circuitry.

Storage, Main Computer Electronic components which can electronically store letters of the alphabet, numbers, and special characters.

Storage, Size of Main Number of bytes comprising main storage.

Storage, Magnetic Core A widely used form of internal computer storage for many years, which consisted of very small ring-shaped pieces of material which could be magnetized in one of two directions.

Storage, Manufacture of The process of converting raw material into electronic components used to store data in the processor unit.

Storage, Vacuum Tubes One of the first methods used to store data electronically in main storage.

Variable Word Length A method of storing data in which each digit, letter of the alphabet, or special character is stored in a single storage location; the number of storage locations required will vary with the size of the field.

NAME_____ DATE_____

Chapter 4
Project 1
Representing numeric data in storage — EBCDIC

Instructions: Darken the bits that would be "on" to represent the numeric values 0 – 9 in EBCDIC.

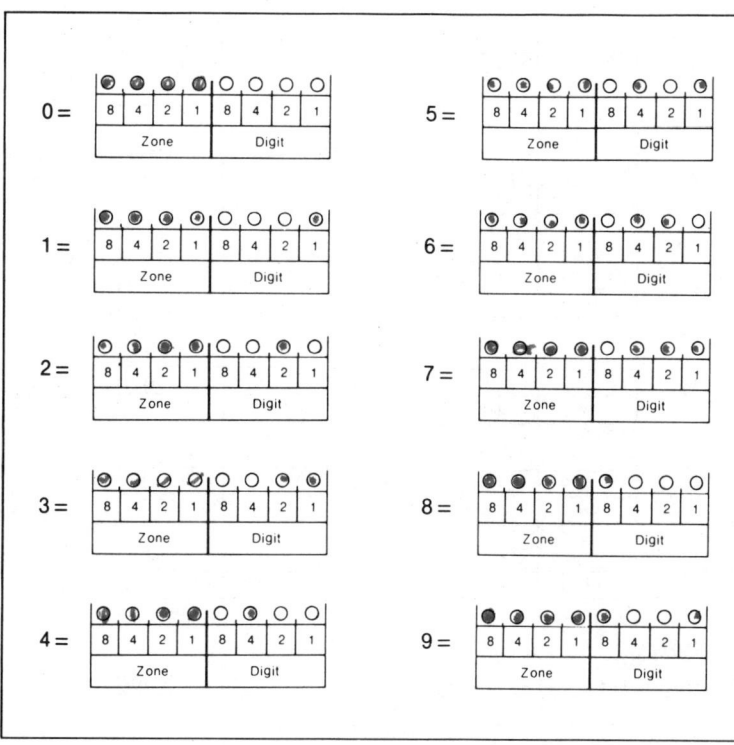

4.5

Chapter 4

Project 2
Representing alphabetic data in storage — EBCDIC

Instructions: Darken the bits that would be "on" to represent the letters of the alphabet A – Z and the indicated special characters in EBCDIC.

A = J = S = $ =

B = K = T = * =

C = L = U = ? =

D = M = V = : =

E = N = W = # =

F = O = X = @ =

G = P = Y = ' =

H = Q = Z = Blank =

I = R =

NAME_____ DATE_____

Chapter 4

Project 3

Representing numeric values in storage — EBCDIC

Instructions: Illustrate how the values displayed on the computer terminals would be recorded in storage using EBCDIC.

Problem 1:

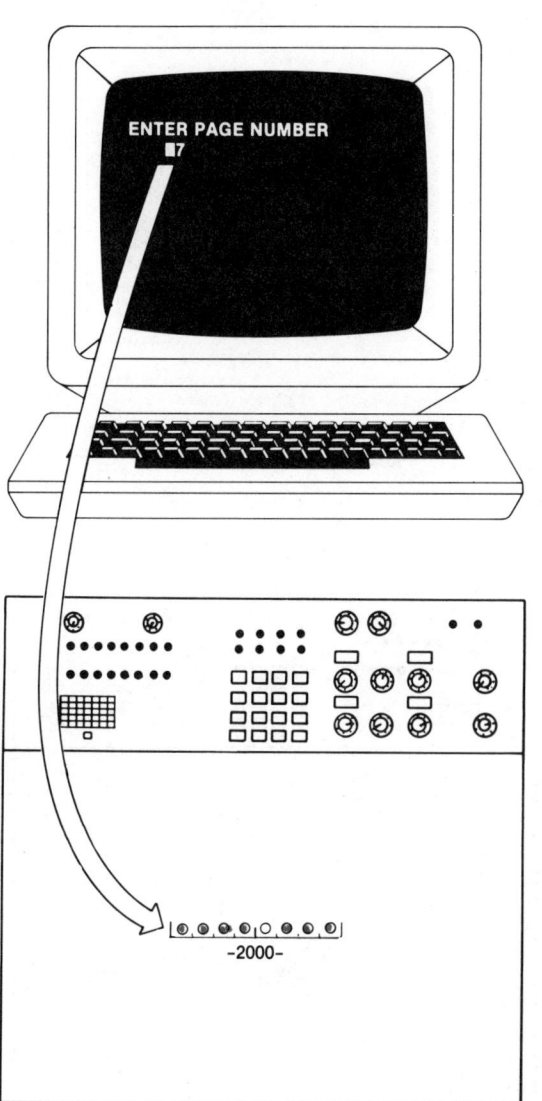

Problem 2:

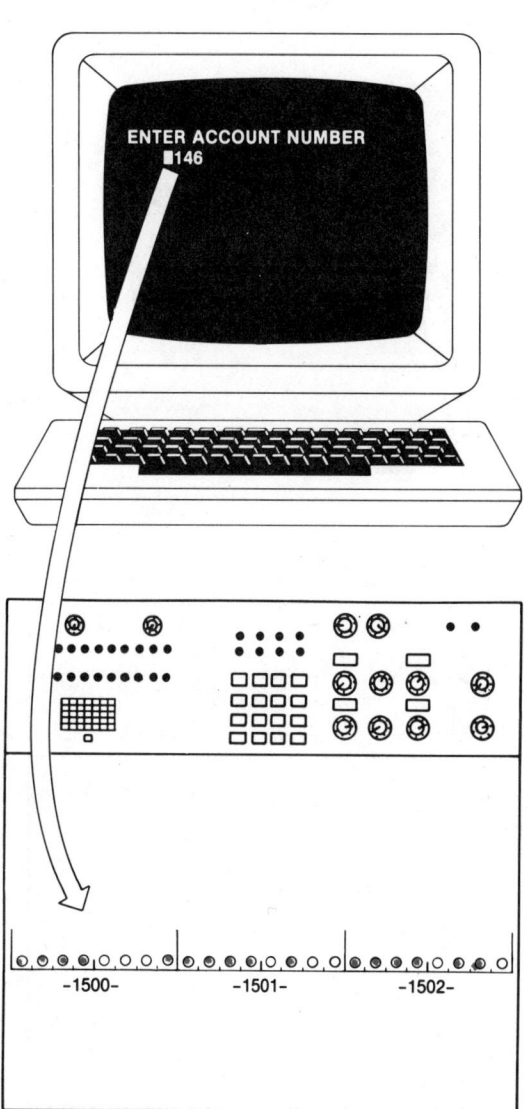

4.7

NAME_____ DATE_____

Chapter 4

Project 4

Representing alphabetic data in storage — EBCDIC

Instructions: Illustrate how the alphabetic data displayed on the computer terminals would be represented in storage using EBCDIC.

Problem 1:

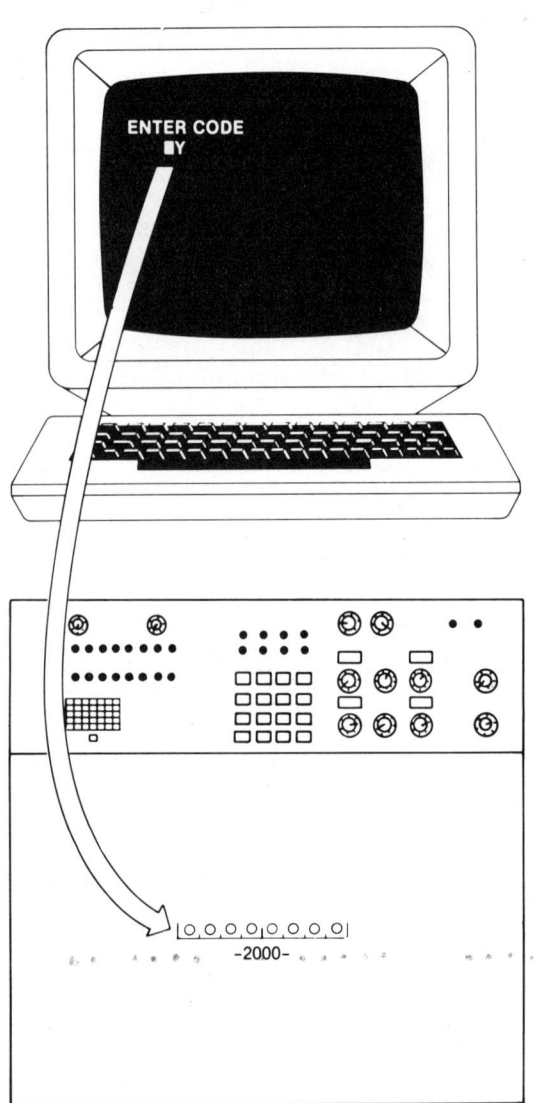

Problem 2:

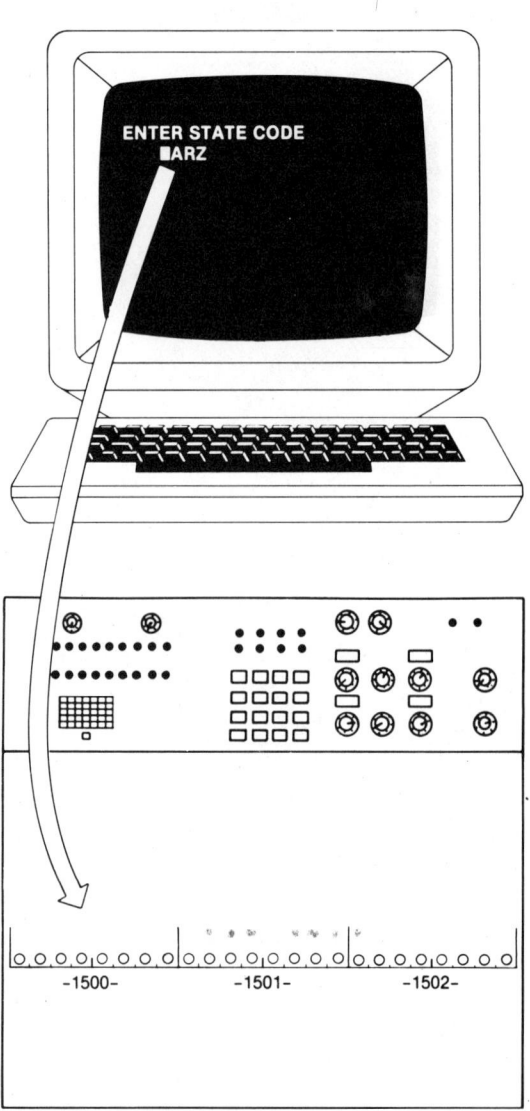

4.8

NAME_____ DATE_____

Chapter 4
Project 5
Representing data in fixed word length machines

Instructions: Illustrate how the numeric value displayed on the computer terminal would be recorded in storage in a fixed word length computer.

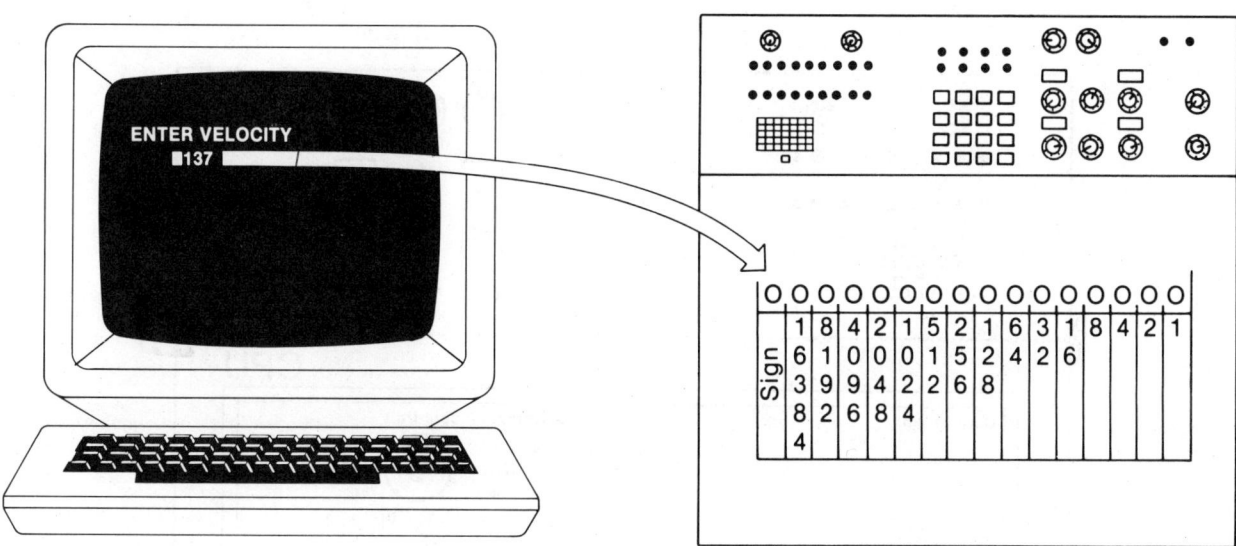

4.9

NAME_____ DATE_____

Chapter 4

Project 6
Executing instructions in a computer

Instructions: Briefly explain the steps that occur when executing a computer instruction as identified by the numbers 1, 2, 3, and 4 in the illustration below.

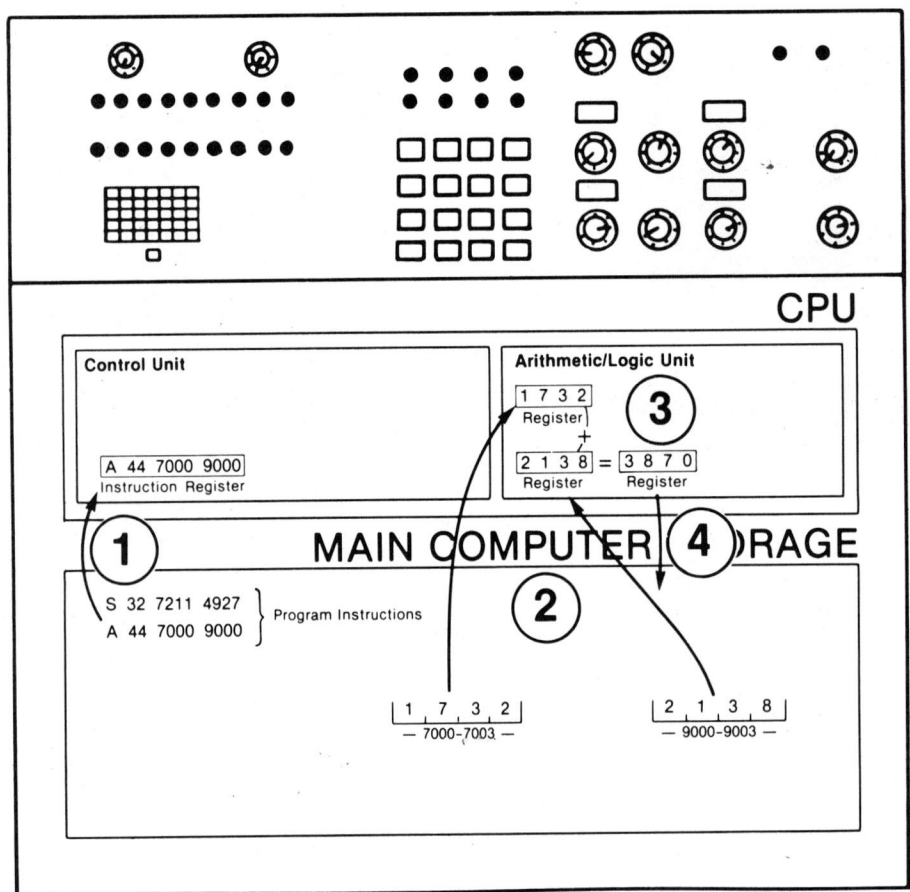

Step 1 _____

Step 2 _____

Step 3 _____

Step 4 _____

4.10

NAME _____ DATE _____

Chapter 4

Project 7
Testing your knowledge — Key Terms

Instructions: Fill in the blanks with the appropriate term from the list of terms on the right side of the page.

B 1. A _**Bit**_ is the smallest unit for storing data.

E 2. A commonly used coding scheme for representing data is _**EBCDIC**_.

C 3. The electronic component which causes processing on a computer to occur by interpreting instructions, performing calculations, moving data, and controlling input/output operations is called the _**CPU**_.

D, A 4. The central processing unit consists of the _**Control unit**_ and the _**ALU**_.

D 5. The _**Control unit**_ consists of the electronic circuitry that directs and coordinates the computer system.

A 6. The electronic circuitry in the central processing unit that controls all arithmetic and logical operations is the _**ALU**_.

R 7. In a _**Variable word length computer**_, a single character is stored in a single addressable location in main computer storage.

L 8. The _**operation code**_ is that portion of an instruction that indicates the operation to be performed.

G 9. An _**instruction register**_ is an area of storage in the central processing unit where machine language instructions are stored and analyzed prior to execution.

F 10. A computer which represents values using a fixed number of bits is called a _**fixed word length computer**_.

P 11. _**Semiconductor memory**_ is a type of memory in which transistors etched on crystals of silicon are used as a storage device.

I 12. One millionth of a second is called a _**microsecond**_.

M 13. _**PROM**_ is a type of memory where the contents can be read but cannot be altered when used as a part of a computer system; yet it can be programmed by the user before being assembled as a part of the system.

N 14. A type of memory in which data can be written into and read from is called _**RAM**_.

O 15. A type of memory in which data can be read from and used but cannot be altered is called _**ROM**_.

A. Arithmetic/Logic Unit (ALU)
B. Bit
C. Central Processing Unit
D. Control unit
E. EBCDIC
F. Fixed word length computer
G. Instruction register
H. Magnetic core
I. Microsecond
J. Millisecond
K. Nanosecond
L. Operation code
M. PROM
N. RAM
O. ROM
P. Semiconductor memory
Q. Vacuum tubes
R. Variable word length computer

4.11

NAME_____   DATE_____

Chapter 4
Project 8
Testing your knowledge — Definitions

Instructions: Briefly define or explain each of the following terms:

1. Bit

2. EBCDIC

3. Addressable storage

4. Operation code

5. Central processing unit

6. Variable word length

7. Fixed word length

8. ROM

9. RAM

NAME_____ DATE_____

Chapter 4

Project 9

Testing your knowledge — True/False Questions

Instructions: Circle the T if the question is true and F if the question is false for each of the true/false questions below and on the following page.

(T) F   1. All data read from an input device must be recorded in main computer storage prior to being processed.

(T) F   2. The basic unit for storing data in main computer storage is the bit (binary digit).

T **(F)**   3. Any digit may be represented in most computer systems by a single bit being "on" or "off."

T **(F)**   4. The extended binary coded decimal interchange code (EBCDIC) uses eight bits to represent a letter of the alphabet and four bits to represent a number.

(T) F   5. In EBCDIC, 8 bits make up a byte.

T **(F)**   6. A byte contains eight addressable storage locations.

T **(F)**   7. Numeric values are represented in EBCDIC by all bits in the zone portion of the byte being "off" and the proper binary value in the digit portion of the byte being "on."

T **(F)**   8. The value zero is represented in EBCDIC by all bits being "off."

T **(F)**   9. The value 10 is represented in EBCDIC by a bit with the place value 8 and a bit with the place value 2 being "on" in a byte.

T **(F)**   10. Special characters such as the dollar sign cannot be recorded in main computer storage because there is no way to represent the dollar sign as a series of on or off bits.

T **(F)**   11. The largest decimal value that can be read from an input record and stored in one byte with EBCDIC is the decimal value 15.

(T) F   12. Alphabetic data requires one byte to represent a character.

T **(F)**   13. A maximum of 64 individual characters can be represented in a byte.

T **(F)**   14. Typical small scale computers will contain a maximum of 80 bytes of storage.

(T) F   15. 16K bytes of storage means that there are approximately 16 thousand bytes of storage.

(T) F   16. 16 megabytes of storage means there are approximately 16 million bytes of storage.

T **(F)**   17. Each bit in main computer storage has a unique address associated with it.

(T) F   18. Once data has been recorded in main computer storage, it can be referenced by its address.

T **(F)**   19. Once a character has been stored in main computer storage, it will remain in that location until it is moved, and no other data can be recorded at that location.

4.13

Testing your knowledge — True/False Questions

T **(F)** 20. When a program reads data into storage, the data must be read into an area in which no other data is currently stored — otherwise an error will occur.

T **(F)** 21. Destructive read in refers to the process of clearing storage to blanks.

(T) F 22. A computer instruction consists of an operation code, a value indicating the number of characters to be processed by the instruction, and the address of the data to be processed.

(T) F 23. The operation code is that portion of the computer instruction that signifies the operation to be performed.

T **(F)** 24. The central processing unit consists of the arithmetic/logic unit, the control unit, and main computer storage.

T **(F)** 25. Data to be used in a calculation must be read directly into the arithmetic/logic unit of the computer for processing to occur.

(T) F 26. With variable word length machines, each number or letter of the alphabet is stored in a single addressable location.

(T) F 27. A fixed word length machine stores data, regardless of size, in a fixed number of consecutive bits in main storage.

T **(F)** 28. The value 132 in a fixed word length computer would be represented by the 1 bit, the 3 bit, and the 2 bit being "on."

T **(F)** 29. Fixed word length computers cannot be used to store alphabetic data.

(T) F 30. Fixed word length computers are commonly used in applications which require many calculations to be performed.

(T) F 31. Access to data stored in semiconductor memory is measured in nanoseconds.

T **(F)** 32. A microsecond is one one-thousandth of a second.

(T) F 33. Magnetic core storage was widely used as main computer storage at one time.

T **(F)** 34. RAM (Random Access Memory) is a form of auxiliary storage.

T **(F)** 35. ROM (Read Only Memory) is used as main computer memory in most computers systems.

NAME_____ DATE_____

Chapter 4

Project 10

Testing your knowledge — Multiple-Choice Questions

Instructions: Circle the correct response to the multiple choice questions below and on the following page.

1. All data read from an input device which is to be processed:

    A. Must first be stored on an auxiliary storage device.
    B. Must first be stored in the central processing unit.
    C. Must first be stored in the control unit.
    D. Must first be stored in main computer storage. *(circled)*

2. In the Extended Binary Coded Decimal Interchange Code (EBCDIC),:

    A. A single bit is called a byte.
    B. 4 bits are called a byte.
    C. 8 bits are called a byte. *(circled)*
    D. 16 bits are called a byte.

3. With EBCDIC, numeric values are represented by:

    A. All bits in the zone portion of the byte being "on" and the proper bits representing the numeric value in the digit portion of the byte being "on." *(circled)*
    B. All bits in the zone portion of the byte being "off" and the proper bits representing the numeric value in the digit portion of the byte being "on."
    C. The proper bits representing the numeric value in either the zone or digit portions of the byte being "on."
    D. The proper bits representing the numeric value in the zone portion of the byte being "on" and all bits in the digit portion of the byte being "off."

4. The value zero is represented in a byte in EBCDIC by:

    A. All bits being "off" in the zone portion of the byte and all bits being "on" in the digit portion of the byte.
    B. All bits being "on" in the zone portion of the byte and all bits being "on" in the digit portion of the byte.
    C. All bits being "on" in the zone portion of the byte and all bits being "off" in the digit portion of the byte. *(circled)*
    D. All bits being "off" in the zone portion of the byte and all bits being "off" in the digit portion of the byte.

5. A computer with 32,000 bytes of storage may be described as having:

    A. 32K. *(circled)*
    B. 32 megabytes.
    C. 32,000K.
    D. 320 megabytes.

6. In computer storage, a unique address is associated with:

    A. Each bit.
    B. Each byte. *(circled)*
    C. Each zone and each digit portion of the byte.
    D. The digit portion of the byte only.

4.15

Testing your knowledge — Multiple-Choice Questions

7. When a program reads data into main computer storage:

    A. The area where the data is to be stored must contain blanks.
    B. The area where the data is to be stored must contain zeros.
    C. The area where the data is to be stored must never have been previously used.
    D. The area where the data is to be stored may contain any values.

8. A computer instruction commonly consists of:

    A. A number which tells the computer the operation to be performed.
    B. An operation code and an entry signifying the type of input device used.
    C. An operation code, a value indicating the number of characters to be processed, and the address of the data to be processed.
    D. An operation code, an entry signifying the type of data to be processed (alphabetic or numeric), and the address of the data.

9. The central processing unit consists of:

    A. The arithmetic/logic unit and the control unit.
    B. Main computer storage and the control unit.
    C. An instruction register and main computer storage.
    D. An instruction register and auxiliary storage.

10. A variable word length machine stores a single character:

    A. In a single addressable location.
    B. In 16 or 32 consecutive bits in main computer storage.
    C. In a single bit.
    D. In a variable number of bits depending upon the size of the number.

11. In a fixed word length computer,:

    A. Each number is stored as a binary value regardless of size.
    B. Each number requires a single byte of storage.
    C. Processing of alphabetic data is not possible.
    D. Answers A and C.

12. Which of the following has not been used as main computer storage?

    A. Vacuum tubes.
    B. Magnetic cores.
    C. Magnetic disk.
    D. Semiconductors.

13. Access time for semiconductor memory is measured in:

    A. Milliseconds.
    B. Microseconds.
    C. Tenths of a second.
    D. Nanoseconds.

14. One form of main computer storage used in microcomputers when storing and processing data is called:

    A. CORE.
    B. ROM.
    C. PROM.
    D. RAM.

4.16

Chapter 4
Project 11
Computer Laboratory Assignment — The Sorting of Records Using a Computer

Description: One of the more burdensome and time-consuming clerical tasks is the sorting of company records. This project is designed to illustrate the capability of the computer to sort records rapidly and accurately in numerical or alphabetical order. Input records which contain a store number, account number, customer number, balance due, and date due will be used to illustrate sorting procedures. These input records are illustrated below.

STORE NUMBER	ACCOUNT NUMBER	CUSTOMER NAME	BALANCE DUE	DATE DUE
25272	263271	JOHNSON	271.54	04/15
25271	262179	JENSOHN	254.36	04/05
25252	315720	HARRVEY	253.59	04/14

A sort program will be used to allow the sorting of these records by store number, account number, customer name, balance due, or date due at the option of the computer terminal operator.

Assignment 1: Analyze the input records in the chart above and manually sort the records in sequence by store number. Record the contents of each of the fields in the chart below after the records are sorted.

STORE NUMBER	ACCOUNT NUMBER	CUSTOMER NAME	BALANCE DUE	DATE DUE

Computer Laboratory Project — The sorting of records using a computer

Assignment 2: The program for this project must be loaded into main computer storage for execution. The method for accomplishing this will vary among different computer systems. After the program is placed in main computer storage, it must be executed. The method for initiating the execution of the program is also dependent upon the type of machine being used. Directions for loading and executing the program must be determined from an instructor or from the computer center. Load the program for the computer laboratory project for Chapter 4 into storage and execute the program. The following display will appear on the terminal. A display of this type is called a "menu" and allows the operator to choose the function to be performed.

```
INTRODUCTION TO COMPUTERS AND
    DATA PROCESSING
SHELLY/CASHMAN...ANAHEIM PUBLISHING CO.
CHAPTER 4 - PROJECT 11
SORTING

SORTING MENU:  1 - SORT ON STORE NUMBER
               2 - SORT ON ACCOUNT NUMBER
               3 - SORT ON NAME
               4 - SORT ON BALANCE
               5 - SORT ON PAYMENT DATE
               6 - RANDOM SORT REQUEST
               7 - END PROGRAM

ENTER MENU SELECTION: ?
```

By entering a number 1 through 7, the appropriate sorting function will be performed. After entering the desired number and depressing the appropriate key, the records before they have been sorted and the records after they have been sorted will be displayed.

Enter the proper number to cause the records to be sorted by Store Number and answer the following questions.

Questions:

1. What is the first record in the file displayed on the terminal after the file has been sorted?

STORE	CUSTOMER	NAME	BALANCE	DATE

2. What is the last record in the file displayed on the terminal after the file has been sorted?

STORE	CUSTOMER	NAME	BALANCE	DATE

3. Have the records been properly sorted by Store Number?

Computer Laboratory Project — The sorting of records using a computer

Assignment 3: Enter the proper number to cause the records to be sorted in alphabetical order by name and answer the following questions.

Questions:

1. What are the names of the first three customers displayed on the terminal?

   _____

   _____

   _____

2. Have the records been sorted in alphabetical order by name?

   _____

Assignment 4: Enter the proper number to cause the records to be sorted on the Balance field and answer the following questions.

Questions:

1. Which customer has the lowest balance? Name _____

   Balance _____

2. Which customer has the highest balance? Name _____

   Balance _____

Assignment 5: By entering a 6, a series of input records will be displayed that can be sorted on any given position.

   Step 1: Enter the value 6 to cause the random sort request to be implemented. Sort the records beginning with column 19 and ending with column 24.

Questions:

1. What value is contained in column 8 of the last record after the records are sorted? _____

2. What values are contained in columns 28 – 30 after the records have been sorted? _____

   Step 2: Enter the value 6 to cause the random sort request to be implemented and then sort the records on various positions to observe the capabilities of the computer sorting program.

Computer Laboratory Project — The sorting of records using a computer

Program Messages

The following table contains error messages that may appear when incorrect entries are keyed into the terminal and the corrective action which should be taken.

ERROR MESSAGE	CAUSE	CORRECTIVE ACTION
INVALID ENTRY-REENTER ENTER MENU SELECTION:?	A numeric value other than 1-7 was entered	Enter a VALUE 1-7 to select the proper function from the menu
?REDO*	A non numeric character was entered when performing menu selection OR A non numeric character was entered when a request for beginning or ending column number was displayed for the random sort	Enter a VALUE 1-7 to select the proper function from the menu OR Enter a valid beginning or ending column number
INVALID COLUMN-REENTER ENTER BEGINNING COLUMN:?	An invalid column number was entered during random sort request	Enter a valid column number
INVALID COLUMN-REENTER ENTER ENDING COLUMN:?	An invalid column number was entered during random sort request	Enter a valid column number
OV ERROR IN _____ *	An excessive number of characters was entered	Begin project again. Reexecute the program and enter the proper values
?EXTRA IGNORED*	A comma was entered as a part of a numeric field. Only the data to the left of the comma will be used and incorrect output will result	Ignore output and redo problem entering the correct numeric values

* These error messages are generated by the system and may vary on different computer systems.

Chapter 4

Project 12
Developing Communication Skills

Instructions: Prepare an oral or written report on one or more of the following subjects.

1. Through library research, obtain a list of manufacturers of computer memory or circuit chips. Write to one or more of the companies to see if you can obtain a "free" sample of a memory chip or circuit board used in a computer. Share the results with the class.

2. Obtain a copy of a personal computing magazine. Research the advertisements to determine the cost of 16K of memory and 32K of memory. Report your findings to the class.

3. Contact Radio Shack and determine the cost of a 4K microcomputer; A 16K microcomputer; A 32K microcomputer. Report your findings to the class.

4. Contact a local computer store selling microcomputers. Write a brief report describing the largest system available. Include the cost of the system and the size of main computer storage.

5. Contact a minicomputer manufacturer such as Digital Equipment, Data General, or Hewlett Packard. Prepare a report describing the smallest system available and the largest system available. Include the cost of the systems and the size of main computer storage available for each.

6. Contact a manufacturer of large mainframes such as IBM, Sperry Univac, or Control Data. Obtain a description of their largest system. Prepare a report summarizing some of its characteristics. Include in the report the cost of the system and the size of main computer storage.

7. Prepare a research report on the future of main computer storage.

8. Research the cost of main computer storage from 1960 to the present. Bring to class documentation specifying the cost of main computer storage in 1960 and the current cost of main computer storage on typical systems.

9. Contact a sales representative from a microcomputer, minicomputer, or large mainframe computer company and ask them to explain their products to the class.

Chapter 4
Answers to selected projects

Chapter 4, Project 7, Testing your knowledge — Key Terms

1. B	4. D, A	7. R	10. F	13. M
2. E	5. D	8. L	11. P	14. N
3. C	6. A	9. G	12. I	15. O

Chapter 4, Project 9, Testing your knowledge — True/False Questions

1. T	8. F	15. T	22. T	29. F
2. T	9. F	16. T	23. T	30. T
3. F	10. F	17. F	24. F	31. T
4. F	11. F	18. T	25. F	32. F
5. T	12. T	19. F	26. T	33. T
6. F	13. F	20. F	27. T	34. F
7. F	14. F	21. F	28. F	35. F

Chapter 4, Project 10, Testing your knowledge — Multiple Choice Questions

1. D	4. C	7. D	10. A	13. D
2. C	5. A	8. C	11. A	14. D
3. A	6. B	9. A	12. C	

Chapter 5
Input to the Computer System

Chapter Objectives

- An understanding of the differences between batch processing systems and transaction-oriented processing systems
- An understanding of punched cards, magnetic tape, and magnetic disk as input media for batch processing systems
- An understanding of dumb and intelligent terminals as input devices for transaction-oriented processing systems
- An understanding of the processing cycles for batch processing systems and transaction-oriented processing systems
- An appreciation of and introduction to the need for editing input data prior to processing the data on computer systems

Chapter Overview

Chapter 5 is designed to provide an overview of the means for providing input to a computer system. In any data processing application, input must occur before any data can be processed and any information can be produced on a computer system.

There are two basic systems used when entering data into a computer. Transaction-oriented systems provide for the entering of data directly into main computer storage for immediate processing. In batch processing systems, source documents which contain the data to be processed are gathered together as a group, and the data is converted to some input medium that will allow the processing of the data as a group.

For many years, a widely used form of input has been the punched card. The punched card contains 80 positions in which numbers, letters of the alphabet or special characters can be recorded. Data to be recorded on the card is placed in predetermined card columns called fields. A device called the keypunch is used to punch holes in the card. To ensure the accuracy of the transfer of data from the source document to the punched cards, a process called verification is used. When verifying data that has been punched, the operator places the cards that have just been punched in a verifier and rekeys the data. As the data is rekeyed, it is compared to the data already punched in the cards. If an error is detected, the machine stops and an error indication is made.

To read cards into the processor unit, a card reader is used. Card readers typically read 200 – 1200 cards per minute. As cards are bulky and cannot be reused, they are being replaced by magnetic tape and magnetic disk as a form of input.

Some input devices record data on magnetic tape instead of punched cards. Magnetic tape as input provides faster reading, easier handling, and is reusable and more economical than punched cards. Other types of modern input devices use floppy disk and magnetic disk to record the data.

For large data entry tasks, key-to-disk shared processor systems are used. With these systems, a number of keyboard consoles are connected through a minicomputer to a large disk storage unit. As data is keyed at the various stations, it is stored on the disks under control of the minicomputer. The data is normally transferred from disks to magnetic tape for processing. Such systems improve productivity, provide for data editing, provide for commonly used fields to be retrieved automatically, and allow statistics to be kept on productivity through the use of the minicomputer. Such systems are expensive and practical only where there are large volumes of data to be recorded.

When processing input data, the data is processed using either local job entry or remote job entry. With local job entry, the input reading devices are located in the computer center. With remote job entry, the input reading devices may be located at some remote site.

With increasingly great frequency, transaction-oriented systems are being used. With these systems, data to be processed is not transcribed onto a machine-readable medium prior to processing. Instead, the data is entered directly into main computer storage for immediate processing. The cathode ray tube (CRT) terminal is frequently used in a transaction-oriented processing system. Some terminals are called "intelligent" because incorporated within the terminal is processing power.

All data being entered into a computer system should be edited to ensure that it is valid. Common tests to edit data include tests to ensure that data is numeric or alphabetic as required, reasonableness tests, consistency tests, and tests to detect transcription and transposition errors.

There are a variety of special input devices. These include optical character readers (OCR) and magnetic ink character recognition devices (MICR). Point of sale terminals are frequently used in retail establishments to capture data at its source; and in the factory, there are a number of data collection input devices that allow data to be captured in an uncontrolled environment. Other types of input include voice input, digitizers, and light pens that allow data to be entered from the face of a CRT.

Chapter 5

Key Terms

Bar Codes Vertical marks or bars on prerecorded tags which can be sensed and read by a machine. The width and combination of vertical lines are used to represent data.

Batch Processing The accumulation and processing of data as a group.

Card Reader A device capable of reading the data stored in a punched card and transmitting it to main computer storage.

Cathode Ray Tube Terminal A device used as a computer terminal which contains a television-like screen for displaying data. Most CRT terminals also have a typewriter-like keyboard.

Check Digit A calculated digit appended to a numeric field to assure validity when referenced in the future.

Data Collection Those operations to obtain data in an uncontrolled environment from those doing the work being reported on.

Data Entry The process of preparing data in some machine-processable form or entering data directly into a computer system.

Data Entry Department The department where data is prepared for processing on a computer system.

Digitizer A data entry device which can scan images and transmit those images as digital impulses to a computer.

Editing Input Data The process of checking to assure the validity of input data.

Field A unit of data within a record.

Floppy Disk An oxide-coated plastic disk about 8" in diameter enclosed in a protective covering that can be used for magnetically storing data.

Floppy Disk Reader A device which can read data stored on a floppy disk.

GIGO Garbage in, garbage out.

Hollerith Code The coding system used to record data on punched cards.

Input Data used for processing on a computer system.

Input Errors Errors that occur when data is converted to a machine-readable form or when data is entered into the computer for processing.

Input/Processing/Output The sequence of events that occurs when data is processed on a computer system.

Input Units Units that are a part of a computer system which present data to the processor unit for processing.

Intelligent Computer Terminal A terminal with the ability to process data using the electronic components within the terminal without the need to access the power of a large computer.

Keypunch A device used to punch holes in cards.

Key-to-Disk Shared Processor System A data entry system in which multiple key stations are used to enter source data into a minicomputer for storage on disk.

Key-to-Diskette A data entry device used to manually record data onto a floppy disk.

Key-to-Tape Data Recorder A data entry device used to manually record data onto magnetic tape.

Light Pen A device which allows data to be entered or altered on the face of a CRT terminal.

Magnetic Ink Character Recognition (MICR) A method used in the banking industry for encoding checks and other documents using a magnetic ink that can be sensed.

Minicomputer A computer system which has smaller computer storage, slower processing speeds, and lower cost than large computer systems.

Optical Character Recognition (OCR) The reading of data by scanning the location or shape of the data on a document.

Optical Scanning Devices Devices that read or otherwise sense data on forms for processing on a computer.

Point of Sale Terminals (POS) Terminals placed at locations where business transactions occur.

Punched Cards A piece of lightweight cardboard capable of storing data in the form of punched holes recorded in predefined locations.

Key Terms

Remote Job Entry Entering jobs in a batch processing system at a location remote from the central computer site.

Tape, Magnetic A ½" wide piece of mylar on which data can be stored electronically. Typical lengths for tape are 600 feet, 1200 feet, and 2400 feet.

Terminal, Dumb A terminal that is used to accept keyed data and transmit that data to a computer with no other processing capabilities.

Terminal, Hard Copy A computer terminal that can produce printed output.

Transaction-Oriented Processing System That type of system in which data is entered into the computer at the time the transaction occurs.

Universal Product Code A code placed on many consumer products to facilitate check out at retail stores.

Verifier A machine used to check the accuracy of cards by rekeying the data which has already been punched.

Voice Input A device that allows vocal input to be accepted and interpreted in a form processable by a computer.

Chapter 5

Project 1
Processing data in a batch processing system

Instructions: The following diagram illustrates the steps that occur when processing data in a batch processing system. Briefly explain each of the steps labeled 1 - 6 in the space provided.

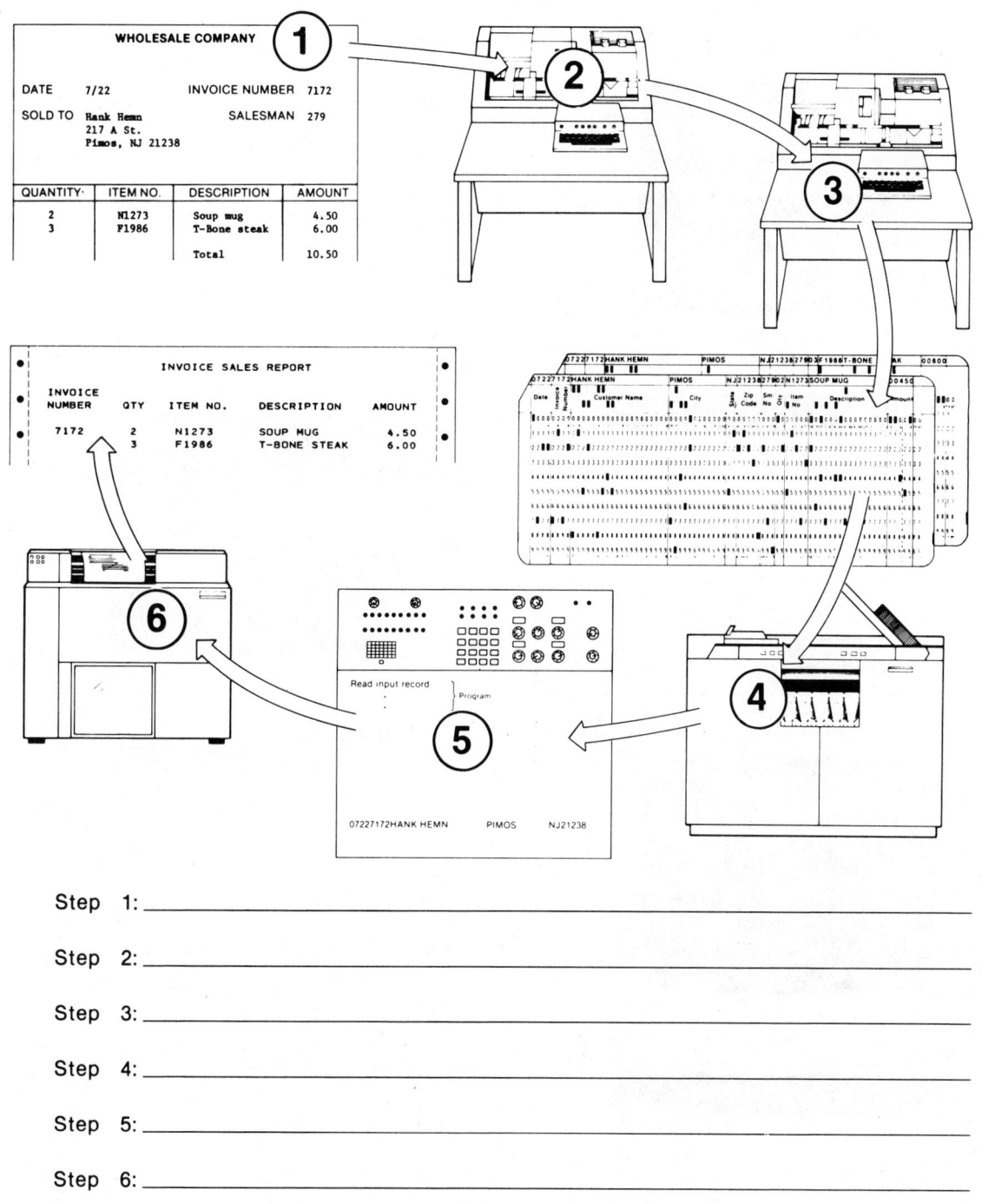

Step 1: _____

Step 2: _____

Step 3: _____

Step 4: _____

Step 5: _____

Step 6: _____

NAME_____ DATE_____

Chapter 5

Project 2

Processing data in a transaction-oriented system

Instructions: The diagram below illustrates the processing steps that occur in a transaction-oriented processing system. Briefly explain each of the steps labeled 1 – 3 in the space provided.

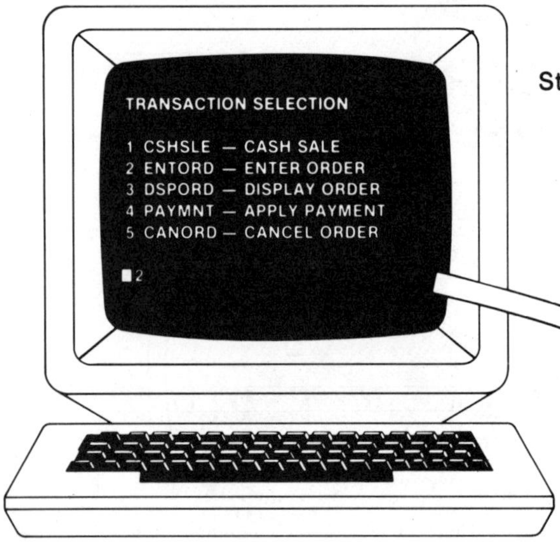

TRANSACTION SELECTION

1 CSHSLE — CASH SALE
2 ENTORD — ENTER ORDER
3 DSPORD — DISPLAY ORDER
4 PAYMNT — APPLY PAYMENT
5 CANORD — CANCEL ORDER

■2

ENTER ORDER INFORMATION

CUSTOMER P.O. R1119
ORDER CLERK: 15
ORDER DATE: 01-09-80
SHIP TO:
  ADDRESS ACE PAINTS
               111 PINE ST
  CITY/STATE: LAKE, CA
  ZIP 90808

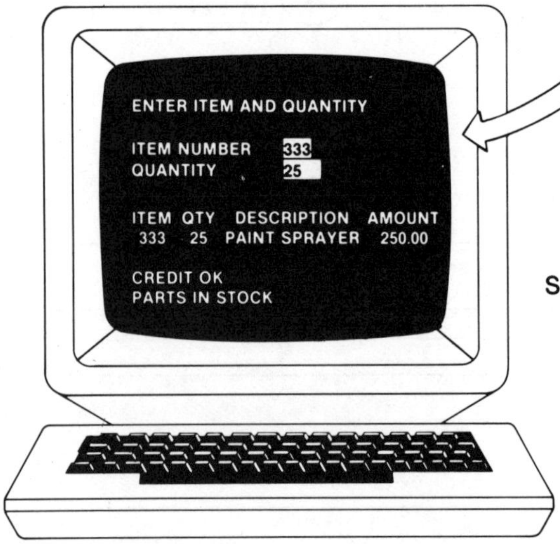

ENTER ITEM AND QUANTITY

ITEM NUMBER 333
QUANTITY 25

ITEM QTY DESCRIPTION AMOUNT
333   25   PAINT SPRAYER   250.00

CREDIT OK
PARTS IN STOCK

Step 1: _____

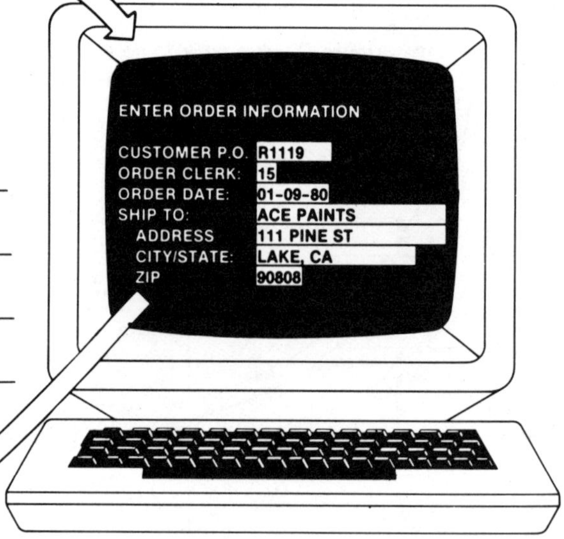

Step 2: _____

Step 3: _____

5.6

NAME _____ DATE _____

Chapter 5

Project 3
Testing your knowledge — Key Terms

Instructions: Fill in the blanks with the appropriate term from the list of terms on the right side of the page.

1. (P) A _transaction oriented system_ is that type of system in which data is entered into the computer at the time the transaction occurs.

2. (B) The processing of data as a group is called _batch processing_.

3. (H) The coding system used on punched cards is called the _Hollerith code_.

4. (J) A _keypunch_ is the input device used to record data on punched cards.

5. (R) A machine used to check punched cards by rekeying data which is already punched is called a _verifier_.

6. (O) A data entry system which uses multiple key stations connected to a minicomputer is called a _shared processor system_.

7. (F) A computer terminal with no internal processing power within the terminal itself is called a _dumb terminal_.

8. (I) A computer terminal with processing power within the terminal is called an _intelligent terminal_.

9. (N) The method of entering jobs in a batch environment at some location distant from the main processor unit is called _remote job entry_.

10. (G) The process of checking to assure the validity of input data is called input _editing_.

11. (E) A _digitizer_ is an input device which can scan images and transmit those images as digital impulses to a computer.

12. (K) A method used in the banking industry for encoding checks and other documents using magnetic ink to provide a method of input is called _MICR_.

13. (L) _OCR_ is the process of reading data by scanning the shape of characters on a document.

14. (M) Terminals which are frequently used in retail stores to capture data at the location where the business transaction occurs are called _point of sale terminals_.

15. (C) The process of capturing input data in an uncontrolled environment, often in factories or warehouses, is called _data collection_.

A. Bar code
B. Batch processing
C. Data collection
D. Data recorder
E. Digitizer
F. Dumb terminal
G. Editing
H. Hollerith Code
I. Intelligent terminal
J. Keypunch
K. MICR
L. OCR
M. Point of sale terminals
N. Remote job entry
O. Shared processor system
P. Transaction-oriented system
Q. Universal product code
R. Verifier

NAME_____ DATE_____

Chapter 5
Project 4
Testing your knowledge — Definitions

Instructions: Briefly define or explain each of the following terms:

1. Batch processing

2. Dumb terminal

3. Editing

4. Hollerith code

5. Intelligent terminal

6. Keypunch

7. Key-to-disk shared processor system

8. MICR

9. OCR

10. Transaction-oriented processing system

NAME_____ DATE_____

Chapter 5

Project 5
Testing your knowledge — True/False Questions

Instructions: Circle the T if the question is true and F if the question is false for each of the true/false questions below and on the following page.

T **(F)** 1. In a batch processing system, data is usually entered directly into a computer by means of a computer terminal as a transaction occurs.

T **(F)** 2. In a transaction-oriented system, the data is gathered together in a group and entered directly into the computer as a single transaction.

T **(F)** 3. The best method to detect errors in input data is by reviewing the output report and comparing the report to source documents.

T **(F)** 4. The punched card was developed in the 1940's by Dr. Herman Hollerith for use as input to computer systems.

(T) F 5. The most widely used form of the punched card can store 80 characters.

T **(F)** 6. A maximum of 40 letters of the alphabet can be recorded on a punched card because a letter of the alphabet requires both a zone and a digit punch.

(T) F 7. Numeric data on a punched card is recorded by a single punch in a given card column.

T **(F)** 8. The length of a field, such as an amount field, will vary from record to record when recorded on a punched card because the number of characters punched is based upon the number of digits on the source document.

T **(F)** 9. Special characters are normally recorded on a punched card just as they are to appear on the printed output.

T **(F)** 10. The placement of the fields on a punched card is determined by the data entry operator who is recording the data. *identified by columns*

(T) F 11. The device used to record data on a punched card is called a keypunch.

T **(F)** 12. The only way to assure the accuracy of punching on a card is by visual verification.

(T) F 13. To read the holes in a punched card, card readers operating in the range of 200 – 1200 cards per minute are used.

(T) F 14. It is estimated that as much as 40% of the budget in some data processing installations is dedicated to data entry.

T **(F)** 15. Card readers operating at 1,000 cards per minute far surpass the ability of the computer to accept the data in main computer storage.

T **(F)** 16. Although punched cards are a relatively slow and bulky form of input, their use as an input medium has continued to increase.

Testing your knowledge — True/False Questions

T F 17. One of the first major efforts to replace punched cards was the development of a data recorder in which data was manually keyed and stored on magnetic tape.

T F 18. Key-to-tape data recorders have several significant advantages over punched cards — tape can be read into main computer storage faster than punched cards, and tape has a higher density than punched cards.

T **F** 19. Most data entry today is accomplished utilizing key-to-tape units.

T **F** 20. Key-to-diskette input devices have the same basic disadvantage as punched cards; that is, once data is recorded on the diskette, it cannot be reused.

T **F** 21. The key-to-diskette system has not gained wide acceptance as a replacement for the keypunch, even though operating characteristics are similar.

T F 22. With key-to-diskette data entry systems, a diskette can store nearly 2,000 card records.

T **F** 23. A disadvantage of the key-to-diskette data entry system is that diskette reading devices are much more expensive than punched card readers.

T **F** 24. One of the most widely used forms of data entry for a transaction-oriented processing system is the key-to-disk shared processor system.

T F 25. One of the most advanced types of data entry devices is the key-to-disk shared processor system in which data is keyed from multiple key stations under control of a minicomputer and stored on magnetic disk.

T F 26. In many key-to-disk shared processor systems, the data on the disk is transferred to magnetic tape prior to being read into the computer.

T **F** 27. Card readers cannot be used as remote job entry stations.

T **F** 28. A "dumb" computer terminal refers to a terminal that is not yet connected to the main processor unit.

T F 29. Intelligent terminals contain a microprocessor and have the ability to process data at the terminal site without the necessity of sending the data to the main computer.

T **F** 30. The difficulty in using computer terminals is that there is no way to edit the input data prior to having the data enter main computer storage for processing.

T F 31. Common editing of input data includes tests to ensure that a field contains only numeric or alphabetic data; reasonableness tests; range tests; and tests for consistency.

T **F** 32. In a transaction-oriented processing system, input editing can only occur if the system contains an intelligent terminal.

T F 33. In OCR systems, the three methods of recording data on the document to be read are: optically readable marks; bar codes; and optically readable characters.

T F 34. Point of sale terminals (POS) are widely used in retail stores to enter data into a computer.

T **F** 35. The ability to speak into a computer system and have the vocal response understood by the computer has not yet been practically implemented in a business environment.

NAME_____   DATE_____

Chapter 5

Project 6
Testing your knowledge — Multiple-Choice Questions

Instructions: Circle the correct response to the multiple choice questions below and on the following page.

1. The type of system in which data is entered directly into main computer storage for immediate processing as the transaction occurs is called:

    A. Local job entry.
    B. Remote job entry.
    C. Transaction-oriented processing.
    D. Batch processing.

2. The punched card can store:

    A. 80 alphabetic or special characters only.
    B. 80 numeric, alphabetic, or special characters.
    C. 80 numeric or alphabetic characters, but no special characters.
    D. 80 numeric characters only.

3. Which of the following best describes the data that would be found on a punched card:

    A. Special characters are not usually found on a punched card.
    B. The decimal point must be recorded on a punched card to allow for decimal alignment.
    C. The dollar sign must be punched on a card if it is to print on a report.
    D. Special characters are normally punched on a card as they appear on the source document.

4. To machine-verify data recorded on a punched card:

    A. The cards must be read into the computer using the card reader.
    B. The cards must be listed on a computer and the output compared to the source document.
    C. The cards are punched twice and searched for double punches to detect inaccurate punching.
    D. The punched cards are placed in a machine called a verifier and the data is rekeyed to detect errors in punching.

5. The advantage of key-to-tape data entry systems as compared to punched cards is that:

    A. Tape can be read into the computer faster than punched cards.
    B. Data can be stored on tape at a greater density than holes in a punched card.
    C. Tape is not as bulky as punched cards.
    D. All of the above.

6. In a key-to-disk shared processor system:

    A. Data is keyed onto disks from multiple key stations under control of a minicomputer. Data on the disk is then processed by the minicomputer to produce the desired output reports.
    B. Data is keyed from multiple stations and stored on individual disks associated with each station.
    C. Data is keyed onto disk from multiple key stations under control of a minicomputer. Data on the disk is then transferred to magnetic tape for processing by the main computer.
    D. Data is keyed into a minicomputer from multiple keystations and processed.

7. Remote job entry refers to:

    A. Preparing input data to be processed in a decentralized data entry department.
    B. Using a computer terminal as a stand-alone computer system.
    C. Inputting data using vocal input through a standard telephone.
    D. Inputting data to a computer system through the use of a card reader or other input device from some remote location using cables or other communications lines.

5.11

Testing your knowledge — Multiple-Choice Questions

8. The primary difference between a "dumb" terminal and an "intelligent" terminal is that the intelligent terminal:

    A. Is directly connected to a minicomputer.
    B. Provides prompting that makes the terminal easy for a nontechnical person to operate.
    C. Has preprogrammed routines built into the hardware to perform input editing of the data as it is keyed into the system.
    D. Has a microprocessor built into the terminal to allow some processing to occur at the terminal.

9. Input editing in a transaction-oriented system with intelligent terminals usually:

    A. Occurs at the terminal site when the data is entered into the terminal.
    B. Occurs within the main computer after data has been keyed and transferred to main storage.
    C. Occurs after the data has been processed on the main computer system.
    D. Occurs when the source documents are reviewed by a control clerk.

10. A terminal operator enters 7765 instead of 7675. An error is detected. This is an example of editing for:

    A. Numeric data.
    B. Transposition. *2 #s are switched*
    C. Consistency.
    D. Reasonableness.

11. The input method used by the banking industry for encoding checks using magnetic ink with machine-readable characters is called:

    A. OCR.
    B. MICR.
    C. UPC.
    D. POS.

12. OCR stands for:

    A. Output character recognition.
    B. Optical character response.
    C. Optical character recognition.
    D. On line character recognition.

13. The codes placed on many consumer products that are optically scanned are called:

    A. OCR.
    B. MICR.
    C. UPC. *universal product code.*
    D. POS.

14. Point-of-sale terminals are usually found in:

    A. Retail stores.
    B. Data entry departments.
    C. Computer centers.
    D. Banks.

15. Vocal input to a computer:

    A. Will never be possible because each person's voice is different.
    B. Is possible but considered to be too costly to have practical application in business.
    C. Has found limited use in some university research centers but as yet has no commercial value.
    D. Is currently feasible and used for some applications.

NAME_____   DATE_____

Chapter 5

Project 7
Computer Laboratory Project — Transaction-Oriented Data Entry

---

Description: This project is designed to acquaint individuals with transaction-oriented data entry. The project consists of entering orders in an order-entry system. The customers and the items which they order will be placed in a data base within the program when an order is entered.

The valid customers for the company using this order entry system and their respective customer numbers are:

Customer Number	Company Name
2673	Aeroflight Co.
3198	Cramer Tools Inc.
4107	Dynamics, Inc.
6439	Dynamite Parts Co.
7718	Elliason Electronics

The items which can be ordered and their item numbers are:

Item Number	Description
2371	Drill Bit
2437	Router Bit
3712	C Clamp
3927	Vise
4436	Level
5563	Pliers
6630	Sockets
6937	Wrench Set
7249	10' Tape
8311	Voltmeter

The program for this project must be loaded into main computer storage for execution. The method for accomplishing this will vary among different computer systems. After the program is placed in main computer storage, it must be executed. The method for initiating the execution of the program is also dependent upon the type of machine being used. Directions for loading and executing the program must be determined from an instructor or from the computer center.

Computer Laboratory Project — Transaction-Oriented Data Entry

After the program is loaded into storage and is executed, the display below will appear on the terminal screeen.

```
INTRODUCTION TO COMPUTERS AND
    DATA PROCESSING
SHELLY/CASHMAN...ANAHEIM PUBLISHING CO.
CHAPTER 5 - PROJECT 7
TRANSACTION-ORIENTED DATA ENTRY

TRANSACTION SELECTIONS

1 - ENTER ORDER
2 - LIST ORDERS
3 - END PROGRAM

ENTER TRANSACTION NUMBER: ?
```

When the above information appears on the screen, the assignments below should be completed.

Assignment 1: An order is to be entered for customer 6439. The customer is ordering 40 vises.

    Step 1: In answer to the message ENTER TRANSACTION NUMBER:, enter the value 1 and then depress the appropriate key to continue. This indicates that an order is to be entered.

    Step 2: When the message CUSTOMER NUMBER: appears on the screen, enter the customer number 6439 and depress the appropriate key to continue.

    Step 3: When the message ITEM NUMBER: appears on the screen, enter the item number corresponding to a vise and depress the appropriate key to continue.

    Step 4: When the message QUANTITY: appears on the screen, enter the value 40 and depress the appropriate key to continue.

    Step 5: The message WHEN FINISHED VIEWING, DEPRESS THE APPROPRIATE KEY TO REVIEW THE ORDER will appear on the screen. The appropriate key should be depressed at that time.

Computer Laboratory Project — Transaction-Oriented Data Entry

Step 6: The following will appear on the screen, with all of the information provided.

```
ORDER APPROVAL

CUSTOMER NUMBER:
CUSTOMER NAME:
ADDRESS:
CITY/STATE:
ITEM NUMBER:
DESCRIPTION:
QUANTITY:
UNIT PRICE:
TOTAL AMOUNT:
IS ALL DATA CORRECT (Y OR N): ?
```

Questions: 1. What is the name of customer number 6439? _____

2. What is the address of Dynamite Parts Co.? _____

3. In what city is Dynamite Parts Co. located? _____

Step 7: After reviewing the order, answer the question IS ALL DATA CORRECT (Y OR N): by entering a Y if the data entered is correct and a N if the data entered is not correct and then depressing the appropriate key to continue. Note that all information appearing on the screen except the customer number, the item number, and the quantity is retrieved from a data base containing customer records and item records. If the data entered is correct and the value Y is entered, the order will be entered into a data base of orders and the menu will reappear on the screen. If the data is not correct and the value N is entered, the order will not be entered into the order data base; instead, the ENTER ORDER INFORMATION message will appear on the screen and the order data should be entered correctly. If the order data has not been entered properly and the value N is used to answer the question, then repeat Steps 2 through 7 until the data is entered properly.

Assignment 2: After the order has been entered, the screen reverts to the transaction selections menu. The transaction number 2 presents a listing of the orders which have been entered thus far.

Step 1: Enter the transaction number 2 and depress the appropriate key to continue.

Question: 1. What is the total amount of the order for Dynamite Parts Co.? _____

5.15

Computer Laboratory Project — Transaction-Oriented Data Entry

Assignment 3: After displaying the listing of orders, depress the appropriate key to continue. The menu will again be displayed. In many data entry applications, there must be provision for errors which are made by the operator. This assignment illustrates some of the errors which can occur in this system.

Step 1: Enter transaction number 1 to enter an order.

Step 2: Enter customer number 2887 in response to the message CUSTOMER NUMBER:.

Questions: 1. What response did you receive when you entered this customer number? _____

2. What can be done to correct this error? _____

Step 3: Enter an order for customer number 2673 for 120 voltmeters.

Questions:

1. What response did you receive when you entered this order? _____

2. What can be done to correct this error? _____

Step 4: Enter a quantity of 57 voltmeters for customer number 2673.

Step 5: Depress the appropriate key to review the order. Enter the value N in response to the question IS ALL DATA CORRECT (Y OR N)? This value should be entered to illustrate the actions taken when the data entered by the operator is not correct.

Question:

1. What took place when the value N was entered? _____
_____

Step 6: The screen should now be ready for you to enter an order. Therefore, enter the following order for 15 of the levels for customer number 7718. Answer Y when you review the order.

Step 7: Enter the transaction number 2 to review the orders which have been entered thus far.

Questions:

1. List the customer numbers which have been entered thus far: _____
_____

2. Why isn't the order for customer number 2673 included in this list? _____
_____

5.16

Computer Laboratory Project — Transaction-Oriented Data Entry

Assignment 4: This assignment is designed to illustrated the typical actions of a data entry operator. Enter the following orders into the system and answer the associated questions:

Step 1: Customer Number 4107; Item Number 2437; Quantity 50

Step 2: Customer Number 3198; Item Number 2371; Quantity 48

Step 3: Customer Number 6439; Item Number 5563; Quantity 68

Step 4: Customer Number 2673; Item Number 3712; Quantity 53

Step 5: Customer Number 7718; Item Number 6630; Quantity 89

Step 6: Customer Number 6439; Item Number 6630; Quantity 58

Questions:

1. What is the total amount owed by customer number 6439 as a result of orders which you have entered? _____

2. How many total items have been ordered for item number 6630? _____

3. Which customer has the highest amount owing? _____

4. Which customer has the lowest amount owing? _____

Computer Laboratory Project — Transaction-Oriented Data Entry

Program Messages

The following table contains error messages that may appear when incorrect entries are keyed into the terminal and the corrective action which should be taken.

ERROR MESSAGE	CAUSE	CORRECTIVE ACTION
INVALID ENTRY — REENTER	An invalid transaction number was entered	Enter a value 1 – 3
INVALID RESPONSE — ENTER Y OR N	A value other than Y or N was entered to answer the question	Enter the value Y or the value N
TABLE IS FULL — ORDER NOT ENTERED NO MORE DATA CAN BE ENTERED. DEPRESS APPROPRIATE KEY TO CONTINUE	A maximum of ten orders can be entered in this program and the maximum has been entered	Terminate the program and begin again
INVALID CUSTOMER NUMBER — REENTER	A customer number not in the customer file has been entered	Enter the correct customer number
INVALID ITEM NUMBER — REENTER	An item number not in the item number file has been entered	Enter the correct item number
INVALID QUANTITY — REENTER	A quantity greater than 99 or less than 1 has been entered	Enter the correct quantity If a customer orders more than 99 items, use two or more orders
?REDO*	An alphabetic character was entered where numeric data is required	Enter a valid numeric value
OV ERROR IN _____*	An excessive number of characters was entered	Begin project again. Reexecute the program and enter the proper values
?EXTRA IGNORED*	A comma was entered as a part of a numeric field. Only the data to the left of the comma will be used and incorrect output will result.	Ignore output and redo problem entering the correct numeric values

* These error messages are generated by the system and may vary on different computer systems.

Chapter 5

Project 8
Developing Communication Skills

Instructions: Prepare an oral or written report on one or more of the following subjects.

1. Visit the school's computing center and determine the various types of input devices that are used for processing student programs. Report your findings to the class.

2. Visit the school's computer center and determine the types of input devices that are used for processing administrative applications. Report your findings to the class.

3. Bring to class an example of a check after it has been processed. Explain the MICR characters at the bottom of the check.

4. Contact a local bank computer center and find out what happens when a check is processed. Be sure to determine the processing that occurs through the use of MICR characters.

5. Bring in an example of a document that will be read using OCR techniques. Explain the document to the class.

6. Many utility companies use optical character reading devices. Contact a company representative to receive an explanation of the processing that occurs when a utility bill is paid.

7. Contact a vendor of vocal input devices and arrange for a lecture/demonstration of their products for the class.

8. Contact the manager of a local grocery store or other retail store that is using portable bar code reading devices and determine how these devices are being used. Prepare a report for the class. Include both favorable and unfavorable reactions.

9. The Universal Product Code is being used in some stores for labeling merchandise, particularly in grocery stores. Using this technique, some stores are advocating eliminating the individual pricing of products. Prepare a report on the use of the universal product code in retail stores.

10. Prepare a report on the current state-of-the-art related to voice input.

Chapter 5
Answers to selected projects

Chapter 5, Project 3, Testing your knowledge — Key Terms

1. P	4. J	7. F	10. G	13. L
2. B	5. R	8. I	11. E	14. M
3. H	6. O	9. N	12. K	15. C

Chapter 5, Project 5, Testing your knowledge — True/False Questions

1. F	8. F	15. F	22. T	29. T
2. F	9. F	16. F	23. F	30. F
3. F	10. F	17. T	24. F	31. T
4. F	11. T	18. T	25. T	32. F
5. T	12. F	19. F	26. T	33. T
6. F	13. T	20. F	27. F	34. T
7. T	14. T	21. F	28. F	35. F

Chapter 5, Project 6, Testing your knowledge — Multiple Choice Questions

1. C	4. D	7. D	10. B	13. C
2. B	5. D	8. D	11. B	14. A
3. A	6. C	9. A	12. C	15. D

Chapter 6
Obtaining Output From the Computer

> **Chapter Objectives**
>
> - An awareness of the types of output available from computer systems
> - An understanding of the types of printers available, their speeds, and their advantages and disadvantages
> - A knowledge of the characteristics of cathode ray tube terminals
> - An understanding of the creation and use of detail, summary, and exception reports
> - An understanding of the use of CRT terminals in transaction-oriented systems for inquiry and the factors to be considered in developing inquiry systems

Chapter Overview

The last step in the basic data processing cycle of input, process, and output is the output step. Chapter 6 provides an overview of the most common types of output used with computer systems of various sizes. Today, there is a wide variety of output devices including printers, computer terminals, plotters, microfilm, and even voice response systems.

One of the most widely used forms of output is the printed report. To produce output reports, a number of different printers are available costing a few hundred dollars to many thousands of dollars. Two common classifications of printers are the method used to place the image on the paper and the speed of the printer.

Printing an image on a page is accomplished by impact printing or non-impact printing. Impact printing is the process where characters are printed by a type font or a hammer striking the paper, ribbon, and character together. Impact printers can be either solid character or dot matrix. Dot matrix characters are formed by a series of dots being used to form a character. Dot matrix printers are relatively inexpensive, but have poorer print quality than solid character printers.

Some non-impact printers use specially coated or sensitized papers that respond to thermal or electrostatic stimuli to form an image. Others use ink jets or xerography to form an image. Such printers are very quiet but do not have the ability to produce multiple copies.

Printers vary greatly in speed. Low speed printers print less than 300 lines per minute; high speed printers are capable of printing 300 – 3,000 lines per minute, and very high speed printers print in excess of 3,000 lines per minute. Some non-impact printers are now capable of printing in excess of 20,000 lines per minute.

In transaction-oriented systems, cathode ray tube terminals are widely used as both input and output devices. CRT terminals are available that can print both upper and lower case letters of the alphabet, display colors, and offer graphic capabilities. Common display controls include reverse video, scrolling, and paging.

Output from a computer can be classified as external output or internal output. Internal output is that form of output which is used within the company. External output is output which will be used outside the company. Special considerations must be given to external output, and preprinted forms are often used.

Computers have great flexibility in the types of printed reports that can be produced. For reports in batch processing systems, they are usually classified as detail printed reports, summary reports, or exception reports. A detail printed report is one in which each input record is examined to determine if it will be printed on the report. A summary report summarizes data from a group of records. The higher within an organization an individual works, the more summarized the data should be. Exception reports are obtained by examining each input record read but printing out only those records which contain "exceptional" conditions, such as very low inventory, excess costs, etc.

In a transaction-oriented processing system, the most common approach for obtaining output is the inquiry. An inquiry is a request from the terminal operator to a computer system for information. The output from a transaction-oriented system must be user oriented; therefore, the system should be easy to use, response time should be brief, prompts should be used, the user entries should be short, and all user entries should be acknowledged. One of the more critical problems in a transaction-oriented system is response time. When using a terminal, it is desirable to have a response time of two seconds.

Computer output microfilm (COM) has significant advantages over the printed report for many applications. These include recording data on the film at a speed of 30,000 lines per minute, the cost of recording is less than the cost of printing, and less space is required to store the output.

In addition to computer printers, terminals, and microfilm, there are many specialized output devices, such as sophisticated graphic display devices, hard copy plotters, and even voice output that controls production machinery.

Chapter 6

Key Terms

Band Printer A type of high-speed printer that uses a rotating belt or band with embossed characters which are struck by a hammer.
Cathode Ray Tube Terminal A device used as a computer terminal which contains a television-like screen for displaying data. Most CRT terminals also have a typewriter-like keyboard.
Chain Printer A type of high-speed printer which contains characters on a rotating chain.
COM (Computer Output Microfilm) A technique used to record output from a computer as very small images on roll or sheet film.
Daisy Wheel Printer A printing device consisting of rotating spokes or arms which contain embossed characters.
Detail Printed Reports A report in which each input record is examined to determine if it will be printed on the report.
Drum Printer A type of high-speed printer that features a cylindrical drum which rotates to position characters for printing.
Electrographic Printer A non-impact printer that uses specially coated paper on which the image is "burned" or formed by various means.
Exception Report A report in which only unusual situations are displayed.
Graphic Display Terminals CRT terminals capable of displaying not only letters of the alphabet and numbers but graphs and drawings as well.
Impact Printers Printing devices which print by some print mechanism striking paper, ribbon, and characters together.
Inquiry A request from a terminal operator to a computer system for information.
Laser Printers Very high-speed printers, printing in excess of 20,000 lines per minute.
Line Printers Printers that print a line at time.
Matrix Printers A printer that forms characters by a series of small dots.
Nonimpact Printers Printers which use a specially coated or sensitized paper that responds to stimuli to cause an image to appear on a form.
Output Information that is produced as a result of processing input data.
Output, External Output used outside a company.
Output, Internal Output used within an organization.
Output Units Units which are a part of a computer system that can display, print, or otherwise make available to people the results of processing data.
Paging The ability to display an entire screen full of data on a CRT terminal under terminal control.
Plotter A device capable of producing drawings as hard copy output from a computer.
Printed Reports Reports which are printed by printers attached to the computer system.
Printers Devices which are connected to the computer system and which can prepare printed reports under the control of a computer program.
Reverse Video The ability to reverse standard display on CRT terminals to highlight characters, words, or lines.
Scrolling The ability to move lines displayed on a CRT terminal screen either up or down.
Serial Printers Printers that print a character at a time.
Summary Reports A report in which one line is printed for each group of records.
Transaction-Oriented Output Output, normally displayed on a CRT terminal in a transaction-oriented processing system.
Voice Output An output device which converts data in main storage to a vocal response understandable by humans.

NAME_____ DATE_____

Chapter 6
Project 1
Identifying types of printers

Instructions: Briefly describe each of the printing mechanisms illustrated below and on the following page.

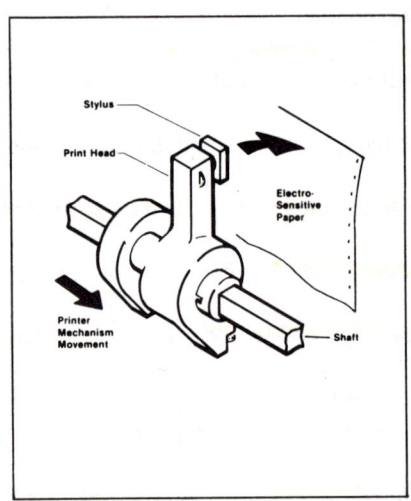

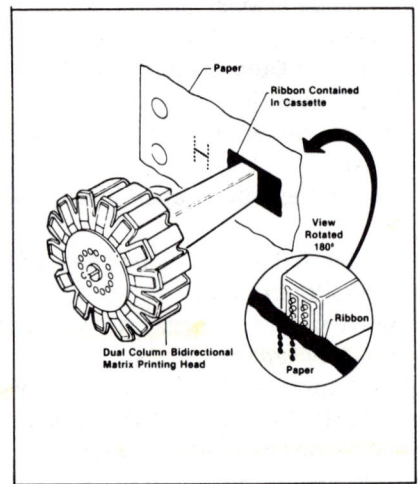

Type: _____   Type: _____

Description: _____   Description: _____

_____   _____

_____   _____

Speed: _____   Speed: _____

Cost: _____   Cost: _____

Identifying types of printers

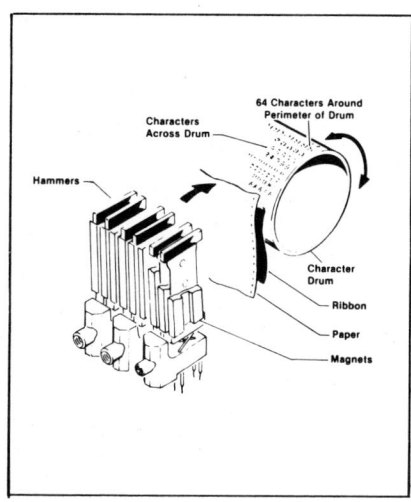 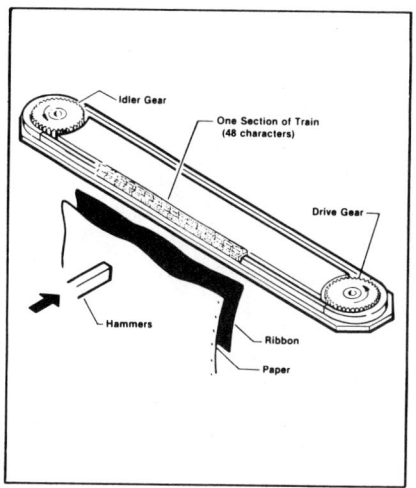

Type: _____   Type: _____

Description: _____   Description: _____

_____   _____

_____   _____

Speed: _____   Speed: _____

Cost: _____   Cost: _____

Identifying types of printers

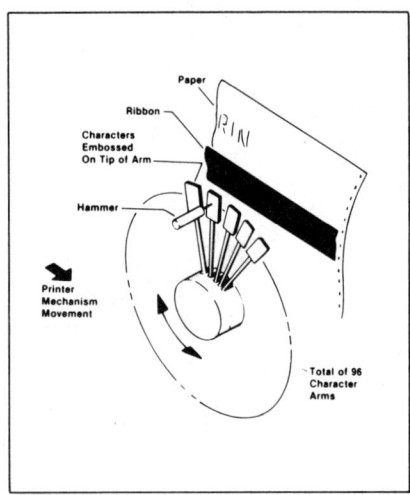 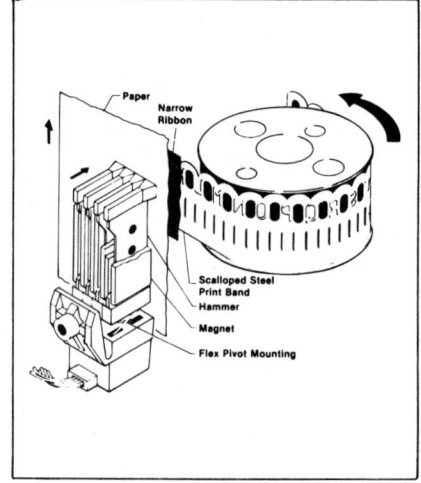

Type: _____   Type: _____

Description: _____   Description: _____

_____   _____

_____   _____

Speed: _____   Speed: _____

Cost: _____   Cost: _____

NAME_____ DATE_____

Chapter 6
Project 2
Testing your knowledge — Key Terms

Instructions: Fill in the blanks with the appropriate term from the list of terms on the right side of the page.

G 1. An _impact printer_ is a device which prints through the use of a printing mechanism striking the paper, ribbon, and character together.

K 2. A printer that forms each character by means of a series of small dots is called a _matrix printer_.

P 3. A _serial printer_ prints a character at a time.

J 4. A _laser printer_ is a very high speed printing device that can print in excess of 20,000 lines per minute.

C 5. A _CRT_ is a device commonly used as a computer terminal and contains a television-like screen for displaying data.

O 6. The ability to move lines displayed on a cathode ray tube screen either up or down is called _scrolling_.

N 7. _reverse video_ is the ability to reverse standard displays on a cathode ray tube terminal to highlight characters, words, or lines.

L 8. _paging_ is the ability to display an entirely new page of data on a cathode ray tube terminal at the operator's request.

H 9. A request from a terminal operator to a computer system for information is called an _inquiry_.

F 10. Output used outside a company is called _external output_.

I 11. Output used within an organization is called _internal output_.

E 12. An _exception report_ is a report in which only unusual situations are displayed.

Q 13. A report in which one line is printed for each group of records is called a _summary report_.

B 14. _COM_ is a technique used to record output from a computer as very small images on roll or sheet film. _(Microfilm)_

M 15. A device capable of producing drawings as hard copy output from a computer is called a _plotter_.

A. Band printer
B. COM
C. CRT
D. Detail printed report
E. Exception report
F. External output
G. Impact printer
H. Inquiry
I. Internal output
J. Laser printer
K. Matrix printer
L. Paging
M. Plotter
N. Reverse video
O. Scrolling
P. Serial printer
Q. Summary report

Chapter 6

Project 3
Testing your knowledge — Definitions

Instructions: Briefly define or explain each of the following terms:

1. COM

2. Matrix printer

3. Paging

4. Plotter

5. Scrolling

6. Serial printer

7. Transaction-oriented output

NAME_____ DATE_____

Chapter 6

Project 4
Testing your knowledge — True/False Questions

Instructions: Circle the T if the question is true and F if the question is false for each of the true/false questions below and on the following page.

T (F) 1. Printers are usually classified by the size of the image or the size of the printer.

(T) F 2. Impact printers use some type of printing mechanism striking the paper, ribbon, and character together to transfer images onto paper.

T (F) 3. Non-impact printers are especially valuable when multiple copies of a report are desired.

T (F) 4. The primary advantage of the dot matrix printer is the high quality of the characters that are printed.

(T) F 5. Dot matrix printers are normally less expensive than solid character printers.

(T) F 6. Some non-impact printers use specially coated or sensitized papers that respond to thermal or electrostatic stimuli to form an image.

(T) F 7. Most low speed printers print a character at a time and are called serial printers.

(T) F 8. Low speed printers are defined as those printers that print less than 300 lines per minute.

(T) F 9. Low speed printers can be purchased for less than $1,000.00.

(T) F 10. Printers operating in the range of 300 – 3,000 lines per minute are called high speed printers.

T (F) 11. For printing speeds in excess of 10,000 lines per minute, microfilm must be used.

(T) F 12. Output from transaction-oriented processing systems is frequently obtained through the use of cathode ray tube terminals.

T (F) 13. A limitation of all CRT terminals is the inability to display upper and lower case letters of the alphabet.

(T) F 14. Graphics (pictures, drawings, and graphs) can be displayed on some CRT devices.

(T) F 15. Reverse video refers to the process of reversing the normal display light on the CRT and is used to format a screen for ease of data entry.

T (F) 16. Scrolling refers to the ability to enter data on any line currently visible on the face of a CRT.

T (F) 17. Paging refers to the ability to display microfiche on the face of a CRT under control of a computer program.

(T) F 18. Internal output is that output which is used within the company.

(T) F 19. External output often requires the use of preprinted forms.

6.9

Testing your knowledge — True/False Questions

T **F** 20. A detail printed report contains all fields from the input record.

T F 21. A detail printed report is one in which each input record is examined to determine if it will be printed on the report.

T **F** 22. The higher in an organization an individual works, the more detailed the output report should be.

T F 23. Summary reports may be generated from input records by printing totals and identifying information only.

T **F** 24. Exception reports should not be prepared for applications such as inventory control because of the need for detailed information, such as the quantity of products on hand for all items.

T **F** 25. A report which contains a salesman number and sales amount from each input record and also contains the total sales of all salesmen is an example of a summary report.

T F 26. Both the systems analyst and the user must be aware of the use of a report, and then design the report in such a way that will make the report most useful.

T **F** 27. An exception report can only be prepared from detailed data.

T F 28. The printed report is the principal form of output in batch systems.

T **F** 29. A disadvantage of transaction-oriented output is that hard copy output cannot be obtained.

T F 30. To obtain output in a transaction-oriented system, an inquiry is commonly used.

T **F** 31. A five to ten second response time is usually adequate in a transaction-oriented processing system.

T F 32. Chain printers have been widely used for many years and can print up to 3,000 lines per minute with relatively good print quality.

T F 33. Typically, band printers can print up to 2,000 lines per minute and feature interchangeable type bands.

T **F** 34. Computer output microfilm records data in very small images and is faster than printed output but is more expensive per page produced.

T F 35. Data can be recorded on microfilm at up to 30,000 lines per minute.

NAME_____ DATE_____

Chapter 6

Project 5

Testing your knowledge — Multiple-Choice Questions

Instructions: Circle the correct response to the multiple choice questions below and on the following page.

1. Impact printers are available that print:

    A. Solid characters only.
    B. Dot matrix characters only.
    C. Electrostatic images.
    D. Solid characters or dot matrix characters.

2. For high quality output reports,:

    A. A dot matrix printer should be used.
    B. A solid character printer should be used.
    C. An electrostatic printer should be used.
    D. A slow speed printer should be used.

3. Serial printers:

    A. Print a line of characters at one time.
    B. Print a page of characters at a time.
    C. Print a character at a time.
    D. Print a word at a time.

4. Low speed printers are available at a cost of:

    A. Less than $100.00.
    B. Less than $1,000.00.
    C. Approximately $5,000.00.
    D. Approximately $10,000.00.

5. Low speed printers print from approximately:

    A. 15 characters per second to 300 lines per minute.
    B. 300 lines per minute to 1,000 lines per minute.
    C. 1,000 to 3,000 lines per minute.
    D. 3,000 to 20,000 lines per minute.

6. High speed printers are available that can print:

    A. A maximum of 1,000 lines per minute.
    B. A maximum of 3,000 lines per minute.
    C. A maximum of 300 lines per minute.
    D. In excess of 50,000 lines per minute.

7. To obtain output in excess of 20,000 lines per minute:

    A. Computer output microfilm can be used.
    B. Dot matrix printers must be used.
    C. Very high speed non-impact printers can be used.
    D. Answers A and C.

Testing your knowledge — Multiple-Choice Questions

8. With CRT devices, a relatively common display is:

    A. 24 lines — 80 characters per line.
    B. 24 lines — 132 characters per line.
    C. 40 lines — 40 characters per line.
    D. 80 lines — 80 characters per line.

9. The term scrolling, when used in reference to a CRT, refers to:

    A. The ability to move lines displayed on the screen either up or down.
    B. The ability to display an entirely new screen full of data if available.
    C. The ability to reverse the normal display light on the screen.
    D. The ability to print a character at any point on the CRT screen.

10. Detail printed reports are normally prepared in any organization for:

    A. Those who need access to the day-to-day operating data of a company.
    B. Management and other high-level personnel, such as the president of a company.
    C. External reporting only.
    D. Internal reporting only.

11. The term "exception report" refers to:

    A. A report which lists unusual conditions derived from the data on input records.
    B. A report produced on demand, as requested by high-level management.
    C. A report which lists totals based upon some control field.
    D. A report which lists totals for a group of records.

12. High-level management personnel should normally receive:

    A. Detail printed reports.
    B. Summary reports.
    C. All internal reports.
    D. All external reports.

13. The most common form of output for batch systems is:

    A. Printed reports.
    B. Data displayed on a CRT.
    C. External output.
    D. Internal output.

14. The most common form of output in a transaction-oriented system is:

    A. The printed report.
    B. Microfilm.
    C. Data displayed on a CRT.
    D. Exception reports.

15. Microfilm is a good form of output when:

    A. Large volumes of output are required.
    B. The production of output at a rapid rate is desirable.
    C. A reduction of storage space for output is desirable.
    D. All of the above.

NAME_____ DATE_____

Chapter 6
Project 6
Computer Laboratory Assignment — Report Formats

Description: This project is designed to acquaint individuals with the varying types of report formats that can be obtained from a single set of data. The terminal operator is placed in the situation of requiring specific information and choosing the report which contains the required information.

The data base for these reports contains sales information for three different stores within a chain of stores. Within each store, there are one or more departments with sales figures; and within each department, there are one or more items which are reported on.

The program for this project must be loaded into main computer storage for execution. The method for accomplishing this will vary between different computer systems. After the program is placed in main computer storage, it must be executed. The method for initiating the execution of the program is also dependent upon the type of machine being used. Directions for loading and executing the program must be determined from an instructor or from the computer center.

Assignment 1: Load the computer program into main computer storage and initiate the execution of the program. When the program is executed, the following menu will appear on the screen.

```
INTRODUCTION TO COMPUTERS AND
    DATA PROCESSING
SHELLY/CASHMAN...ANAHEIM PUBLISHING CO.
CHAPTER 6 - PROJECT 6
REPORT FORMATS

REPORT MENU
1 - DETAILED REPORT
2 - STORE SUMMARY
3 - DEPARTMENT SUMMARY
4 - ITEM SUMMARY
5 - STORE/DEPT SALES REPORT
6 - HIGH DEPARTMENT REPORT
7 - LOW STORE REPORT
8 - END PROGRAM
ENTER REPORT SELECTION: ?
```

6.13

Computer Laboratory Project — Report Formats

Step 1: You are the inventory control manager who requires a detailed report of all items sold for the chain of stores. In response to the message ENTER REPORT SELECTION, enter the number of the report which you feel will give you the required information and depress the appropriate key to continue.

Questions:

1. How many robes did department 143 in store 14 sell? _____

2. Which department in which store sold the most bicycles? Dept. _____ Store _____

3. What was the total amount taken in for the sale of item number 640 in department 446 of store 18? _____

Step 2: After viewing the screen and answering the questions, depress the appropriate key to continue.

Step 3: You are the head buyer for all of the stores; and as part of your responsibilities, you must approve the purchase of all items for all of the stores. In order to make these approvals, you need to know how many of each type of item is sold. In response to the message ENTER REPORT SELECTION, enter the number of the report which you feel will give you the required information and depress the appropriate key to continue.

Questions:

1. How many bats were sold? _____

2. What was the total amount received from the sale of T-shirts? _____

3. How many of item 431 were sold? _____

4. What item generated the largest amount of dollar sales? _____

Step 4: After viewing the screen and answering the questions, depress the appropriate key to continue.

Step 5: You are the president of the chain of stores and you wish to know the volume of sales for each store. In response to the message ENTER REPORT SELECTION, enter the number of the report which you feel will give you the required information and depress the appropriate key to continue.

Questions:

1. Which store had the highest sales? _____

2. Which store sold $1,943.00 worth of merchandise? _____

Step 6: After viewing the screen and answering the questions, depress the appropriate key to continue.

Computer Laboratory Project — Report Formats

Step 7: You are the vice-president in charge of department sales. You must know the total sales for each department in the chain of stores. In response to the message ENTER REPORT SELECTION, enter the number of the report which you feel will give you the required information and depress the appropriate key to continue.

Questions:

1. Which department had the highest sales? _____

2. Which department sold $1,116.50 worth of merchandise? _____

Step 8: After viewing the screen and answering the questions, depress the appropriate key to continue.

Step 9: You are the marketing manager and must constantly review the performances of the departments and stores in order to determine which of them requires marketing assistance and which of them has done an outstanding job so that they can be properly recognized in the company newsletter. Therefore, you must know the department which had the highest sales so they can be mentioned in the newsletter; and you must also know the store that had the lowest sales so you can determine the proper marketing approach for the store. Choose the reports which you feel will give you this information and enter the appropriate report numbers. This information is contained on two different reports.

Questions:

1. Which department had the highest sales? _____

2. What were the sales of the highest department? _____

3. What were the sales of the store which sold the least? _____

Step 10: After viewing the reports and answering the questions, depress the appropriate key to continue.

Step 11: As chief financial officer of the chain of stores, it is critical that you know the sales of each department within each store. The individual item sales are not important to you. In response to the message ENTER REPORT SELECTION, enter the number of the report which you feel will give you the required information and depress the appropriate key.

Questions:

1. What was the total revenue of department 227 in store 10? _____

2. What was the total sales of department 143 in store 14? _____

3. In which store did department 446 sell the most? _____

4. Which department in which store sold the least? _____

Step 12: After viewing the report and answering the questions, depress the appropriate key to display the report menu. Enter the value 8 to terminate the program.

Computer Laboratory Project — Report Formats

Program Messages

The following table contains error messages that may appear when incorrect entries are keyed into the terminal and the corrective action which should be taken.

ERROR MESSAGE	CAUSE	CORRECTIVE ACTION
INVALID SELECTION — REENTER	A numeric value other than 1 - 8 was entered for the report selection	Enter a value 1 - 8 to select the appropriate report or to terminate the program
? REDO *	A non numeric character was entered when performing menu selection	Enter a VALUE 1 - 8 to select the proper function from the menu
OV ERROR IN _____ *	An excessive number of characters was entered	Begin project again. Reexecute the program and enter the proper values
?EXTRA IGNORED*	A comma was entered as a part of a numeric field. Only the data to the left of the comma will be used and incorrect output will result	Ignore output and redo problem entering the correct numeric values

* These error messages are generated by the system and may vary on different computer systems.

Chapter 6
Project 7
Developing Communication Skills

Instructions: Prepare an oral or written report on one or more of the following subjects.

1. Obtain a list of printers used with the computer system at your school. Determine the type of printers used and their speeds.

2. Obtain samples of reports which have been generated from solid character printers, dot matrix printers, and inexpensive non-impact printers. Prepare a display for the class. (Your local computer store should be able to supply you with these samples.)

3. Most utility companies send out statements using a computer generated output. Analyze the statements. What type of printer was used? Share your findings with the class.

4. Visit your local computer store to determine the least expensive printer available for a microcomputer. Bring in a sample of the output for the class, and give a brief report concerning the advantages, disadvantages, or any limitations of the printer.

5. Ink jet printing technology is a newer form of printing technology used on some systems. Prepare a research report on ink jet technology.

6. Obtain a copy of the output generated from a manufacturer of word processing systems. What type of printing device was used? Analyze the output in terms of print quality.

7. Some authorities say that the need for the printed report for the internal reporting requirements of a business is no longer necessary or desirable in most situations because of the availability of computer output microfilm. Prepare a report on computer output microfilm and its use in business.

8. Obtain a sample of output generated from plotters.

9. Some microcomputer systems are now available that generate voice output. Contact a representative of the local computer store and arrange for a demonstration of a system which has voice output available.

10. Prepare a list of applications in which voice output could be useful. Use your imagination!

Chapter 6
Answers to selected projects

Chapter 6, Project 2, Testing your knowledge — Key Terms

1. G	4. J	7. N	10. F	13. Q
2. K	5. C	8. L	11. I	14. B
3. P	6. O	9. H	12. E	15. M

Chapter 6, Project 4, Testing your knowledge — True/False Questions

1. F	8. T	15. T	22. F	29. F
2. T	9. T	16. F	23. T	30. T
3. F	10. T	17. F	24. F	31. F
4. F	11. F	18. T	25. F	32. T
5. T	12. T	19. T	26. T	33. T
6. T	13. F	20. F	27. F	34. F
7. T	14. T	21. T	28. T	35. T

Chapter 6, Project 5, Testing your knowledge — Multiple Choice Questions

1. D	4. B	7. D	10. A	13. A
2. B	5. A	8. A	11. A	14. C
3. C	6. B	9. A	12. B	15. D

Chapter 7
Auxiliary Storage and File Organization

Chapter Objectives

- An understanding of the need for auxiliary storage
- An understanding of the storage and access of data stored on magnetic tape
- An understanding of the sequential and random access methods
- An understanding of the file organization methods — sequential, relative or direct, and indexed
- A familiarization with the auxiliary storage devices and media used for both large and small computer systems

Chapter Overview

Chapter 7 is designed to develop an understanding of the common types of auxiliary storage and file organization techniques. Two major considerations when evaluating auxiliary storage are an analysis of the media on which the data is stored and the manner in which the data is organized and accessed.

Magnetic tape is one of the most widely used forms of auxiliary storage. Data is recorded on magnetic tape in the form of magnetic spots that can be read and transferred into main computer storage. Reels of ½ inch tape, 2,400 feet in length, are commonly used. EBCDIC is the coding scheme most widely used for magnetic tape. In this system, nine horizontal channels are used to vertically record the bits that represent the character. Eight channels represent the eight bits in the byte, and the ninth channel is used for a parity bit. Data on magnetic tape can be stored at densities of 800 bits per inch, 1,600 bits per inch, and 6,250 bits per inch. Data can be transferred from magnetic tape into main storage at rates from 15,000 characters per second to 1,250,000 characters per second, depending upon the speed at which the tape moves past the read/write heads on the tape unit and the density of the data recorded on the tape.

Records are stored sequentially on magnetic tape and must be separated by an interblock gap approximately .6 inch wide to allow for the starting and stopping of the tape. To provide for more efficient use of tape and faster reading and writing speeds, records may be blocked on tape; that is, two or more records are placed on tape between interblock gaps to form a physical record. Magnetic tape is often used in systems for backing up magnetic disk files.

Another widely used form of auxiliary storage is magnetic disk. Disks are composed of a series of platters mounted to form a disk pack. These disk packs rotate under read/write heads to read or record data on the surface of each disk. A concentric circular recording position on the disk is called a track. The number of tracks on a disk surface can vary from 200 to over 800. Two methods are used to physically organize data on the disk — the cylinder method and the sector method. The cylinder method uses the concept of a cylinder as the basic reference point. To reference a record using the cylinder method, a program must specify the cylinder number, recording surface number, and record number. With the sector method, each track is divided into individual storage locations called sectors. Each sector can hold a specified number of characters and can be referenced.

A mass storage device is also available as auxiliary storage. This device consists of a data cartridge two inches in diameter and four inches in length housing a strip of magnetic tape. The cartridge is stored in a series of honeycomb-like cells. Up to 472 billion characters can be stored on this device. Retrieval time is very slow — approximately 3 to 8 seconds.

Magnetic bubble memory is also a newer form of auxiliary storage and offers very high density.

Sequential access means that data is retrieved from a file stored on auxiliary storage, one record after another in a predetermined sequence. Rapid retrieval of any given record is not possible with sequential access. Where rapid retrieval of any record is required, random access is used. Random access allows records to be retrieved without reading any other record in the file. Magnetic tape must use sequential access. Magnetic disk can use either sequential or random access. Random access provides relatively rapid access to any record in a file.

Two major types of processing can be performed on data stored on auxiliary storage: data retrieval and file updating. When files are updated, three functions can be performed: additions, deletions, and changes. Files can be updated either sequentially or randomly. With sequential file updating, a new master file is created containing the updated data. With random updating, a new file is not created; the updated record is written back into the same location in the file.

Data can be stored on auxiliary storage in one of three logical file organizational ways. These are sequential, relative, or indexed organization. In a relative file, records are stored in relative locations within the file based upon some key. Random access is normally used with relative files. Records stored in an indexed file are stored in an ascending sequence or descending sequence by a key. In addition, an index is created when the file is built which contains the key for each of the records in the file and a disk address of the records. Data can be accessed either sequentially or randomly when indexed files are used.

For small scale computers, floppy disk, disk cartridges, and tape cassettes are used as forms of auxiliary storage. For larger systems, disk packs capable of storing millions of characters are used. Some of the packs are removable; others are fixed.

Chapter 7

Key Terms

Access Arms, Magnetic Disk The mechanism that positions read-write heads over tracks on magnetic disk storage devices.

Actuator The access arm on a disk storage unit that swings in and out over the proper location.

Auxiliary Storage Devices Devices, generally magnetic tape and magnetic disk, on which data can be stored for use by computer programs; also known as secondary storage.

Blocking The storing of two or more logical records on magnetic tape or disk to form a physical record for the purpose of more efficiently storing and processing the records.

Bubble Memory A type of memory which is composed of small magnetic domains formed on a thin crystal film of synthetic garnet.

Cylinder The amount of data that can be read with a single positioning of an access arm on a magnetic disk.

Data Management Programs Programs supplied as a part of a system's software that handle such operations as the blocking and deblocking of records, accessing files, etc.

Direct Access Storage Device An auxiliary storage device on which data can be stored and retrieved in any order, sequentially or randomly.

Direct or Relative File Organization A file in which records are stored in a location based upon the key found in the record.

Disk Cartridge A type of removable disk storage commonly containing a single disk for recording and retrieving data.

Disk Drive A device consisting of a spindle on which a disk pack can be mounted for electronically storing data.

Disk Pack A unit which consists of multiple metal platters connected to a common hub. Each platter is coated with a metal oxide on which data can be electronically stored.

File A collection of one or more records.

File Organization The methods used to organize records so that they are accessible by computers.

File Updating The processing of additions, deletions, and changes against a master file.

Indexed File Organization A file organization method in which records are stored in ascending or descending sequence and are referenced by an index which permits sequential or random retrieval.

Interblock Gap A blank space typically .6 inch wide that separates records or groups of records on magnetic tape.

Logical Record Individual records stored on an auxiliary storage device.

Magnetic Disk A form of auxiliary storage in which data is stored on rotating disk.

Mass Storage Devices Very large-scale auxiliary storage devices.

Master Files Those files which reflect the current status of a business.

Millisecond One thousandth of a second.

Parity Check A checking method in which a bit is associated with each character stored so that all characters will contain an odd (or even) number of bits.

Physical Record A group of records placed together on an auxiliary storage device.

RAMAC One of the first magnetic disk storage devices introduced by IBM in the mid-1950's.

Random Access The ability to retrieve records in a file without reading any previous records.

Random File Updating The process of updating files in which each master record is individually retrieved without searching through each master record sequentially.

Sector A series of individual storage areas on magnetic disk.

Sequential Access Data retrieved from a file, one record after another in a predetermined sequence.

Sequential File Updating The processing of additions, deletions, and changes against a sequential file.

Sequential Files Those files in which records are stored one after another, normally in ascending or descending sequence, based upon some control field.

Key Terms

Tape, Magnetic A ½" wide piece of mylar on which data can be stored electronically. Typical lengths for tape are 600 feet, 1200 feet, and 2400 feet.

Tape Coding, Magnetic The coding structure used to represent data on magnetic tape.

Tape Density, Magnetic The number of characters per inch that can be recorded on magnetic tape; common densities include 800, 1600, or 6250 bytes per inch.

Tape Reels A plastic container on which magnetic tape is stored for processing on a computer system.

Track, Magnetic Disk The concentric recording positions on magnetic disk.

Updating The process in which files are changed, with additions, deletions, and changes, to reflect the latest information.

NAME_____ DATE_____

Chapter 7

Project 1

Magnetic Tape — Data transfer rates

Instructions: The speed at which magnetic tape is moved past the read/write heads of a tape drive varies from 12.5 inches per second to 200 inches per second, and the density of magnetic tape varies from 200 bytes per inch to 6,250 bytes per inch. The speed at which data is transferred into main computer storage can be obtained by multiplying the tape transport speed by the density of the data stored on magnetic tape. The chart below illustrates the tape transport speed and density of a number of widely used magnetic tape drives. Calculate the data transfer rate of each unit.

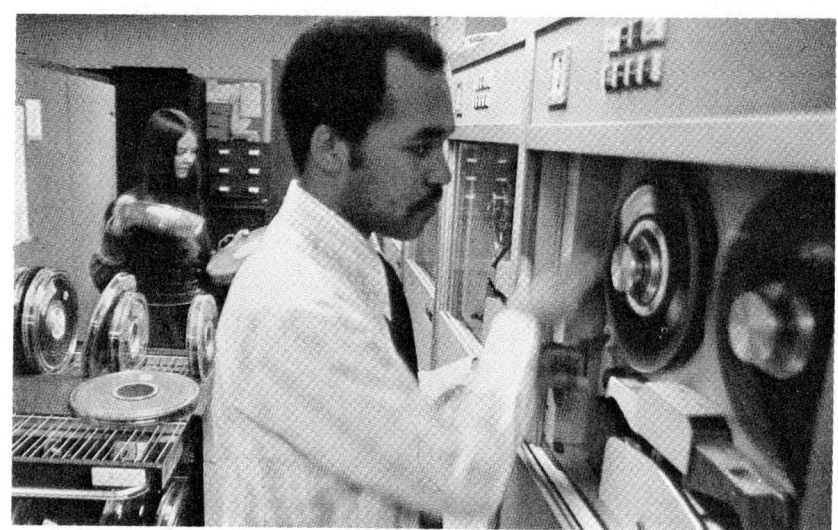

MODEL	TAPE SPEED (Inches per second)	DENSITY (BYTES PER INCH)	DATA TRANSFER RATE
1	75	800	
5	125	800	
7	125	1600	
9	200	1600	
10	200	6250	

NAME_____ DATE_____

Chapter 7

Project 2
Floppy disks — Storage capacity

Instructions: The storage capacity of floppy disks varies greatly. Generally, floppy disks come in two versions: an 8-inch disk and a 5¼-inch disk. Various storage capacities are possible with each type. Normally, more than one disk drive can be attached to a computer system at one time. For many microcomputers, the maximum number of units which can be attached is four.

With one widely used 5¼-inch mini-disk, there are 35 tracks on the diskette numbered from track 0 to track 34. Each track is divided into 10 sectors. Each sector can hold 256 bytes of data. The chart below summarizes some of the characteristics of this unit.

Complete the chart by filling in the blanks to determine the storage capacity.

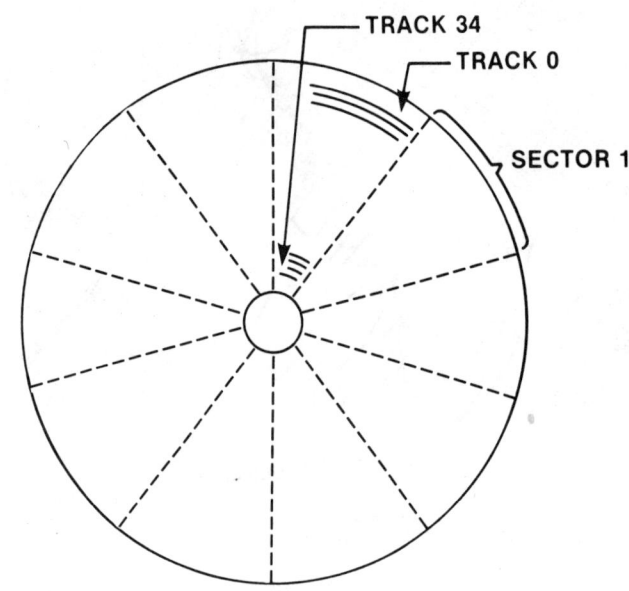

CHARACTERISTICS
OF
5¼" MINI FLOPPY DISK

DISK ROTATION SPEED	AVERAGE ACCESS TIME (MILLISECONDS)	DATA TRANSFER RATE	NUMBER OF TRACKS	NUMBER OF SECTORS PER TRACK	NUMBER OF BYTES PER SECTOR	NUMBER OF BYTES PER TRACK	NUMBER OF BYTES PER DISKETTE	TOTAL SYSTEM CAPACITY (4 DISK DRIVES ON LINE)
300 R.P.M	100	12,500 BYTES PER SECOND	35	10	256	_____	_____	_____

7.6

NAME_____ DATE_____

Chapter 7

Project 3

8-inch sealed disks — Storage capacity

Instructions: The 8-inch sealed disks can be used as high capacity, reliable fixed-disk drives for microcomputer and minicomputer systems. Such disk drives offer considerably larger data capacity and faster access than multiple floppy disk drives. Capacities typically range from 8 to 25 megabytes. An illustration of a typical 8-inch disk drive is illustrated below with some of its characteristics.

Complete the chart by filling in the blanks to determine the storage capacity of the unit.

CHARACTERISTICS OF 8" RIGID DISK DRIVES

DISK ROTATION SPEED	AVERAGE ACCESS TIME (MILLISECONDS)	NUMBER OF TRACKS	NUMBER OF BYTES PER TRACK	NUMBER OF BYTES PER DISK SURFACE	NUMBER OF READ/WRITE HEADS (DISK SURFACES)	TOTAL STORAGE CAPACITY
2964 R.P.M.	70	244	12,000	_____	4	_____

7.7

NAME_____ DATE_____

Chapter 7

Project 4
Removable disk packs — Storage capacity

Instructions: One widely used removable magnetic disk storage unit consists of disk packs that contain 10 magnetic disks mounted on a rotating shaft. Each disk is 14" in diameter. As the disk packs are removable, unlimited storage is possible; however, the disk packs must be mounted on the disk drives to be directly accessible by the computer.

The chart below summarizes some of the characteristics of one widely used disk drive and related disk packs.

Complete the chart by filling in the blanks to determine the storage capacity.

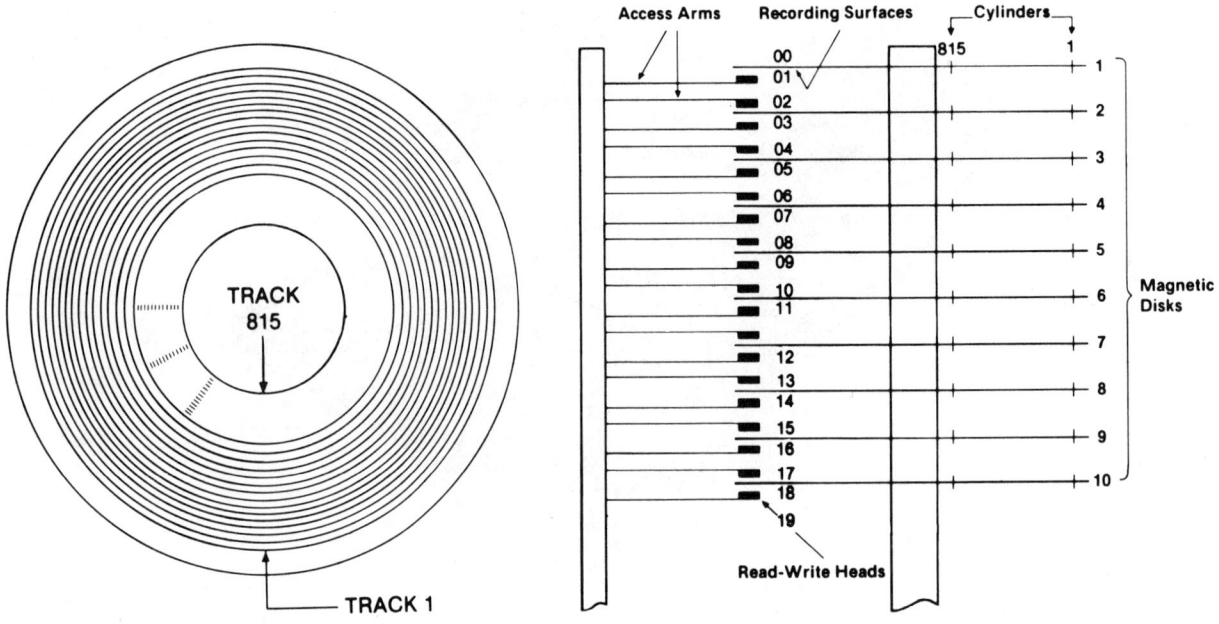

DISK ROTATION SPEED	AVERAGE ACCESS TIME	DATA TRANSFER RATE	NUMBER OF DISKS	RECORDING SURFACES	BYTES PER TRACK	CYLINDER CAPACITY (multiply recording surfaces times bytes per track)	TRACKS PER SURFACE	DISK CAPACITY (Multiply cylinder capacity times number of tracks per surface)	SYSTEM CAPACITY (8 units may be attached on-line to the computer)
3,600 R.P.M.	28.5 MILLISECONDS	806,000 BYTES PER SECOND	10	19	13,440	?	815	?	?

7.8

Chapter 7
Project 5
Sequential file updating

Instructions: The diagram below illustrates the steps that occur when updating a sequential file. Briefly explain the process that occurs and indicate the contents of the updated master file by filling in the blank spaces on the new customer master file.

TRANSACTION FILE			
ACTION	CODE	CUSTOMER NUMBER	COMPANY NAME
Add	A	1135	ACE INC.
Delete	D	2241	ELECTRO CO.
Name Change	C	3771	MART CORP.

MASTER FILE	
CUSTOMER NUMBER	COMPANY NAME
1001	ABBOT CO.
2241	ELECTRO CO.
3771	MART & SONS

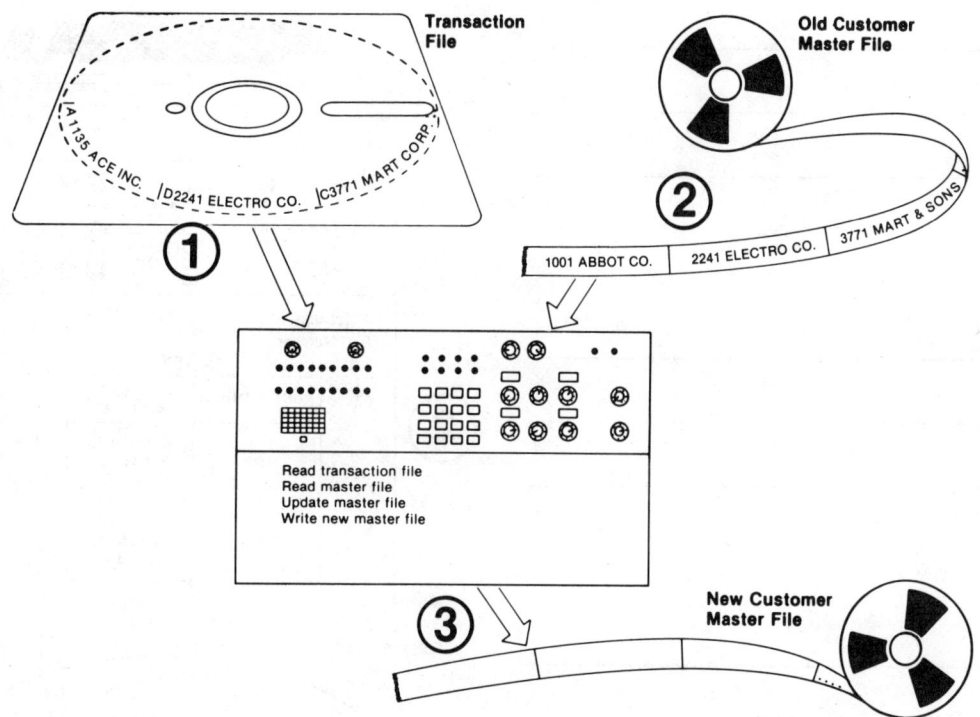

Step 1 _____

Step 2 _____

Step 3 _____

7.9

Chapter 7

Project 6
Indexed files — random retrieval

Instructions: The following diagram illustrates the steps that occur when randomly retrieving a record using an indexed file. Briefly explain each of the steps labeled 1, 2, 3, and 4.

STEP 1: _____

STEP 2: _____

STEP 3: _____

STEP 4: _____

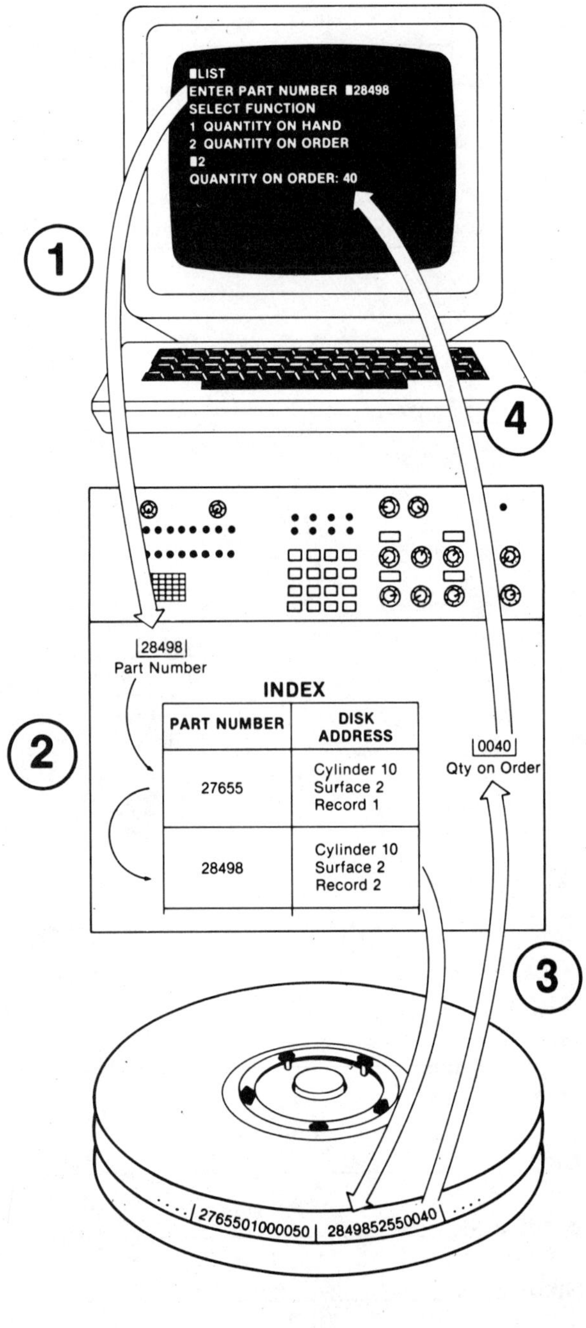

7.10

NAME_____ DATE_____

Chapter 7

Project 7
Testing your knowledge — Key Terms

Instructions: Fill in the blanks with the appropriate term from the list of terms on the right side of the page.

P 1. Auxiliary storage using magnetic tape and magnetic disk is also known as **secondary storage**.

B 2. The storing of two or more logical records on magnetic tape between interblock gaps to form a physical record is called **blocking**.

C 3. A **cylinder** is defined as the amount of data that can be read with a single positioning of an access arm on a magnetic disk.

E 4. A **direct access storage device** is a type of auxiliary storage device in which data can be stored and retrieved in any order, sequentially or randomly.

D, O 5. A type of file organization in which records are stored in a location based upon the key found in the record is called **direct** or **relative** file organization.

F 6. A **disk cartridge** is a removable form of disk storage commonly containing a single disk for storing of data.

G 7. A **disk pack** is a unit which consists of multiple metal platters connected to a common hub with each platter being coated with a metal oxide on which data can be electronically stored.

H 8. The process of making additions, deletions, and changes to a master file is called **file updating**.

I 9. **Indexed** file organization is a method in which records are stored in ascending or descending sequence and are referenced by an index which permits sequential or random retrieval.

J 10. An **interblock gap** is a blank space that separates records or groups of records on magnetic tape.

L 11. The accessing of data on magnetic disk is often measured in **milliseconds** or thousandths of a second.

M 12. The ability to retrieve records in a file without reading any of the previous records is called **random access**.

Q 13. Data retrieved from a file one record after another in a predetermined sequence is called **sequential access**.

R 14. Files in which records are stored one after another in either ascending or descending sequence are called **sequential files**.

S 15. The concentric recording positions on a magnetic disk are called **tracks**.

A. Auxiliary storage
B. Blocking
C. Cylinder
D. Direct
E. Direct access storage device
F. Disk cartridge
G. Disk pack
H. File updating
I. Indexed
J. Interblock gap
K. Microseconds
L. Milliseconds
M. Random access
N. Random file
O. Relative
P. Secondary storage
Q. Sequential access
R. Sequential files
S. Tracks

NAME_____ DATE_____

Chapter 7

Project 8
Testing your knowledge — Definitions

Instructions: Briefly define or explain each of the following terms:

1. Blocking

2. Cylinder

3. Direct or relative file organization

4. Interblock gap

5. Indexed organization

6. Sector

7. Tape density

8. Updating

NAME_____   DATE_____

Chapter 7

Project 9
Testing your knowledge — True/False Questions

Instructions: Circle the T if the question is true and F if the question is false for each of the true/false questions below and on the following page.

T **(F)** 1. Main computer storage and magnetic disk are the two most widely used forms of auxiliary storage.

(T) F 2. Magnetic disk storage is sometimes called secondary storage.

T **(F)** 3. Magnetic disk storage was developed before magnetic tape storage.

(T) F 4. Data is recorded on magnetic tape in the form of magnetic spots that can be read and transferred into main computer storage.

(T) F 5. The Extended Binary Coded Decimal Interchange Code (EBCDIC) is often used as the scheme for encoding data on magnetic tape.

T **(F)** 6. One of the most common densities of magnetic tape is 160 characters per inch. *800, 1600, 6250*

(T) F 7. The data transfer rate of a magnetic tape unit is calculated by multiplying the number of characters per inch on tape by the speed at which the tape moves past the read/write heads. *TR = S × D*

(T) F 8. Because of the density of magnetic tape, some systems can transfer data into main computer storage at rates in excess of one million characters per second.

(T) F 9. Records are stored on magnetic tape sequentially and are separated by an interblock gap.

T **(F)** 10. Blocking records on magnetic tape allows the tape to be used more efficiently but decreases the speed at which the data can be read into main computer storage.

T **(F)** 11. The use of magnetic tape has increased substantially in the past five years.

T **(F)** 12. Magnetic tape cannot be used to store a backup file for records stored on another media such as magnetic disk.

(T) F 13. An advantage of magnetic disk over magnetic tape is that magnetic disk provides for direct or random access to data.

T **(F)** 14. To read data stored on disk or write data onto a disk, access arms or an actuator with read/write heads touching the surfaces of the disk are used to sense the magnetic impulses on the disk.

(T) F 15. The basic recording positions on a disk surface consist of a series of concentric recording positions called tracks.

(T) F 16. A cylinder of data refers to the number of tracks that can be referenced by a single positioning of the access arms.

7.13

Testing your knowledge — True/False Questions

T **F** 17. On some disk storage devices, data is stored in sectors. A sector is a single track of data that can be located by an address.

T **F** 18. When data is referenced on a disk using the sector method, a track number, a sector number, and a record number must be specified.

T F 19. Mass storage devices are available which can store over 400 billion characters of data on data cartridges containing strips of magnetic tape.

T F 20. Bubble memory is expected to augment or even replace magnetic disk as a form of auxiliary storage in the future.

T F 21. The major limitation of the sequential access method is that rapid retrieval of any given record in a file is not possible.

T F 22. Sequentially accessed files are most often used in batch processing systems.

T F 23. Random access means that any record stored in a file can be retrieved without reading any other record in the file.

T F 24. In most transaction-oriented systems, randomly accessed files are mandatory.

T **F** 25. The ability to retrieve data both randomly and sequentially is usually not possible on most computer systems.

T F 26. When updating a file, three operations are performed: additions are made to the file; deletions are made from the file: and changes are made to the file.

T F 27. Sequential file updating requires the creation of a new master file.

T **F** 28. With random file updating, the master records are retrieved randomly but the transaction records must be retrieved sequentially.

T F 29. Relative files, sometimes called direct files, are created by storing the records in a file on disk based upon a key value found in the record.

T **F** 30. Data stored in a relative file can only be retrieved randomly.

T F 31. With indexed file organization, records are stored in ascending or descending sequence on a disk and are retrieved through the use of an index which is created when the file is loaded.

T F 32. Records in an indexed file can be retrieved either sequentially or randomly.

T **F** 33. Random retrieval of data in an indexed file is much faster than with a random or direct file.

T F 34. Data management programs which perform operations such as blocking and deblocking of records are normally supplied as a part of the operating system and relieve the application programmer of these tasks.

T **F** 35. On small scale computer systems, the floppy disk is the only widely used form of auxiliary storage.

NAME_____   DATE_____

Chapter 7

Project 10

Testing your knowledge — Multiple-Choice Questions

Instructions: Circle the correct response to the multiple choice questions below and on the following page.

1. The two most commonly used forms of auxiliary storage are:

    A. Magnetic tape and main computer storage.
    B. Magnetic disk and main computer storage.
    C. Magnetic tape and magnetic disk.
    D. Magnetic tape and mass storage devices.

2. Common densities of magnetic tape are:

    A. 800, 1600, and 6250 bytes per inch.
    B. 80, 160, and 625 bytes per inch.
    C. 80,000, 160,000, and 625,000 bytes per inch.
    D. 8, 16, and 625 bytes per inch.

3. Magnetic tape with a density of 800 characters per inch and a tape transport speed of 200 inches per second would have an effective transfer rate of:

    A. 320,000 characters per second.
    B. 1,600 characters per second.
    C. 32,000 characters per second.
    D. 160,000 characters per second.

4. Interblock gaps are placed between one or more records on magnetic tape:

    A. To allow for the starting and stopping of the tape drive during reading and writing.
    B. To separate files on tape.
    C. To separate fields on tape.
    D. To allow the operator to mount the tape between undivided records for reader retrieval.

5. Where it is necessary to have random access to data,:

    A. Magnetic tape can be used if data is arranged in sequence.
    B. Magnetic tape cannot be used except for random updating.
    C. Magnetic disk is used.
    D. Both A and C.

6. The circular recording positions on a single disk surface are called:

    A. Cylinders.
    B. Sectors.
    C. Tracks.
    D. Records.

7. When using the cylinder method for storing data on a disk, with a single positioning of an access arm:

    A. A cylinder of data can be accessed.
    B. All records can be accessed.
    C. All sectors can be accessed.
    D. One file can be accessed.

7.15

Testing your knowledge — Multiple-Choice Questions

8. On magnetic disk units, access to data is possible in approximately:

    A. 50 milliseconds.
    B. 50 microseconds.
    C. 500 milliseconds.
    D. 500 microseconds.

9. Magnetic bubble memory:

    A. Retains data when power is turned off.
    B. Can store millions of characters in a very small space.
    C. Has fast access time.
    D. All of the above.

10. When using magnetic tape as a form of auxiliary storage:

    A. Records can only be accessed if they are in ascending or descending order.
    B. Records can be accessed sequentially or randomly.
    C. Records can only be accessed randomly.
    D. Records can only be accessed sequentially.

11. Which of the following functions are performed when updating a file?

    A. Adding, sorting, and deleting records from a file.
    B. Adding, sorting, and changing records in a file.
    C. Sorting, deleting, and changing records in a file.
    D. Adding, deleting, and changing records in a file.

12. With sequential file updating:

    A. A new master file must be created.
    B. New data is recorded on the old transaction file.
    C. New data is recorded over previous records in the old master file.
    D. The new master file is printed and then reloaded when needed.

13. With direct or relative file organization:

    A. Records are loaded into adjacent positions on tape or disk.
    B. The location of the record in the file is based upon a key value found in the record.
    C. Records are loaded into alternative positions on the disk.
    D. Records are loaded into alternative tracks on the disk.

14. With indexed file organization:

    A. Records are stored in an ascending or descending sequence based upon the key of the record, and an index is created to allow reference to the data randomly or sequentially.
    B. Records are loaded in random sequence; an index is created to allow reference to the data sequentially.
    C. Records are loaded in ascending or descending sequence based upon the key in the record, and an index is created which can only reference data randomly.
    D. Records are loaded sequentially and can only be referenced sequentially through an index but can be referenced directly through the key of the records.

15. Small scale computer systems use which of the following types of auxiliary storage?

    A. 8-inch sealed disk units capable of storing 20 million characters.
    B. Disk cartridges.
    C. Floppy disks.
    D. All of the above.

Chapter 7

Project 11

Computer Laboratory Project — Inquiry

Description: This project is intended to illustrate the use of an inquiry to obtain information from a computer system. The application is a bank inquiry system. Four types of inquiries are possible: 1) An inquiry to obtain a customer's name, address, and account number using the customer name as the key for the inquiry; 2) An inquiry to obtain a customer's name, address, and account number using the account number as the key for the inquiry; 3) An inquiry to obtain the account balance using the account number as the key for the inquiry; 4) An inquiry to obtain the current month's activity using the account number as the key for the inquiry.

The program for this project must be loaded into main computer storage for execution. The method for accomplishing this will vary among different computer systems. After the program is placed in main computer storage, it must be executed. The method for initiating the execution of the program is also dependent upon the type of machine being used. Directions for loading and executing the program must be determined from an instructor or from the computer center.

After the program is loaded into main computer storage and is executed, the menu illustrated below will appear on the screen.

```
INTRODUCTION TO COMPUTERS AND
    DATA PROCESSING
SHELLY/CASHMAN...ANAHEIM PUBLISHING CO.
CHAPTER 7 - PROJECT 11
INQUIRY
        INQUIRY TYPES:
1 - NAME, ADDRESS, ACCOUNT NUMBER-
    KEY IS NAME
2 - NAME, ADDRESS, ACCOUNT NUMBER-
    KEY IS ACCOUNT NUMBER
3 - ACCOUNT BALANCE-KEY IS ACCOUNT
    NUMBER
4 - CURRENT MONTH'S ACTIVITY-KEY
    IS ACCOUNT NUMBER
5 - NO MORE INQUIRIES
        ENTER INQUIRY TYPE ?
```

The menu shown above contains the selections which are available for the inquiry application. The message ENTER INQUIRY TYPE? asks for the number of the inquiry to be processed.

Computer Laboratory Project — Inquiry

When the value 1 is entered in response to the message, the system will ask for the name of the customer. After the name is entered, the display illustrated below will appear.

```
INQUIRY TYPE: 1
LAST NAME: HANSON

NAME: HANSON, HAROLD T.
ADDRESS: 2963 ELLIOT AVE. ANAHEIM, CA
ACCOUNT NUMBER: 26381

WHEN FINISHED VIEWING, DEPRESS
    THE APPROPRIATE KEY ?
```

Note that an inquiry type 1 supplies the customer name, customer address, and customer account number.

When the value 2 is entered in response to the message, the system will ask for the account number. After the account number is entered, the display shown below will appear.

```
INQUIRY TYPE: 2
ACCOUNT NUMBER: 26381

NAME: HANSON, HAROLD T.
ADDRESS: 2963 ELLIOT AVE. ANAHEIM, CA
ACCOUNT NUMBER: 26381

WHEN FINISHED VIEWING, DEPRESS
    THE APPROPRIATE KEY ?
```

Note that the same information is obtained from a type 2 inquiry as is obtained from a type 1 inquiry, but that the key is the account number instead of the last name of the customer.

When the value 3 is entered in response to the message, the system will ask for the account number. After the account number is entered, the display below will appear.

```
INQUIRY TYPE: 3
ACCOUNT NUMBER: 35790

ACCOUNT NUMBER: 35790
CURRENT BALANCE: $23,515.64

WHEN FINISHED VIEWING, DEPRESS
    THE APPROPRIATE KEY ?
```

Computer Laboratory Project — Inquiry

Note that inquiry 3 supplies the account balance.

When the value 4 is entered in response to the message, the system will ask for the account number. After the account number is entered, the display below will be shown on the screen.

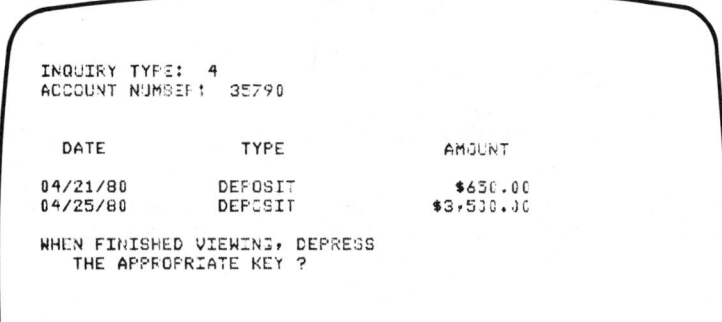

From the example above, it will be noted that inquiry type 4 returns the date, type, and amount of the account activity during the month. The two types of activities are deposits and withdrawals.

If the value 5 is entered in response to the message, the program is terminated.

Assignment 1: You have been hired as a customer service representative at the bank using the inquiry system just described. Your primary responsibility is to answer queries from bank customers and from bank executives concerning the accounts of the customers. After becoming acclimated to the environment, you begin to receive phone calls.

Step 1: Ms. Adams calls and tells you that she is filling out a credit application and cannot remember her account number. She asks for her account number.

Questions:

1. You have been directed that before any information is given out over the telephone, you should verify that the person calling is who they say they are. You are to do this by asking for the person's address and verifying it from information in the computer system. What is Ms. Adams' address?

   _____

2. What is Ms. Adams' account number? _____

Step 2: Juan Gonzalez calls and asks what his account balance is. He tells you his account number is 46338.

Questions:

1. What information do you use to verify that Mr. Gonzalez's account number is 46338?

   _____

2. What is the balance of Juan Gonzalez's account? _____

7.19

Computer Laboratory Project — Inquiry

Step 3: Jane Wilkerson, a vice-president of the bank in charge of loan approval, calls. She is performing a credit check on Lawrence L. Lambert and wants to know the balance in the account of Mr. Lambert and the amount of activity in the account during the current month. She is not sure of the account number.

Questions:

1. What is the balance in the account of Lawrence L. Lambert? _____

2. How many deposits and withdrawals has Mr. Lambert made during the current month? ____

Step 4: Juan Gonzalez, account number 46338, calls you back and states that the balance you gave him does not correspond to the balance he calculates. He asks you if you can tell him the amount of his deposit on April 7.

Questions:

1. Did a transaction occur on April 7? _____

2. If so, what type of transaction was it? _____

3. What amount was involved? _____

Step 5: Norma Chablinski calls you and she seems upset. She claims that she made a deposit of $55,273.26 on April 2 and a withdrawal of $50,050.72 on April 8. Yet she claims that the balance she calculates does not correspond to a balance on her account given her by another operator yesterday. She asks you to find out what the problem is.

Questions:

1. What is Norma Chablinski's account number? _____

2. What information do you use to verify who is calling you? _____
   _____

3. Did Ms. Chablinski make a deposit on April 2? _____

4. If the answer to number 3 is yes, for what amount? _____

5. Was a withdrawal made on April 8? _____

6. If the answer to number 5 is yes, for what amount? _____

7. What can you tell Ms. Chablinski concerning the reasons that the balance she calculates does not correspond to the actual balance? _____
   _____

Step 6: Mr. Michael Jackson calls you to verify his balance, which he claims is $3,657.98.

Question:

1. What response will you give Mr. Jackson? _____

Computer Laboratory Project — Inquiry

Assignment 2: You should have noticed in Assignment 1 that the response times to your inquiries varied; that is, the responses to your inquiries were not immediate as has been the case in previous chapters. This delayed response time is built into the program to allow you to experience different response times.

Question:

1. What were your initial reactions when the response from the computer system was not immediate? Did you think perhaps the computer system was not working properly? What would be your advice to a systems analyst designing an inquiry system concerning response times? _____

_____

_____

Program Messages

The following table contains error messages that may appear when incorrect entries are keyed into the terminal and the corrective action which should be taken.

ERROR MESSAGE	CAUSE	CORRECTIVE ACTION
INVALID TYPE — REENTER	A inquiry type other than 1 - 5 was entered	Enter a valid inquiry type
NAME NOT IN FILE	A customer name was entered that is not in the customer file.	Enter a valid customer name
ACCOUNT NUMBER NOT IN FILE	An account number which is not in the account file has been entered	Enter a valid account number
? REDO *	An alphabetic character was entered where numeric data is required	Enter a valid numeric value
OV ERROR IN _____ *	An excessive number of characters was entered	Begin project again. Reexecute the program and enter the proper values
?EXTRA IGNORED*	A comma was entered as a part of a numeric field. Only the data to the left of the comma will be used and incorrect output will result	Ignore output and redo problem entering the correct numeric values

* These error messages are generated by the system and may vary on different computer systems.

Chapter 7

Project 12
Developing Communication Skills

Instructions: Prepare an oral or written report on one or more of the following subjects.

1. Prepare a research report on the historical development of magnetic tape as a form of auxiliary storage.

2. Prepare a report on the historical development of magnetic disk as a form of auxiliary storage. Be sure to include storage capacities of the various forms of disks as they evolved and the cost per byte of storage from the earliest to the most modern devices.

3. Prepare a report on the use of magnetic bubble memory as a form of auxiliary storage.

4. Contact a local computer store or a manufacturer of microcomputers and determine the type of auxiliary storage available for their systems. What is the cost of auxiliary storage, and what is the storage capacity? Share your findings with the class.

5. Contact the manufacturer of a small scale business computer system to obtain information regarding the type of auxiliary storage systems available including their cost and capacity.

6. Contact the manufacturer of large scale computer systems and determine the types of auxiliary storage systems available for their largest system. Prepare a report for the class.

7. Contact the data processing manager of a large bank in your locality to determine if and how magnetic tape is being used with their computer system.

8. If your school has a computer center, contact the data processing manager to obtain information about the type of auxiliary storage used. Obtain the technical data related to each type, such as the density of the magnetic tape, the capacity of the disk, and related data.

9. Contact the data processing manager of a local computer installation and determine the type of file organization techniques they use for various applications.

10. Prepare a research report of the various types of floppy disk systems that are available. Include in this report the types of drives, storage capacities, and costs.

11. Review current data processing periodicals for advertisements related to auxiliary storage devices that are being offered.

Chapter 7
Answers to selected projects

Chapter 7, Project 7, Testing your knowledge — Key Terms

1. P	4. E	7. G	10. J	13. Q
2. B	5. D,O	8. H	11. L	14. R
3. C	6. F	9. I	12. M	15. S

Chapter 7, Project 9, Testing your knowledge — True/False Questions

1. F	8. T	15. T	22. T	29. T
2. T	9. T	16. T	23. T	30. F
3. F	10. F	17. F	24. T	31. T
4. T	11. F	18. F	25. F	32. T
5. T	12. F	19. T	26. T	33. F
6. F	13. T	20. T	27. T	34. T
7. T	14. F	21. T	28. F	35. F

Chapter 7, Project 10, Testing your knowledge — Multiple Choice Questions

1. C	4. A	7. A	10. D	13. B
2. A	5. C	8. A	11. D	14. A
3. D	6. C	9. D	12. A	15. D

Chapter 8
Data Communications

Chapter Objectives

- A basic knowledge of the components of a modern data communications network
- A knowledge of line speeds and modes of transmission
- A knowledge of line configurations
- An understanding of ways to establish contact when using various line configurations
- An introduction to data communications networks
- A knowledge of computer operations in a data communications environment

---

Chapter Overview

Data communications is becoming increasingly important in a modern data processing environment. It is estimated that over 90 percent of the computers sold or leased have data communications capabilities. A basic data communications configuration consists of the following: a terminal; a modem to convert digital data to an analog form so that the data can be transmitted over communications lines; a communications channel such as a telephone line; a modem at the receiving end of the communications lines to convert the analog signals to digital signals; a communications control unit that monitors the communications lines and controls the data which is sent over the lines; and the computer system which processes the data.

Computer terminals may be CRT's, hard copy terminals, or even small computer systems. To provide for the portability of terminals, a special type of modem called an acoustic coupler is used. There are a number of different types of communication channels used to transmit data over long distances. These channels include telephone lines, coaxial cables, microwave transmission, satellite communications, and fiber optics. The communications control unit interfaces between the modem and the computer system. Its purpose is to provide a path for data transfer between the computer system and the data communications network. Sophisticated communications control units are called front-end processors. They are programmable and can control the network, relieving the main computer of these tasks.

There are three grades of communications channels. They are low speed or narrow band, medium speed or voice grade, and high speed or broadband channels. Low speed channels have a bit transmission rate of 40 to 300 bits per second. Medium speed channels transmit from 300 to 9,600 bits per second. High speed channels transmit in excess of 9,600 bits per second.

Two modes of transmission are used when transmitting data: asynchronous transmission and synchronous transmission. With asynchronous transmission, one character at a time is transmitted, with each character preceded by a start bit and followed by a stop bit. With synchronous transmission, characters are transmitted as a group based upon a timing mechanism. Synchronous transmission is used where fast transmission is required.

Types of lines include simplex, half-duplex, and full-duplex. A simplex line allows data to be transmitted in one direction only. A half-duplex line permits transmission in both directions, but not at the same time; and full-duplex lines transmit in both directions at the same time. ASCII is a commonly used data communications code.

Two common types of line connections are point-to-point and multidrop. In a point-to-point connection, each terminal is connected to the computer by an individual line. A multidrop line has multiple terminals on a single line. However, only one terminal at a time can transmit even though more than one terminal can receive. Contact is established on a multidrop line by polling and addressing.

Leased lines may be obtained that provide for a permanent circuit used to connect a terminal with a computer system; or switched lines may be used in which contact is made through established voice telephone lines and networks by dialing.

Communications facilities may be combined in a variety of ways to form a network. A star network contains a central computer system and one or more terminals connected to the computer system. A ring network provides for a series of computer systems communicating with one another. A ring network is useful when all of the processing is not done at a central site.

A variety of devices is available to improve the efficiency of a data communications network. Two common devices are multiplexers and concentrators. A multiplexer is an electronic device which can divide a channel capable of a certain speed into multiple channels of a slower speed. A concentrator is a minicomputer that can accept information from any terminal over slow-speed lines and transmit the data to the main computer over a high-speed line.

The ability of computer systems to process multiple applications in the same processor unit occurs through the use of multiprogramming. Multiprogramming is defined as the concurrent execution of two or more programs on one computer system. Most data communications programs are executed in a computer system which uses multiprogramming.

Data communications lines are made available by common carriers. A common carrier is a company or organization which contracts with state or federal governments to carry the property of others at regulated charges. There are approximately 3,000 common carriers in the United States, with the dominant carriers being American Telephone and Telegraph and Western Union.

Since terminals use common telephone lines for access to data, unauthorized access to data is a challenging problem to the industry.

Chapter 8

Key Terms

Acoustic Coupler A special type of modem which allows a standard telephone headset to be attached to a terminal to allow the transmission of data.

Addressing, Data Communications A technique used in data communications networks to establish contact with a remote terminal.

ASCII Code American Standard Code for Information Interchange: a seven bit code widely used in data communications.

Asynchronous Transmission in Data Communications The transmission of a single character at a time preceded by a start bit and followed by a stop bit.

Channel An electronic device associated with a computer system that controls the physical transfer of data between the input/output device and main computer storage.

Channels, Communication The lines or data links over which data is transmitted including standard telephone lines, coaxial cables, microwave transmission, satellite, and fiber optics.

Common Carrier A company or organization which contracts with state or federal governments to carry the property of others.

Concentrator A device which accepts information from many terminals over slow-speed lines and transmits the data to the main computer over a high-speed line.

Data Communications The transmission of data from one location to another using communications channels such as telephone lines, coaxial cables, microwaves, or other means.

Fiber Optics Technology based upon light-weight, smooth hair-like strands of transparent material used for transmission of data and sound at high rates of speed.

Front-end processor A sophisticated programmable communications control unit consisting of a computer designed to handle communication functions to relieve the main computer of these tasks.

Full-Duplex Line A data communications channel that allows data to be sent in both directions at the same time.

Half-Duplex Line A channel that allows data to be sent in both directions, but not in both directions at the same time.

Interrupt An electronic signal which indicates to the central processing unit that the transfer of data between an input or output device and storage has been completed.

Leased Line A permanent communications channel used to connect a terminal with a computer system.

Line Speed The speed at which data is transmitted over communications channels.

Microwave Transmission The transmission of data through open space on a line of sight path.

Minicomputer A computer system which has smaller computer storage, slower processing speeds, and lower cost than a large computer system.

Modem A device which accepts a digital signal and converts it to an analog signal or accepts an analog signal and converts it to a digital signal.

Multidrop Lines A communication network in which more than one terminal is on a single line connected to the computer.

Multiplexer An electronic device which divides a channel of a certain speed into a series of channels of a slower speed.

Multiprogramming The concurrent execution of two or more computer programs on one computer system.

Networks, Data Communications A system composed of one or more computers and terminals.

Point-to-Point Line A direct communication line between a terminal and a computer system.

Polling A method used in data communications networks in which each terminal is interrogated in sequence to determine if there is data to be sent.

Ring Network A network in which there is no central computer, but a series of computers which communicate with one another.

Testing your knowledge — Key Terms

Satellite, Communications Communications relay stations positioned thousands of miles above the earth, used in transmission of data from and to earth stations.

Simplex Lines A channel which allows data to be transmitted in one direction only.

Star Networks A network which contains a central computer and one or more terminals connected to the computer system.

Supervisor A program that is part of the operating system that controls and schedules the resources of a computer system.

Switched Line A type of data communications line in which connection is established with a computer over a regular telephone network.

Synchronous Transmission Transmission of data based upon a timing mechanism in which data is transmitted at fixed intervals.

Terminals, Data Communication A terminal used in a data communication system for the transmission and reception of data. These terminals may consist of CRT terminals, small computer systems, or other types of I/O devices.

NAME_____ DATE_____

Chapter 8

Project 1
Identifying the components
of a data communications system

Instructions: Briefly describe the function of each of the components of a data communications system as illustrated below and identified by the numbers 1 – 6.

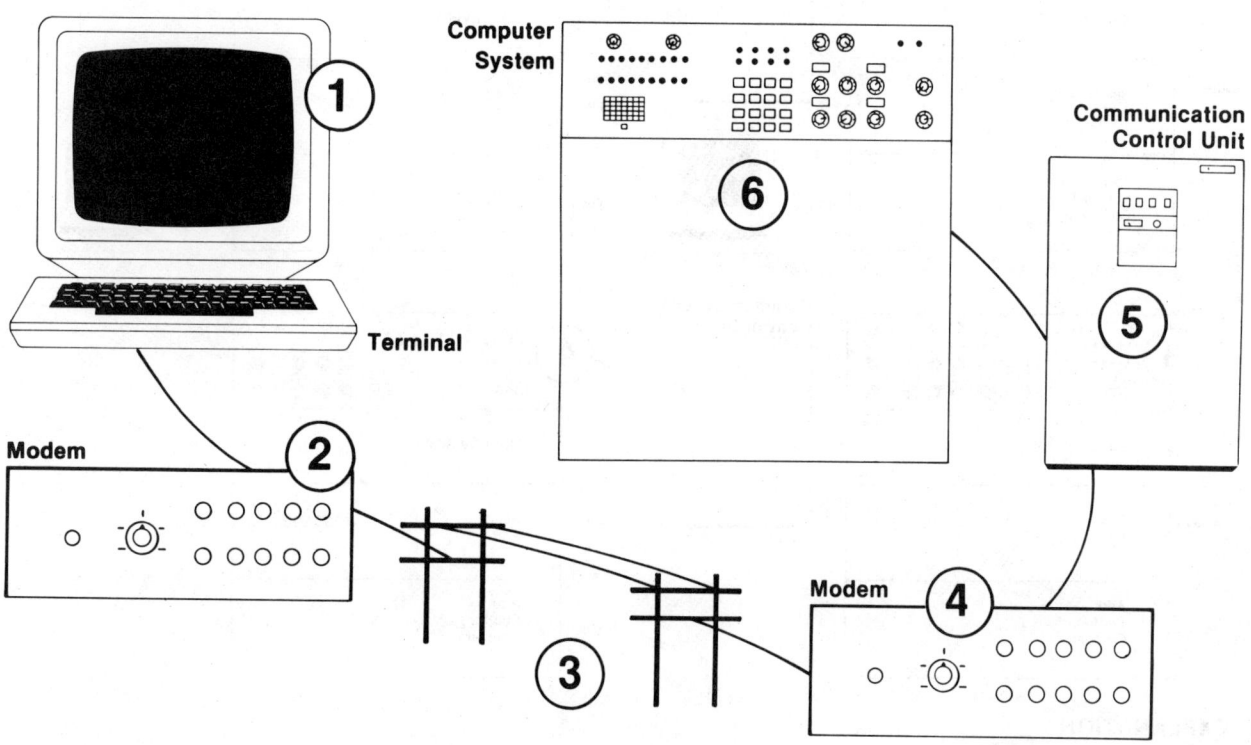

EXPLANATION

1. _____
2. _____
3. _____
4. _____
5. _____
6. _____

8.5

NAME_____ DATE_____

Chapter 8
Project 2
Multiprogramming

Instructions: Briefly explain the operations that occur in a multiprogramming environment as illustrated by the diagram below.

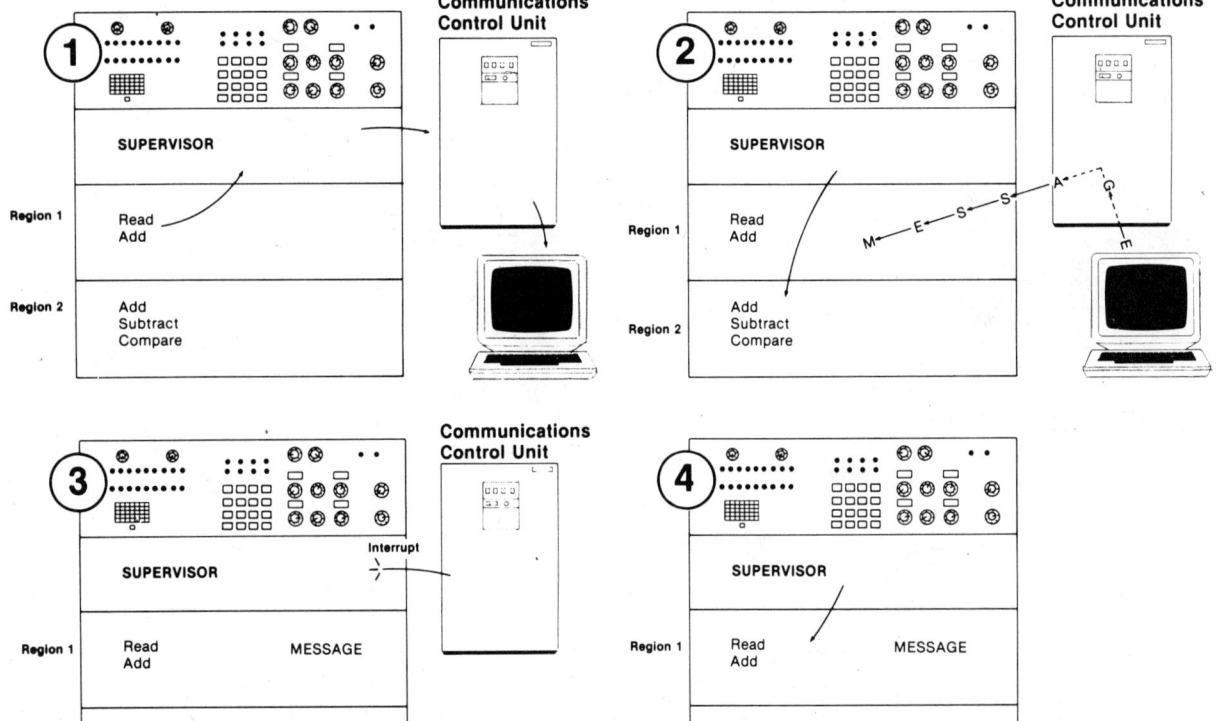

EXPLANATION

1. _____

_____

2. _____

_____

3. _____

_____

4. _____

_____

8.6

NAME_____ DATE_____

Chapter 8
Project 3
Testing your knowledge — Key Terms

Instructions: Fill in the blanks with the appropriate term from the list of terms on the right side of the page.

M 1. The device used to convert digital impulses to analog impulses is called a __Modem__.

D,G,L,X,E 2. Data communications channels include __coaxial cable__, __fiber optics__, __comm. satellites__, __microwave__ and __telephone lines__.

H 3. A sophisticated communications control unit specifically designed to handle data communications tasks is called a __front end processor__.

C 4. The transmission of one character at a time preceded by a start bit and followed by a stop bit is called __asynchronous transmission__.

J 5. A __half-duplex__ line allows data to be sent in both directions, but not at the same time.

B 6. The __ASCII__ code is widely used in data communications.

N 7. A __Multidrop__ line has more than one terminal on a single line connected to a computer system.

V 8. A __switched__ line is used to establish contact through the use of a regular voice telephone network.

R 9. The technique used by a computer system to establish contact on a multidrop line when a terminal has data to send is called __polling__.

A 10. To send data to a terminal in a multidrop line, __addressing__ is used.

U 11. A __star network__ contains a central computer system and one or more terminals connected to the computer system.

S 12. The network that utilizes a series of computer systems to communicate with one another is called a __ring network__.

O 13. The electronic device which can effectively divide a channel capable of a certain speed into multiple channels of a slower speed is called a __multiplexer__.

F 14. A __concentrator__ is a minicomputer located at the terminal side of a long distance line used to reduce line costs by accepting information from many terminals over slow speed lines and transmitting the data to the computer over a high speed line.

A. Addressing
B. ASCII
C. Asynchronous transmission
D. Coaxial cable
E. Communication satellites
F. Concentrator
G. Fiber optics
H. Front-end processor
I. Full-duplex
J. Half-duplex
K. Leased line
L. Microwave
M. Modem
N. Multidrop
O. Multiplexer
P. Multiprogramming
Q. Point-to-point
R. Polling
S. Ring network
T. Simplex channel
U. Star network
V. Switched
W. Synchronous transmission
X. Telephone lines

NAME_____ DATE_____

Chapter 8

Project 4
Testing your knowledge — Definitions

Instructions: Briefly define or explain each of the following terms:

1. Acoustic coupler

2. Asynchronous transmission

3. Concentrator

4. Front-end processor

5. Half-duplex channel

6. Modem

7. Multiplexer

8. Polling

9. Synchronous transmission

NAME_____   DATE_____

Chapter 8
Project 5
Testing your knowledge — True/False Questions

Instructions: Circle the T if the question is true and F if the question is false for each of the true/false questions below and on the following page.

(T) F   1. The ability to remotely communicate with a calculating machine was first demonstrated by Dr. George Stibitz in 1940 at Dartmouth College.

T **(F)**   2. Data can be transmitted in a digital form over telephone lines to a computer for processing in most communications systems.

(T) F   3. A modem is required to convert analog signals to a digital form at the receiving end of a data communications facility.

T **(F)**   4. Acoustic couplers are used to convert vocal responses on a telephone line to digital impulses which can be processed by a computer.

(T) F   5. Standard telephone lines are widely used for transmitting data in data communications systems.

(T) F   6. Coaxial cables are high quality communications lines that are usually laid under the ground or the ocean.

(T) F   7. Microwave systems transmit data on a line of sight path and provide a much faster transmission rate than do telephone lines.

T **(F)**   8. Communication satellite systems are used primarily for transmitting data very rapidly over short distances.

(T) F   9. Fiber optics as a communications channel is very lightweight compared to wire cables and also offers increased speed in transmission.

T **(F)**   10. A communications control unit interfaces between the terminal and the modem and is used to improve bit transmission speed.

(T) F   11. A front-end processor is a sophisticated minicomputer specifically designed to handle data communications tasks.

T **(F)**   12. The use of a front-end processor in a data communications system reduces the amount of work which can be accomplished by the main computer system.

(T) F   13. Low speed communications channels can transmit data at speeds of 40 to 300 bits per second.

(T) F   14. High speed communications channels permit transmission rates in excess of 9,600 bits per second.

T **(F)**   15. Transmission in which each character is preceded by a start bit and followed by a stop bit is called synchronous transmission.

Testing your knowledge — True/False Questions

T **F** 16. Asynchronous transmission is normally used in applications where rapid transmission of data is required.

T **F** 17. A half-duplex line allows data to be sent in both directions at the same time.

T F 18. A major advantage of full duplex lines is that no turnaround is required to reverse the direction of transmission.

T F 19. The ASCII code utilizes seven bits to represent data and is widely used in data communications.

T **F** 20. Where multiple terminals are used in a data communications system, point-to-point lines are the least expensive system.

T **F** 21. A multidrop line has more than one terminal on a single line, and all can transmit simultaneously.

T F 22. A leased line provides a permanent circuit used to connect a terminal with a computer system.

T F 23. A switched line establishes contact through the regular voice telephone network.

T **F** 24. Polling is used on a switched line when a terminal operator desires to transmit data to the computer.

T F 25. In a multidrop configuration, addressing is used to send data to a particular terminal.

T **F** 26. In a multidrop configuration, data can only be received by a single terminal at one time.

T **F** 27. A star network can only contain point-to-point lines.

T **F** 28. A ring network utilizes a central computer system encircled by a ring of terminals attached with point-to-point lines.

T F 29. A multiplexer is an electronic device which can effectively divide a channel capable of a certain speed into multiple channels of a slower speed.

T **F** 30. The capacity of a high speed line from a concentrator to the host computer is always more than the total capacity of all of the lines feeding into the concentrator.

T **F** 31. Most host computers in a data communications system must have all of their resources used for data communications tasks and other processing is not usually possible.

T F 32. Multiprogramming is the concurrent execution of two or more programs on one computer system.

T **F** 33. Multiprogramming is possible because most computers now contain more than one CPU.

T F 34. Data communications programs are usually input/output bound.

T F 35. The Carterfone decision said that modems and equipment from various manufacturers could be used on AT&T telephone systems.

8.10

NAME_____   DATE_____

Chapter 8

Project 6
Testing your knowledge — Multiple-Choice Questions

Instructions: Circle the correct response to the multiple choice questions below and on the following page.

1. The basic components of a data communications system include:

    A. A terminal, a communications channel, a communications control unit, and the computer system.
    B. A terminal, a modem, a communications channel, a communications control unit, and the computer.
    C. A terminal, a modem, a communications channel, a modem, a communications control unit, and a computer system.
    D. A terminal, a communications channel, a modem, a communications control unit, and the computer.

2. A modem is used to:

    A. Accept digital signals and convert them to analog signals.
    B. Accept analog signals and convert them to digital signals.
    C. Accept a digital signal from several channels and transmit the data at a fast rate.
    D. Both A and B.

3. The purpose of a communications control unit is to:

    A. Interface between the terminal and the communications channel to improve transmission speed.
    B. Interface between the terminal, the communications channel, and the computer.
    C. Interface between the modem and the computer system to assemble bits into a character for processing, perform error recovery, and other data communications tasks.
    D. Interface between the modem and the computer system for the purpose of converting analog signals to digital impulses for processing on the computer.

4. A front-end processor is:

    A. A part of the main computer's processor unit.
    B. A minicomputer specifically designed to control the data communications network and perform data communications tasks to relieve the main computer from the need to perform these functions.
    C. That portion of the main computer system that performs input/output operations.
    D. That portion of the main computer system that controls all input entering into the system.

5. High speed communications channels operating in excess of 9,600 bits per second are normally used for:

    A. Transmitting data from one terminal operator to another.
    B. Transmitting data from one terminal operator to a main computer.
    C. Transmitting data from the computer to a terminal.
    D. Computer-to-computer communications.

6. With asynchronous transmission:

    A. One character at a time is transmitted based upon a timing impulse.
    B. One record at a time is transmitted based upon a timing impulse.
    C. One character at a time is transmitted with each character identified by a start and stop bit.
    D. One record at a time is transmitted with each record identified by a start and stop bit.

7. Asynchronous transmission is normally used for:

    A. Computer-to-computer communications.
    B. Applications requiring fast transmission.
    C. Applications in which terminals are used to enter data a character at a time.
    D. Both A and C.

8.11

Testing your knowledge — Multiple-Choice Questions

8. Transmitting data in which the beginning and the end of a character are identified by a timing mechanism is called:

    A. Multiplexing.
    B. Asynchronous transmission.
    C. Synchronous transmission.
    D. Broadband transmission.

9. The type of communications channel that allows data to be transmitted in both directions, but not at the same time is called:

    A. Simplex.
    B. Half-duplex.
    C. Duplex.
    D. Broad band.

10. ASCII is:

    A. A coding system that uses 7 bits to represent data and is widely used in data communications.
    B. A coding system that uses 8 bits to represent data and is widely used in data communications.
    C. The only coding system that can be used for transmitting data along a communications channel.
    D. A replacement for EBCDIC in modern computer systems.

11. When point-to-point lines are used:

    A. The terminal is connected directly to the computer system on a single line.
    B. Multiple terminals are connected by a single line to the computer system.
    C. Two terminals are connected directly via communications lines to allow operator-to-operator communication.
    D. Data can be transmitted in one direction only.

12. The method used on a multidrop line to determine if a terminal has data to transmit to a computer is called:

    A. Addressing.
    B. Polling.
    C. Multiplexing.
    D. Concentrating.

13. The purpose of a multiplexer is to:

    A. Combine multiple slow channels into one fast channel.
    B. Allow multiple terminals to use a single communications channel.
    C. Effectively divide a channel capable of a certain speed into multiple channels of a slower speed.
    D. Concentrate bits into a stream that can be transmitted as a unit without a start and stop bit.

14. The device used at the terminal side of a communications line to reduce line costs by accepting information from many terminals over slow speed lines and transmitting the data to the main computer system over a high speed line is called a:

    A. Communications satellite.
    B. Microwave channel.
    C. Multiplexer.
    D. Concentrator.

15. Multiprogramming is defined as:

    A. The concurrent execution of two or more computer programs on one computer system.
    B. The concurrent execution of two or more computer programs on multiple computer systems.
    C. The concurrent execution of two or more computer programs in a star network.
    D. The concurrent execution of two or more computer programs in a ring network.

Chapter 8

Project 7
Computer Laboratory Assignment — Airline Reservations

Description: This project is designed to acquaint students with reservation systems that are commonly found in the airline industry, the hotel industry, and other industries as well. This project is an airline reservation system in which the flights available can be displayed, reservations can be made, a list of the passengers on a given flight can be obtained, and seat assignments can be made.

The program for this project must be loaded into main computer storage for execution. The method for accomplishing this will vary among different computer systems. After the program is placed in main computer storage, it must be executed. The method for initiating the execution of the program is also dependent upon the type of machine being used. Directions for loading and executing the program must be determined from an instructor or from the computer center.

After the program is loaded into main computer storage and is executed, the display illustrated will be shown.

```
INTRODUCTION TO COMPUTERS AND
    DATA PROCESSING
SHELLY/CASHMAN...ANAHEIM PUBLISHING CO.
CHAPTER 8 - PROJECT 7
AIRLINE RESERVATIONS

TASK SELECTION

1 - DISPLAY FLIGHTS
2 - MAKE RESERVATION
3 - LIST PASSENGERS
4 - MAKE SEAT ASSIGNMENT
5 - END PROGRAM

ENTER SELECTION: ?
```

From the task selection menu, it can be seen that one of five values should be entered to select the desired task.

When the value 1 is entered, the flight information for flights from Los Angeles to San Francisco will be displayed on the screen.

Computer Laboratory Project — Airline Reservations

When the value 2 is entered in response to the message ENTER SELECTION, the flight reservation information illustrated below is displayed on the screen.

```
ENTER FLIGHT NUMBER: ?
ENTER PASSENGER NAME: ?

RESERVATION CONFIRMED -
    PASSENGER:
    FLIGHT:
    LEAVE LAX:
    ARRIVE SF:

WHEN FINISHED VIEWING, DEPRESS
    THE APPROPRIATE KEY TO CONTINUE ?
```

The first two lines in the screen above are printed one at a time so that the desired flight number and the passenger name can be entered by the terminal operator. If there are seats on the desired flight, the confirming information is displayed. If not, a message is printed indicating the flight is full.

When the value 3 is entered, a list of the passengers with flight reservations is displayed.

When the value 4 is entered in response to the message ENTER SELECTION, the seat selection information illustrated below is displayed, as well as a schematic of the airplane seats from which a seat selection is made.

```
SEAT ASSIGNMENTS

ENTER PASSENGER NAME: ?
ROWS 1 - 4 ARE NON-SMOKING
ENTER SEAT: ?
SEAT    GIVEN
  TO PASSENGER
WHEN FINISHED VIEWING, DEPRESS
    THE APPROPRIATE KEY TO CONTINUE ?
```

The first line is printed and then the operator can enter the name of the passenger requesting the seat assignment. If the passenger has a reservation, the seat can then be selected. If the seat is unoccupied, the seat will be assigned to the passenger. If the seat is occupied, another selection must be made.

When the value 5 is entered in response to the message ENTER SELECTION, the program is terminated.

Computer Laboratory Project — Airline Reservations

Assignment 1: You have just been hired as a reservation specialist by an airline which services Los Angeles and San Francisco. This airline uses the reservation system previously described. You will be making reservations for passengers calling in on the telephone. You have been directed that when a passenger requests a reservation, the passenger's name should be entered as first initial-last name (example: G. SHELLY). Load and execute the reservation program.

   Step 1: Ms. L. Aimes calls you and asks what flights you have from Los Angeles to San Francisco and what time they leave. Display the appropriate screen and answer the following questions.

Questions:

   1. What is the earliest flight in the morning from Los Angeles to San Francisco? _____ What time does it leave? _____

   2. In order to arrive in San Francisco at 4:00 p.m., what flight should be taken? _____

   Step 2: Ms. Aimes informs you she would like to take the flight that leaves at 12:00 p.m. Enter the proper data to reserve a seat for her on this flight.

Questions:

   1. What flight is Ms. Aimes requesting? Flight Number _____

   2. What is your answer to Ms. Aimes concerning her reservation? _____

   _____

   Step 3: Ms. Aimes then informs you that she will take the flight which arrives in San Francisco at 4:00 p.m.

Questions:

   1. What is the flight number of the flight Ms. Aimes has requested? _____

   2. What is your answer to Ms. Aimes concerning her reservation? _____

   _____

Computer Laboratory Project — Airline Reservations

Step 4: During the day, the following passengers call to make reservations. If the flight they request is full, they decide to make other travel plans.

Name	Flight
J. Buttre	109
F. Hupptre	105
P. Lonnette	109
O. Nique	109
E. Areewt	105
P. Guinot	109
F. Yew	109
I. Huiski	107
T. Knight	109
W. Killinon	109
H. Lawten	107

Enter the reservations for those people whose requested flights are not full.

Step 5: Your supervisor has just called you on the telephone and requested the number of people who have reservations. Request the appropriate task to display the passenger names and answer her question.

Question:

1. How many passengers have reservations? _____

Assignment 2: You have been promoted from a reservation specialist to an airline counter executive. Your primary responsibility is to make seat assignments for passengers. You work at the airport.

Step 1: Mr. T. Knight approaches your desk and requests a seat for his trip on flight 109. Request the proper task to make a seat assignment for Mr. Knight.

Question:

1. What seats are available for the flight? (Note: all the available seats are displayed in the upper right corner of the screen) _____

_____

Step 2: When finding out that all seats were available, Mr. Knight chooses seat 3C. Enter the data to make a seat assignment of 3C for Mr. Knight.

Step 3: Ms. O. Nique is next in line. She requests a seat on the aisle in the nonsmoking section.

Questions:

1. What seats are available for Ms. Nique. _____

2. Why isn't seat 3C shown on the screen? _____

Step 4: From the choices you offer her, Ms. Nique requests seat 4D. Enter the data to make a seat assignment of 4D for Ms. Nique.

Computer Laboratory Project — Airline Reservations

Step 5: Mr. Killinon is next in line. He requests a window seat in the smoking section.

Question:

    1. What seats are available for Mr. Killinon? _____

Step 6: Mr. Killinon requests seat 6A. Enter the data to make a seat assignment of 6A for Mr. Killinon.

Step 7: Mrs. P. Lonnette is next in line and she informs you she is quite superstitious. She always flies in seat 3C. She wishes seat 3C for this flight.

Questions:

    1. Upon viewing the available seats, what can you tell Mrs. Lonnette about seat 3C? _____

    _____

Step 8: Mrs. Lonnette notes rather vehemently that she does not believe the picture you showed her of the available seats and insists that you enter seat 3C for her. Do so.

Question:

    1. What message did you receive that you can show Mrs. Lonnette? _____

    _____

Step 9: Mrs. Lonnette reluctantly agrees to seat 3D. Make this seat assignment for her.

Step 10: Mr. H. Litton is next in line. He requests a window seat in the nonsmoking section. Upon seeing the seats available, he requests seat 4E.

Question:

    1. What must you tell Mr. Litton when you enter his seat selection? _____

    _____

Step 11: Upon finding out his predicament, Mr. Litton advises you to make a reservation for him on Flight 109. Proceed to do this.

Step 12: After his reservation is made, Mr. Litton again requests seat 4E. Make this seat selection for him.

Question:

    1. How many seats are now available for other passengers? _____

Step 13: Terminate the program.

8.17

Computer Laboratory Project — Airline Reservations

Program Messages

The following table contains error messages that may appear when incorrect entries are keyed into the terminal and the corrective action which should be taken.

ERROR MESSAGE	CAUSE	CORRECTIVE ACTION
INVALID TASK — REENTER	A task selection number other than 1–5 was entered	Enter a valid task selection number
INVALID FLIGHT NUMBER — REENTER FLIGHT NUMBER	An invalid flight number was entered	Enter a valid flight number or enter the value 9 to return to task selection
ENTER FLIGHT NUMBER		This message is not an error message. If, however, you do not know the valid flight number, enter the value 9 to return to task selection
FLIGHT IS FULL ENTER NEW FLIGHT NUMBER OR THE VALUE 9 IF NO FLIGHT IS DESIRABLE	The flight entered is full	Enter a new flight number or enter the value 9 to return to task selection
INVALID PASSENGER NAME — REENTER	A passenger name was not entered or the passenger name was longer than 18 characters	Enter a valid passenger name
FLIGHT IS FULL — THERE ARE NO MORE FLIGHTS FROM LAX TO SF TODAY	There are no more seats on Flight 109 — reservations have been made for the 30 available seats	No more reservations can be made. Seat assignments and other activities can be done. To make reservations, end the program and then re-execute it.
SEAT ENTERED IS NOT AVAILABLE — REENTER	Either an invalid seat number or a seat number already assigned has been entered	Enter the seat number of an available seat
PASSENGER HAS NO RESERVATION — SEAT CANNOT BE RESERVED	The passenger name entered for seat selection is not in the list of passengers having reservations for the flight	Return to task selection; and either make a reservation for the passenger or make a seat selection using a valid name
? REDO *	An alphabetic character was entered where numeric data is required	Enter a valid numeric value
OV ERROR IN _____ *	An excessive number of characters was entered	Begin project again. Reexecute the program and enter the proper values
?EXTRA IGNORED*	A comma was entered as a part of a numeric field. Only the data to the left of the comma will be used and incorrect output will result	Ignore output and redo problem entering the correct numeric values

* These error messages are generated by the system and may vary on different computer systems.

Chapter 8

Project 8
Developing Communication Skills

Instructions: Prepare an oral or written report on one or more of the following subjects.

1. One of the fastest growing areas in data communications is satellite communications. Prepare a report on the current state-of-the-art technology relative to the use of satellites in transmitting data.

2. In most cities, earth stations for communication satellites can be seen atop buildings. Survey your community to observe which companies have earth stations. Upon locating an earth station, contact a member of the company to determine the use of the earth station. Report your findings to class.

3. Contact a sales representative from a data communications supplier and request a demonstration or lecture regarding the use of their products.

4. Determine what data processing periodicals are available which are devoted to data communications. Request the school librarian to order these periodicals for the reference library.

5. Contact the data processing manager at your school to determine the type of communications network being used. Prepare a report describing the terminals, networks, and related data communications equipment.

6. Some microcomputer systems provide for limited data communications capabilities. Contact the local computer store to determine the data communications capabilities of several of their widely used microcomputers.

7. When transmitting data via satellite communications, the unauthorized accessing of this data is a challenging problem. Data encryption is advocated as a possible solution to this problem. Prepare a report on data encryption as used with data communications.

8. Prepare a research report on the Carterfone decision.

9. Review one of the widely read periodicals in data processing. Prepare a list of the data communications equipment that is currently being advertised.

10. Prepare a report on the use of fiber optics as a communications channel.

Chapter 8
Answers to selected projects

Chapter 8, Project 3, Testing your knowledge — Key Terms

1. M
2. D, E, G, L, X
3. H
4. C
5. J
6. B
7. N
8. V
9. R
10. A
11. U
12. S
13. O
14. F

Chapter 8, Project 5, Testing your knowledge — True/False Questions

1. T
2. F
3. T
4. F
5. T
6. T
7. T
8. F
9. T
10. F
11. T
12. F
13. T
14. T
15. F
16. F
17. F
18. T
19. T
20. F
21. F
22. T
23. T
24. F
25. T
26. F
27. F
28. F
29. T
30. F
31. F
32. T
33. F
34. T
35. T

Chapter 8, Project 6, Testing your knowledge — Multiple Choice Questions

1. C
2. D
3. C
4. B
5. D
6. C
7. C
8. C
9. B
10. A
11. A
12. B
13. C
14. D
15. A

Chapter 9
Data Base and Distributed Data Processing

> **Chapter Objectives**
>
> - An understanding of the interrelationships of data within an organization
> - A knowledge of the reasons for a data base
> - A basic knowledge of the components of a data base and how data is stored and accessed in a data base
> - An understanding of the concepts of distributed data processing
> - An understanding of the need for distributed data bases and a basic knowledge of the methods used

Chapter Overview

The key to successfully using computing power in a company is to analyze the needs of the company and then organize both the data and the computing power in such a way that it reflects the structure of the company. One method of doing this is through the use of a data base. A data base is a collection of data which can be used by more than one application.

When data is stored in sequential, relative, or indexed files, each record in the file contains limited data about a single entity. If four files are used in a company, the data within each of the files is often interrelated, and there is data redundancy; that is, the same data is stored in more than one file. Thus, changes which occur would require all related files to be changed.

To combat problems of data redundancy, program dependence on data, and data dependence on computer hardware, the concept of a data base was introduced in the 1960's. When a data base is organized and stored on auxiliary storage, application programs can reference data in the data base independently of how the data is stored and organized. A data base is created, accessed, and updated by a data base management system. The data base management system consists of a series of programs written by a computer manufacturer or a software vendor that provides for: 1) Establishment of data relationships within the data base; 2) Data independence; 3) Comprehensive data security; 4) Recovery capabilities; 5) Query language capability. The data base administrator has the responsibility for managing the data within a company.

A hierarchical data base, sometimes called a tree structure, is composed of a hierarchy of elements. An element is a data record which contains application-oriented data. The data is retrieved by moving along the paths of the hierarchy according to a request from the program.

In a network data base, independent files are established for each major element of data; and the elements are linked together through the use of pointers in the records which point to other records in other files. To establish the network data base, a data base schema must be defined which identifies the relationships among the data which is to be stored in the data base. This is done by a data definition language.

Single files are sometimes called flat files. When comparing a flat file to a data base, the data base eliminates redundant data and updating is considerably simplified. The ability to retrieve data is also enhanced with the data base through the use of query languages. Data base management systems are found on large computers, minicomputers, and even some microcomputers.

Major reasons for developing data bases are to reduce data redundancy, to allow data to be referenced by multiple applications without the programs being data dependent, and to allow the data to be stored and accessed independently of the type of auxiliary storage being used. Security and controlled access to data is also possible. A major disadvantage of data base systems is that the development and control of a data base is a difficult and complex task.

Data communications capabilities have been used in recent years to develop networks consisting of a large centralized computer and many smaller minicomputers located in the area where the processing is required. This concept is called distributed data processing. Advantages include more system reliability, lower communications costs, improved employee productivity, and more timely information.

When using distributed data processing on some systems, all of the data is kept at the central computer system. A second approach, called the shared technique, places most of the data in the data base on the large central computer with parts of this data base duplicated at the remote sites. A third method allows each remote site to have its own data base that contains data required for its operation. This data is not duplicated at the central site. Thus, distributed data processing involves not only the distribution of computing power but also requires an organized distribution of the data which is required.

Chapter 9

Key Terms

Centralized Departments An organizational structure in which computer power is concentrated in a single location.

Data Base A collection of interrelated data stored together with a minimum of redundancy to serve multiple applications.

Data Base, Hierarchical A data base in which there is a fixed relationship between the elements in the hierarchy.

Data Base, Network A data base in which each of the elements is linked to the others through pointers.

Data Base Administrator The person who is responsible for creating, updating, and controlling access to a data base.

Data Base Management System A series of programs which is used to establish a data base, update the data base, and query the data base.

Data Definition Language A language that is a part of a data base system which allows for the definition of files and records, and their relationships.

Distributed Data Base The concept of distributing portions of a data base at remote sites where the data is most frequently referenced.

Distributed Data Processing The distribution of computing power and data using minicomputers at locations where processing is required.

Minicomputer A computer system which has smaller computer storage, slower processing speeds, and lower cost than large computer systems.

Query Language A language provided as a part of data base management systems that provides for easy access to data in a data base.

NAME_____ DATE_____

Chapter 9

Project 1
Distributed data bases

Instructions: Describe the characteristics of the distributed data base systems illustrated by the diagrams below.

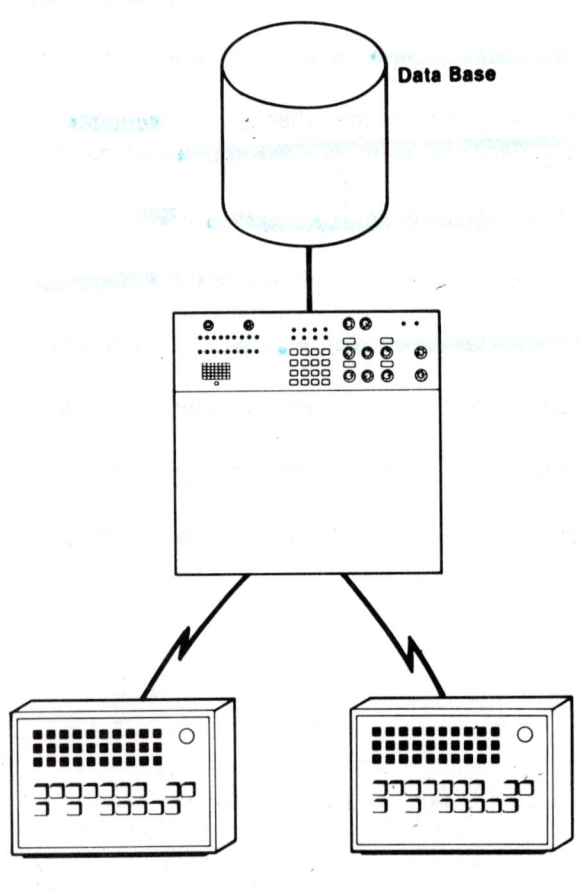

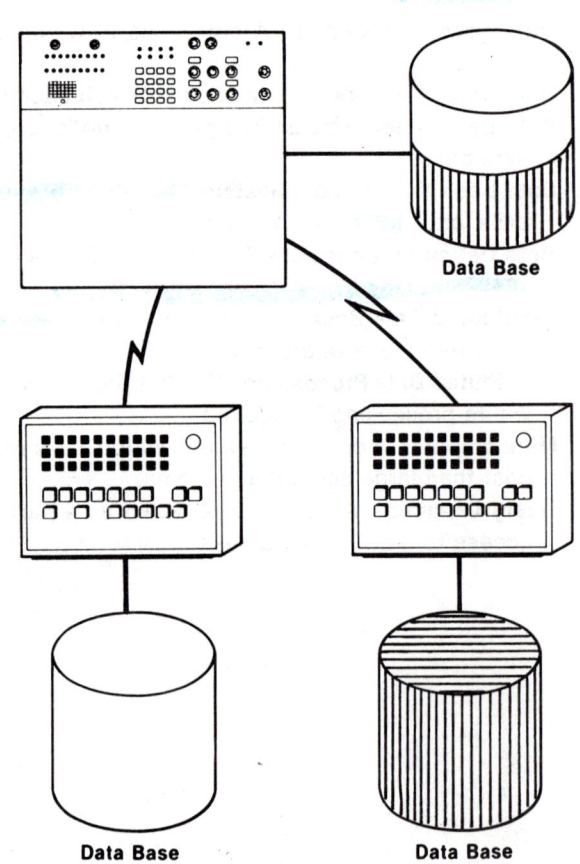

EXPLANATION:

_____

_____

_____

_____

_____

_____

EXPLANATION:

_____

_____

_____

_____

_____

_____

NAME_____ DATE_____

Chapter 9

Project 2

Testing your knowledge — Key Terms

Instructions: Fill in the blanks with the appropriate term from the list of terms on the right side of the page.

A 1. A __data base__ is a collection of data which can be used by more than one application.

N 2. The term used to describe the same data being stored in more than one file is data __redundancy__.

C 3. A data base is created, accessed, and updated by a __data base man sys__.

B 4. A __data base adm__ has the responsibility for managing the data within a company or organization.

H 5. The type of data base called a tree structure is the __hierarchical__ data base.

L 6. A __network__ data base provides for the establishment of individual files linked together through the use of pointers in the records which point to other records in the file.

O 7. The data base __schema__ identifies the relationships among the data which is to be stored in the data base.

D 8. To specify the relationships which exist in a data base, a __data def lang__ is used.

P 9. That portion of a data base required by a program is called the __subschema__.

C,M 10. A __data base man sys__ is used to logically search a data base and request specific I/O functions from the data management programs.

G 11. Single files are sometimes called __flat files__.

M 12. A __query language__ is a very high-level language which allows users to specify their information requirements without requiring the use of programmers.

F 13. __distrib data proc__ is the concept in which data communications capabilities are used to develop networks consisting of a large centralized computer system and many smaller minicomputers which are located in the area where processing is required.

E 14. A __distrib data base__ refers to the type of data base in which there is a distribution of portions of the data base at remote sites where the data is most frequently referenced.

I,J,K 15. Data base management systems are used on _____, _____, and _____.

A. Data base
B. Data base administrator
C. Data base management system
D. Data definition language
E. Distributed data base
F. Distributed data processing
G. Flat files
H. Hierarchical
I. Large computers
J. Microcomputers
K. Minicomputers
L. Network
M. Query language
N. Redundancy
O. Schema
P. Subschema

9.5

NAME_____ DATE_____

Chapter 9
Project 3
Testing your knowledge — Definitions

Instructions: Briefly define or explain each of the following terms:

1. Data base

2. Hierarchical data base

3. Network data base

4. Data base administrator

5. Data definition language

6. Distributed data base

7. Distributed data processing

8. Query language

NAME_____ DATE_____

Chapter 9

Project 4
Testing your knowledge — True/False Questions

Instructions: Circle the T if the question is true and F if the question is false for each of the true/false questions below and on the following page.

(T) F   1. The data base is one method of organizing data so that it corresponds to the needs and structure of a company.

T **(F)**   2. An advantage of separate files is that there is normally no interrelationships among the data.

T **(F)**   3. Data redundancy is the term used to describe common data which is stored in more than one record.

(T) F   4. When there is redundant data on files, the management of that data is often a difficult and error-prone activity.

T **(F)**   5. An advantage of redundant data is that the updating of files containing the data is greatly simplified.

(T) F   6. A data base may be defined as a collection of interrelated data stored together with a minimum of redundancy to serve multiple applications.

T **(F)**   7. A data base is created, accessed, and updated by programming in a low-level language.

(T) F   8. A data base management system is used to establish data relationships within a data base; and to provide for data independence, security, and recovery capabilities.

(T) F   9. A query language is normally a part of a data base management system.

(T) F   10. The data base administrator usually has the responsibility for managing the data within a company.

(T) F   11. There are two major types of data base organizations in use today — hierarchical and network.

T **(F)**   12. A network data base is sometimes called a tree structure and is composed of a hierarchy of elements which contain application-oriented data.

T **(F)**   13. A hierarchical data base is a data base in which individual files are established for each major element of data, and these elements are linked together through the use of pointers in the records which point to other records in the file.

(T) F   14. To establish a data base, a data base schema must be defined which identifies the relationships among the data which is to be stored in the data base.

(T) F   15. A data definition language is used to specify the relationships of data in a data base and to build the data base on the direct access device.

(T) F   16. That portion of a data base required by a program is called a subschema.

9.7

Testing your knowledge — True/False Questions

T **F** 17. To search the data base and request specific I/O functions, the programmer must write instructions in some low-level language.

T **F** 18. Defining the subschema of a data base is the responsibility of the user.

T **F** 19. Flat files refer to those files used in a data base system.

T F 20. When using a data base, redundant data is often eliminated and the update process simplified.

T F 21. A query language is a very high-level language which allows the user to specify informational requirements without the use of a programmer.

T **F** 22. Data base management systems are found only on large computers.

T **F** 23. A disadvantage of the use of a data base is the lack of security.

T F 24. An advantage of the data base is that access to data is relatively easy.

T F 25. The ability to define the data that should be in the data base and to establish logical relationships among the data is a skill which presents significant challenges to the data base administrator.

T F 26. In a decentralized approach to data processing, when a department requires a computer, it is placed in that department under control of that department.

T **F** 27. The centralized approach to data processing has been found to result in the most efficient means of responding to the needs of users and few problems have been encountered.

T **F** 28. Timesharing allows a user at a remote terminal to interact with the computer system provided the system is not being used for batch processing.

T **F** 29. In distributed data processing systems, individual minicomputers are placed in various departments; and a large centralized computer is not usually required.

T **F** 30. Distributed data processing systems offer less system reliability because of the use of a number of computers.

T F 31. On some distributed data processing systems, data to be accessed must be requested from the central computer system.

T F 32. Most of the data will be contained in the data base of the central computer when using a shared technique of distributed data base, and parts of the data base will be duplicated at the remote sites.

T **F** 33. In a distributed data processing system in which data is kept at the central computer, communications costs are substantially reduced.

T **F** 34. Data contained in a data base at a central computer should never be duplicated at the remote site.

T F 35. A possible method of using a data base in a distributed data processing system is to allow each remote site to have its own data base.

9.8

NAME_____   DATE_____

Chapter 9

Project 5

Testing your knowledge — Multiple-Choice Questions

Instructions: Circle the correct response to the multiple choice questions below and on the following page.

1. When separate files of data are used within an organization:

    A. The data within each of the files is usually unrelated.
    B. The data within each of the files is usually interrelated.
    C. There may be a great deal of data redundancy.
    D. Both B and C occur.

2. A collection of interrelated data stored together with a minimum of redundancy to serve multiple applications is the definition of:

    A. Single files.
    B. Flat files.
    C. Multiple files.
    D. A data base.

3. Which of the following is not a capability of a data base management system?

    A. Low-level language capability to access the data base.
    B. Provision for establishment of data relationships within the data base.
    C. A query language.
    D. Data security and recovery capabilities.

4. The individual or group responsible for determining what data should be in the data base and the relationships among the data is the:

    A. User.
    B. Data processing manager.
    C. Computer operator.
    D. Data base administrator.

5. The major types of data base organization are:

    A. Direct and distributed.
    B. Sequential, relative, and indexed.
    C. Hierarchical and network.
    D. Tree and hierarchical.

6. A data base schema:

    A. Defines the elements in a table.
    B. Defines that portion of the data base for use by a program.
    C. Defines the type of data base access.
    D. Defines the relationships among the data which is to be stored in the data base.

7. When using a data base as compared to flat files:

    A. There is less data redundancy with data bases, and file updating is simplified.
    B. There is less data redundancy with data bases, but file updating is more complex.
    C. There is less data redundancy with flat files, and file updating is simplified.
    D. There is less data redundancy with flat files, and file updating is more complex.

Testing your knowledge — Multiple-Choice Questions

8. With the use of a query language:

    A. Users can specify their informational requirements through the use of a low-level language.
    B. Users can specify their informational requirements through the use of a very high-level language.
    C. Programmers must write instructions in the query language to allow access to data.
    D. Users can specify their informational requirements through the use of a very high-level language, provided calculations are not required.

9. Data base management systems are available on:

    A. Large computers.
    B. Minicomputers.
    C. Microcomputers.
    D. All of the above.

10. When using a data base management system:

    A. Security of data is decreased, but access to data is increased.
    B. Security of data is decreased, and access to data is decreased.
    C. Security of data is increased, but access to data is decreased.
    D. Security of data is increased, and access to data is increased.

11. A major disadvantage of data base systems is that:

    A. The speed of processing is substantially decreased.
    B. The development and control of a data base is a difficult and complex task.
    C. The amount of data stored is limited.
    D. The amount of data accessed is limited.

12. The ability to use a remote terminal and to interact with a computer system in such a way that it appears to the user that no one else is using the system is called:

    A. Timesharing.
    B. Distributed data processing.
    C. Centralized processing.
    D. Multiprocessing.

13. Distributed data processing is the concept in which:

    A. A large central computer handles all processing needs.
    B. One or more minicomputers are used to handle all processing needs.
    C. Intelligent terminals are used in a timesharing mode.
    D. A network is developed consisting of a large centralized computer system and a number of smaller minicomputers which are located in the areas where processing is required.

14. In most distributed data processing systems:

    A. There is more system reliability.
    B. A single computer system is used.
    C. Employee productivity is decreased.
    D. Access to a data base is difficult.

15. In distributed data processing systems:

    A. The data base is stored at the central computer site.
    B. Portions of the data base at the central computer are duplicated at remote sites.
    C. Each remote site has its own data base.
    D. All of the above can occur.

Chapter 9
Project 6
Developing Communication Skills

Instructions: Prepare an oral or written report on one or more of the following subjects.

1. Prepare a report on distributed data processing.

2. Prepare a report on the organizational implications in a business resulting from the use of a distributed data processing system.

3. Contact a local computer store to determine if any of their microcomputer systems contains a data base management system. Discover the cost and capabilities of the software.

4. Prepare a research report on the advantages and disadvantages of the hierarchical data base as compared to the network data base.

5. Relational data bases are a newer type of data base advocated by some computer scientists. Prepare a research report on the current developments of relational data bases.

6. Contact one of the major software vendors of data base systems and prepare a detailed report on the capabilities of their query language.

7. In the middle and late 1960's, management information systems using data bases were touted as the solution to many corporations' problems concerning processing large amounts of data. For the most part, these systems failed. Consult technical journals of that era and write a report about why they failed. Contrast the failures in the middle and later 1960's with the considerable successes being found with data base systems now.

8. What effect could new technologies such as bubble memory have on the way data is stored and processed. Research this topic and prepare an oral report for class.

9. What happens in a distributed data processing network when a computer system containing some required data is down or is not accessible? Are there any ways to overcome or solve this problem? Consult technical journals and document the responses of industry to this problem.

10. One problem which users of data bases frequently encounter is that pointers in the data base are, in error, destroyed or rendered unusable. Therefore, there may many times be data in a data base which is not accessible because pointers do not point to it. Visit a local installation which utilizes a network data base system and discuss this problem with the data base administrator. Report to the class on your findings.

Chapter 9
Answers to selected projects

Chapter 9, Project 2, Testing your knowledge — Key Terms

1. A	4. B	7. O	10. C	13. F
2. N	5. H	8. D	11. G	14. E
3. C	6. L	9. P	12. M	15. I, J, K

Chapter 9, Project 4, Testing your knowledge — True/False Questions

1. T	8. T	15. T	22. F	29. F
2. F	9. T	16. T	23. F	30. F
3. F	10. T	17. F	24. T	31. T
4. T	11. T	18. F	25. T	32. T
5. F	12. F	19. F	26. T	33. F
6. T	13. F	20. T	27. F	34. F
7. F	14. T	21. T	28. F	35. T

Chapter 9, Project 5, Testing your knowledge — Multiple Choice Questions

1. D	4. D	7. A	10. D	13. D
2. D	5. C	8. B	11. B	14. A
3. A	6. D	9. D	12. A	15. D

Chapter 10
Systems Analysis and Design

Chapter Objectives

- An understanding of the structure of the data processing department and its function within the organization
- An understanding of the five phases utilized in a system project
- A familiarity with the tools used in systems analysis and design, including data flow diagrams and systems flowcharts
- A knowledge of the major business systems applications

Chapter Overview

Chapter 10 is designed to provide an understanding of the organizational structure of the typical data processing department; to explain the steps to be undertaken in conducting a systems project; and to provide a brief overview of the business systems found in most organizations.

Any system is made up of a series of procedures which are defined as logical steps by which all repetitive actions are initiated, performed, controlled, or completed. Thus, a system is composed of a network of related procedures designed to perform a specific task.

There are three primary reasons for the use of computer systems: 1) Reduce costs; 2) Produce more timely information; 3) Improve customer service.

Most systems are designed by members of the data processing department. Within the data processing department, there are three groups — systems, programming, and operations. In the late 1950's, most applications were accounting in nature, and the director of data processing reported to a member of top management who was concerned with the financial aspects of the business. Today, the position of director of data processing has frequently become a top management position on the vice-presidential level. As a profession, data processing has risen in status. With the widespread use of data bases, a position called the data base administrator has developed in many organizations. This individual frequently serves in a staff position reporting to the vice-president of information systems. Today, in a distributed data processing environment, some companies are providing systems and programming support at the level where the computer power is located rather than in a centralized department.

The job of the systems analyst is to analyze, design, and implement systems using a computer. The steps in conducting a system project can be broken down into a series of specific phases: Phase 1 — Initiation of the system project and the preliminary investigation; Phase 2 — Detailed system investigation and analysis; Phase 3 — System design; Phase 4 — System development; Phase 5 — System implementation and evaluation.

The purpose of the preliminary investigation is to determine if a problem or request for assistance warrants further investigation. The primary method of conducting the preliminary investigation is through the personal interview of managerial and supervisory personnel. One of the most important aspects is to uncover the true nature of the problem. The outcome of the preliminary investigation should be a report to management indicating the nature of the problem and a recommendation concerning further action.

After the preliminary investigation comes the detailed system investigation and analysis. During this phase, a detailed investigation takes place to determine WHAT is taking place in the current system with an analysis as to WHY the procedures are occurring. Basic fact gathering techniques include the interview, questionnaires, gathering the current system documentation, and personal observations of current procedures. To document the system, a data flow diagram is often used. Once the detailed investigation and analysis has been completed, a presentation will be given to management recommending one or more approaches to solving the problem.

The system design phase is involved with the design of the new system. Steps are designing the system output, designing the system input, designing the files, data base, and processing methods, and presenting the system design to management and users for approval. In defining the output requirements, the analyst is concerned with what information is needed by the users of the new system. It is not the responsibility of the systems analyst to tell the users what type of output they are going to receive. The analyst should be aware that there are many types of output including the printed report, microfilm, CRT terminals, plotters, and even audio response units. When designing system input, the analysts must decide what media is to be used, how data is to enter the system, how it can be captured at its source, the volume of input, and how often is it necessary to input the data. If transaction-oriented processing is used, the analyst must determine what response time is necessary and if hard copy is required or if CRT terminal output will be satisfactory.

When designing system files, the analysts must determine the data which is to be stored on auxiliary storage. As a first step, the analyst will develop a data dictionary that contains a list of the various data elements required for the system; the attributes of the data, the points in the system where the data is required, the type of access required for the data (random or sequential), the amount of activity, and amount of data to be stored. When designing the system processing, the design tool frequently used is the system flowchart.

An important aspect of any system design is the design of a set of controls to ensure the accuracy of the processing and to prevent computer-related fraud. Controls are source document control, input control, processing control, and output control. An audit trail must be established that enables any input record or process executed to be traced back to the original source data. Backup is also an important consideration. A backup is merely a copy of a file, typically stored on magnetic tape. Backup is very critical in a transaction-oriented system, and consideration must be given for restarting the system.

The final step in the system design phase is the presentation to management and users. Approval at all levels is very important.

Phase 4 systems development tasks are the establishment of a project development and implementation plan, development of detailed programming specifications, programming and testing the system, and preparing final documentation of the system.

The implementation and evaluation of the system is the final phase in the system project. When converting to a new system, either direct or parallel conversion may be used. Direct conversion would only be used with simple systems. The major disadvantage of parallel conversion is that a complete duplication of effort is required. After conversion, the new system should be evaluated to determine if it is producing the desired results at the costs anticipated and the maintenance factors involved.

Although the computer has virtually unlimited use in business, common applications are order entry, inventory control, accounts receivable, accounts payable, general ledger, and payroll.

Chapter 10

Key Terms

Accounts Payable The amount of money a company owes to other companies in payment of bills for merchandise or services.

Accounts Receivable Money owed by customers of a company for merchandise sold or for services rendered on a charge basis.

Audit Trail Provides the ability to trace any processing back to the original source data.

Backup File A copy of a current file used if the current file is destroyed.

Computer Operator An individual who operates the computer system.

Computer Programmers People who design, write, test, and implement the programs which process data on a computer system.

Controls, System The method used to assure that only valid data is accepted and processed on a computer.

Data Flow Diagram A diagramming technique used to graphically illustrate the flow of data through a system.

Data Processing Department The department in a company that is commonly made up of systems, programming, and operations.

Data Processing Manager The individual who is in charge of and manages a data processing department.

Data Base Administrator The person who is responsible for creating, updating, and controlling access to a data base.

Direct Conversion At a given date, the old system ceases to be operational and the new system is placed into use.

Distributed Data Processing The distribution of computing power and data using minicomputers at locations where processing is required.

Documentation, Program The detailed recording of the facts about a program through supporting materials and within the program itself.

Editing Input Data The process of checking to assure the validity of input data.

Gantt Chart A charting technique used to illustrate schedule deadlines and milestones.

General Ledger System The system used to provide a complete historical record of all financial transactions of a company.

Inventory Control The method used to keep track of merchandise available for sales.

Maintenance, System An ongoing process after a system has been implemented to correct errors and make changes as required to meet changing needs.

Order Entry System The system which defines the procedures used when processing an order.

Parallel Conversion Processing data in both the old system and the new system and comparing results.

Payroll System The system used to pay employees for services rendered.

Program Development Cycle The well-defined sequence of steps in writing a program that includes review of specifications, design, code, test, and document.

Preliminary Investigation That phase of a system project undertaken to determine if a problem warrants further study.

Printer Spacing Chart A preprinted form to assist in designing output reports.

Printers Devices which are connected to the computer system and which can prepare printed reports under the control of a computer program.

Procedures A series of logical steps by which all repetitive actions are initiated, performed, controlled, or completed.

Programming The process of writing instructions for a computer.

Programming Manager The person in charge of the programming group in a data processing department.

System Project, Conducting The steps in conducting a systems project can be broken down into a series of phases: initiation of the project; detailed investigation; design; development; implementation and evaluation.

System A series of related procedures designed to perform a specific task.

Systems Analysis The process of analyzing existing systems for the purpose of evaluating possible improvements in methods and procedures.

Systems Analysts People who design and develop systems which will be implemented on a computer system.

System Design That phase of a system project in which the new system is created.

System Development That phase of a system project concerned with scheduling, programming, and documenting a system.

System Flowchart A series of symbols designed to graphically illustrate the procedural steps in a system.

System Implementation and Evaluation That phase of a system project that is concerned with the conversion to the new system.

System Investigation That phase of a system project concerned with fact gathering and analyzing the existing system.

Systems Manager The person who is in charge of the systems analysis and design group within a data processing department.

Test Data Data created to test the reliability of a program.

Testing, Program The process of checking to assure that a program produces reliable and accurate results.

NAME_____   DATE_____

Chapter 10
Project 1
Systems analysis and design

Description: The local chamber of commerce consists of business persons throughout the community who are pledged to honest and reliable service. A file of current members containing their names, addresses, phone numbers, and types of business they represent is maintained on a standard 4 X 5 inch card file. An example of a record of one of the members is illustrated below.

```
NAME          Robert A. Sharpe
COMPANY NAME  Sharpe's Auto Repair
ADDRESS       1123 Ocean Blvd.
CITY          Belmont          STATE  CA     ZIP CODE  92632
PHONE NUMBER  551-5283
TYPE OF BUSINESS  Auto Repair
```

The chamber of commerce frequently receives inquiries from members of the community relative to the names of business persons who are members of the chamber of commerce and the service they perform. For example, a call may be received from an individual requesting the names of all auto repair shops in town that are represented by a member of the chamber of commerce. Another service of the chamber of commerce is to provide a list of the membership to other cities and approved charitable and political organizations.

A letter was received by the board of directors stating that the services of the chamber of commerce had severely deteriorated in the last several months because on two separate occasions, inquiries had been made concerning the services of some of the members; and on both occasions, the information was not accurate. The first, a request for electricians, resulted in a list of the names of three individuals — two of whom had moved over two years ago and were no longer working in the community. On the second, the name of one of the newer members of the chamber of commerce was omitted from the list. This individual is considering resigning from the chamber of commerce according to the letter received.

You have been called in as a consultant to design a computerized system that will provide for the production of lists of members of the chamber of commerce upon request, and will also provide for the handling of all requests for information relative to the membership and the type of business service they provide.

A minicomputer with CRT terminals, 200 million bytes of auxiliary storage, two magnetic tape units, and a high speed printer are available for your use.

Systems Analysis and Design

Phase 1: Initiation of the systems project and the preliminary investigation

In preparing for the preliminary investigation, it has been determined that the chamber of commerce has 12 paid employees. Sylvia Lock is the Executive Director and is responsible for managing the overall operation of the chamber of commerce. Reporting to Sylvia Lock is George Hamm, Vice-President in charge of local affairs, and Betty Simply, Vice-President in charge of state and federal affairs. Bruce Lane is Director of Membership, and Wilma Mae Brown is Director of Community Relations. Bruce Lane and Wilma Mae Brown report to George Hamm. There is one secretary assisting George Hamm, Bruce Lane, and Wilma Mae Brown. The secretary, Susan Statts, reports directly to George Hamm. Working for Bruce Lane, Director of Membership, is the Assistant Director of Membership, Marilyn Seymour, and the Assistant Director, Special Events, Evette Francosi.

Reporting to Betty Simply, Vice-President in charge of state and federal affairs, is Lulu Chow, Director of Research and Development, and Samuel Feinberg, Director of Governmental Affairs. There is one secretary, Coleen O'Shea, assisting Betty Simply, Lulu Chow, and Samuel Feinberg. Coleen O'Shea reports directly to Betty Simply. Lupe Gomez is the executive secretary and receptionist for the Executive Director, Sylvia Lock.

Serving in a nonpaying, advisory capacity is a board of directors consisting of six members of the chamber of commerce from the community.

Assignment 1: Preparing an organizational chart
Prepare an organizational chart of the chamber of commerce similar to the organizational chart illustrated on page 10.5 of the textbook.

Assignment 2: Conducting the preliminary investigation

Questions:

1. Analyze the organizational chart. List below the individuals whom you should interview when conducting the preliminary investigation.

   _____
   _____
   _____
   _____
   _____

2. State the objective of the preliminary investigation. _____
   _____
   _____

Systems Analysis and Design

    3. List the specific questions that you would ask and of whom you would ask them.

_____

_____

_____

_____

    4. Conduct the interviews (contact the instructor for the method used to conduct the interview).

    5. Prepare a memorandum giving your recommendations relative to the findings of the preliminary investigation. Follow the format contained on page 10.9 of the textbook.

Phase 2: Detailed system investigation and analysis

Upon review of the recommendation as a result of the preliminary investigation, approval has been given to conduct a detailed systems investigation and analysis of the inquiry and reporting system of the chamber of commerce.

Assignment 3: The detailed systems investigation and analysis

Questions:

    1. Prepare a list of the steps to be taken in the detailed systems investigation and analysis.

_____

_____

_____

_____

    2. Review the organizational chart previously developed. List the individuals to be interviewed during the detailed investigation (See "Operating Documents" on page 10.8 for further information concerning jobs performed by specific personnel).

_____

_____

_____

_____

Systems Analysis and Design

3. Prepare a list of specific questions to be asked of each of the individuals to be interviewed.

4. Conduct the interview (contact the instructor for the method of conducting the interview).

5. Prepare a written report summarizing the information gained from each of the interviews.

Operating Documents

As a result of the interviews, it has been determined that two basic documents are used in the system under study. One set of documents consists of the file of 4 X 5 inch cards which contain the individual's name, address, phone number, and type of business. The other form is the typed listing of the members of the chamber of commerce. A sample of these forms is illustrated below.

```
NAME          Robert A. Sharpe
COMPANY NAME  Sharpe's Auto Repair
ADDRESS       1123 Ocean Blvd.
CITY  Belmont        STATE  CA     ZIP CODE  92632
PHONE NUMBER  551-5283
TYPE OF BUSINESS  Auto Repair
```

```
                          BELMONT
                    CHAMBER OF COMMERCE

COMPANY NAME         ADDRESS           CITY                       TYPE OF BUSINESS   OWNER/MEMBER

Sharpe's Auto Repair 1123 Ocean Blvd.  Belmont, CA 92632  551-5283  Auto Repair       Robert A. Sharpe
Computer Haven       1109 Pacific Dr.  Belmont, CA 92631  841-4320  Computer Sales    Lester L. Finley
```

The Assistant Director of Membership, Marilyn Seymour, maintains the card file of members of the chamber of commerce and handles all inquiries. Requests for membership lists are handled by George Hamm's secretary, Susan Statts.

Systems Analysis and Design

Assignment 4: Detailed systems investigation — system documentation

Prepare a data flow diagram to document the inquiry system and the system to handle the processing of the membership lists. Then prepare a narrative explaining the data flow diagrams.

Assignment 5: Presentation of findings

Prepare a memorandum containing your recommendations for the improvement of the existing systems under study. Follow the format illustrated on page 10.13 of the textbook.

Phase 3: System design

Assignment 6: List the steps that are to occur in the systems design phase of the system study and then answer the questions below.

Questions:

1. What information must be produced from the new system? List each major output, such as "Inquiry Response," and then list each item of information which will be contained in that output.

2. After all of the various types of output have been determined and the contents have been listed, design each output report or output screen using the technique illustrated on page 10.15 of the textbook.

3. What data will be input to the new system? List each major input, such as "Inquiry Data," and then list each item of information which will be entered within that major input category.

Assignment 7: After all of the various types of input have been determined and the contents have been listed, design the manner in which the data will enter the new system. For example, if an inquiry is to be used, design the format of the CRT screen, the format of the prompts, and any other material which must be used to properly enter data into the computer system.

Assignment 8: For each major item of input, list the input editing which must be performed to ensure that only valid data enters the new system. Describe for each item what constitutes valid data and what constitutes invalid data. Specify the tests which will be performed on each item of data.

Assignment 9: Develop a data dictionary for any files or data bases which must be designed for the new system. Include a description of the data item, the size of the data item (i.e. number of characters required, etc.), the type of data (alphanumeric, numeric, etc.), and the relationships among the elements of data in the files or data bases.

Systems Analysis and Design

Assignment 10: Design the records which will be placed in the files or data bases required for the new system.

Assignment 11: Draw a system flowchart of the processing which will occur in the new system. Be sure to show the flow of data through the system, which files must be available for each process, what input data will be input to the process, and what output will be produced.

Assignment 12: Prepare an oral presentation explaining the design of the new system and the advantages the new system will offer.

Phase 4: System development

Assignment 13: Prepare a Gantt Chart illustrating schedule deadlines and milestones for the tasks to be undertaken during the system development phase of the systems project.

Phase 5: Implementation and evaluation

Assignment 14: Prepare a report describing the method of conversion to be used when changing from the old system to the new system.

Chapter 10

Project 2

Testing your knowledge — Key Terms

Instructions: Fill in the blanks with the appropriate term from the list of terms on the right side of the page.

1. (L) __Procedures__ are a series of logical steps by which all repetitive actions are initiated, performed, controlled, or completed.

2. (H, N, P) Most data processing departments consist of __operations__, __programming__, and __systems__.

3. (Q) Individuals who design systems are called __sys. analysts__.

4. (M) __Programmers__ are responsible for writing the instructions for the computer system which will cause the data to be processed.

5. (C) The __data base adm__ is responsible for developing and maintaining the data base, controlling the data base, and even controlling who has access to the data within the business organization.

6. (J) That phase of the system project which is concerned with determining if a problem warrants further investigation and analysis is called the __prelim inves__.

7. (F) That phase of a system project that is concerned with determining WHAT and WHY is called __invest + analysis__.

8. (E) A __data flow diag__ is used to graphically illustrate the flow of data through a system.

9. (K) The __printer spacing chart__ is used to design the format of the printed report.

10. (D) A __data dictionary__ contains a list of the various data elements required for the system, the attributes of the data, and other information.

11. (O) A __sys flow chart__ illustrates the actual steps which will occur in the system and the devices which will be used.

12. (A) The term used to describe the ability to trace an input record or process back to the original source data is __audit trail__.

13. (B) A copy of an existing file is called a __backup__ file.

14. (G) A __Gantt__ chart is used to graphically illustrate schedule deadlines and milestones.

15. (I) __Parallel__ conversion consists of processing data in both the old and new systems simultaneously and comparing the results.

A. Audit trail
B. Backup
C. Data base administrator
D. Data dictionary
E. Data flow diagram
F. Detailed system investigation and analysis
G. Gantt
H. Operations
I. Parallel
J. Preliminary investigation
K. Printer spacing chart
L. Procedures
M. Programmers
N. Programming
O. System flowchart
P. Systems
Q. Systems analysts

10.11

NAME_____ DATE_____

Chapter 10
Project 3
Testing your knowledge — Definitions

Instructions: Briefly define or explain each of the following terms:

1. System

2. Procedure

3. Data flow diagram

4. System flowchart

5. Audit trail

6. Direct conversion

7. Parallel conversion

NAME_____ DATE_____

Chapter 10

Project 4

Testing your knowledge — True/False Questions

Instructions: Circle the T if the question is true and F if the question is false for each of the true/false questions below and on the following page.

T **(F)** 1. A system is defined as a series of logical steps by which all repetitive actions are initiated, performed, controlled, or completed. *Procedure*

T **(F)** 2. The primary reason for the use of a computer in business is to improve the speed at which calculations are performed.

(T) F 3. Most data processing departments consist of three primary groups: systems, programming and operations.

T **(F)** 4. Today, the director of data processing usually reports to some financial officer within the organization, such as the vice-president of finance.

(T) F 5. Data processing has risen in status in most organizations during the past twenty years.

T **(F)** 6. The data base administrator, who is responsible for developing and maintaining the company data base, reports to the programming staff.

T **(F)** 7. In distributed data processing environments, systems analysts, programmers, and operations personnel work in a centralized department supporting the main computer system.

(T) F 8. The conversion of a manual system to a computerized system is one of the primary reasons for developing a new system.

(T) F 9. Prior to making a full-scale commitment to design and implement a system, a preliminary investigation is undertaken to determine if a problem warrants further investigation.

T **(F)** 10. An important aspect of the preliminary investigation is to document the flow of data through the system.

T **(F)** 11. The outcome of the preliminary investigation is a preliminary design of the new system.

(T) F 12. The detailed system investigation and analysis is intended to to determine WHAT is taking place and WHY the procedures found are occurring.

T **(F)** 13. The basic fact-gathering technique utilized in the detailed system investigation is the interview with high-level management to determine what should be taking place.

(T) F 14. The data flow diagram is used to graphically illustrate the flow of data through the system.

(T) F 15. Upon completion of the detailed investigation, a presentation will be given to management recommending one or more approaches to solving the problem.

T **(F)** 16. The first step in the system design phase is to design the system input.

10.13

Testing your knowledge — True/False Questions

T **(F)** 17. It is the responsibility of the systems analyst to define for the user the type of output to be received from a new system because most users lack an understanding of computerized processing.

T **(F)** 18. During the system design phase of a system project, the design of a printed report is the only consideration when reviewing output requirements because other forms of output can only be considered with management approval.

(T) F 19. The method of entering data into the system will depend upon whether batch processing or transaction-oriented processing is to be used.

(T) F 20. A data dictionary contains a list of the various data elements required for the system and the attributes of the data.

T **(F)** 21. The system flowchart shows the actual data which will appear in each output report.

(T) F 22. The serial numbering of source documents is a form of source document control.

(T) F 23. In batch processing systems, key verification is an important form of input control.

T **(F)** 24. Editing of data cannot occur in a batch system.

T **(F)** 25. The production of a detailed report from each record is called an audit trail.

(T) F 26. Backup files on magnetic disk are frequently created using magnetic tape.

T **(F)** 27. Backup files are not possible on transaction-oriented systems because the status of the files is constantly changing.

T **(F)** 28. Users are not normally involved in system design approval — only top management is consulted.

T **(F)** 29. The Gantt Chart is used to document the logic within a program.

T **(F)** 30. The programming specifications developed by the systems analyst do not contain detailed descriptions of the processing that is to occur as this must be defined by the programmer during the coding of the program.

T **(F)** 31. Testing a program can only be done by using the actual data employed in the processing applications of a company.

T **(F)** 32. Direct conversion should be performed on large complex systems to avoid excessive costs.

(T) F 33. With parallel conversion, both the old system and the new system are operated simultaneously and the results compared.

T **(F)** 34. A post implementation evaluation should be conducted only if difficulties are encountered during system testing.

T **(F)** 35. A well designed system should never encounter the need for system maintenance, as maintenance implies system errors.

NAME_____   DATE_____

Chapter 10

Project 5

Testing your knowledge — Multiple-Choice Questions

Instructions: Circle the correct response to the multiple choice questions below and on the following page.

1. A series of logical steps by which all repetitive actions are initiated, performed, controlled, or completed is the definition of:

    A. A system.
    B. A procedure.
    C. A program.
    D. An operation.

2. The primary reasons for the widespread use of computers in a business organization are to:

    A. Improve the speed of calculation and reduce the number of scientific employees.
    B. Improve the speed of calculation and reduce the number of total employees.
    C. Reduce costs, produce more timely information, and improve customer service.
    D. Improve the speed of calculations, reduce the number of office workers, and reduce the work week.

3. Most data processing departments consist of:

    A. Data entry, data control, and systems groups.
    B. Systems, programming, and data entry groups.
    C. Systems, programming, and data control groups.
    D. Systems, programming, and operations groups.

4. The individual responsible for developing and maintaining the data base is the:

    A. Systems analyst.
    B. Programmer.
    C. Computer operator.
    D. Data base administrator.

5. The phases in conducting a system project are:

    A. Preliminary investigation, detailed system investigation, system design, system development, and system implementation.
    B. Preliminary investigation and the design of input, processing and output.
    C. Preliminary investigation, system design, programming, testing, and implementation.
    D. Preliminary investigation, presentation to management, and system implementation.

6. One of the most important aspects of the preliminary investigation is to:

    A. Analyze the present system and document the data flow.
    B. Interview low-level personnel to determine what specific problems exist.
    C. Interview managerial and supervisory personnel to attempt to uncover the true nature of the problem.
    D. Develop a new system design if deemed necessary.

7. The outcome of the preliminary investigation should be:

    A. A system flowchart of the new system.
    B. A report to workers defining new job duties if necessary.
    C. A report to management indicating the nature of the problem, and a recommendation concerning the need for further action.
    D. A new or modified design of the existing system.

10.15

Testing your knowledge — Multiple-Choice Questions

8. During the detailed system investigation, the aim should be to:

    A. Determine WHAT is taking place and WHY the procedures are being performed.
    B. Design the new system.
    C. Program the new system.
    D. Both A and B.

9. A data flow diagram is used to:

    A. Define the logic used in a computer program.
    B. Define the flow of data as the data is processed by a series of programs.
    C. Graphically illustrate the flow of data through a system.
    D. Graphically illustrate the various input/output, processing, and auxiliary storage devices that are used as data flows through a system.

10. Which is the proper sequence of activities to be performed during the system design phase of a system project?

    A. Design the input, output, and files and make a presentation to management.
    B. Design the files, input, and output and make a presentation to management.
    C. Design the output, input, and files and make a presentation to management.
    D. Make a presentation to management and design the input, output, and files.

11. When designing the output, the systems analyst:

    A. Should design the output that is needed by the operations department.
    B. Should design the output in conjunction with the programmer assigned to the project.
    C. Should design the output in conjunction with the user.
    D. Assigns the design of the output to the programmer, who develops a printer spacing chart.

12. Controls are established in a system to:

    A. Simplify the programming process and document the system.
    B. Ensure the accuracy of the processing and prevent computer-related fraud.
    C. Document the system and improve the speed of data entry.
    D. Document the system and provide for approval of the system design.

13. The term used to describe the method by which any input record or processing executed on the computer system can be traced back to the original source data is:

    A. Source document control.
    B. Input control.
    C. Processing control.
    D. Audit trail.

14. Programming specifications should include:

    A. A brief description of the system and a system flowchart.
    B. The format of the input, output, and files to be processed.
    C. A detailed description of the processing that is to take place.
    D. All of the above.

15. With direct conversion of a system,:

    A. At a given date, the old system ceases to be operational; and the new system is placed into use.
    B. The new system is tested using actual operating data from a company; and when the results have been verified with the results of the old system, the new system is placed into use.
    C. The old system and the new system process data simultaneously, and the results are compared.
    D. Only minor changes are made in the system that is already operational.

Chapter 10
Project 6
Developing Communication Skills

Instructions: Prepare an oral or written report on one or more of the following subjects.

1. Contact the data processing manager of a local computer installation and obtain an organizational chart of the data processing department for that company.

2. Review current newspaper ads for job opportunities in data processing. Prepare a report for the class regarding the types of jobs available, pay scales, and experience required.

3. Datamation, Infosystems, and other data processing periodicals produce yearly salary surveys of data processing positions. Obtain a copy of the latest salary survey, and prepare a report for the class.

4. There are many employment agencies that specialize in the placement of data processing personnel. Contact one of these agencies and arrange for a guest speaker to talk to the class about job opportunities.

5. Prepare a research report on the topic of structured analysis and design.

6. Contact the data processing manager of a local company to determine if it would be possible to obtain the documentation for one of their systems for review by the class.

Chapter 10
Answers to selected projects

Chapter 10, Project 2, Testing your knowledge — Key Terms

1. L
2. H, N, P
3. Q
4. M
5. C
6. J
7. F
8. E
9. K
10. D
11. O
12. A
13. B
14. G
15. I

Chapter 10, Project 4, Testing your knowledge — True/False Questions

1. F
2. F
3. T
4. F
5. T
6. F
7. F
8. T
9. T
10. F
11. F
12. T
13. F
14. T
15. T
16. F
17. F
18. F
19. T
20. T
21. F
22. T
23. T
24. F
25. F
26. T
27. F
28. F
29. F
30. F
31. F
32. F
33. T
34. F
35. F

Chapter 10, Project 5, Testing your knowledge — Multiple Choice Questions

1. B
2. C
3. D
4. D
5. A
6. C
7. C
8. A
9. C
10. C
11. C
12. B
13. D
14. D
15. A

Chapter 11
Program Design and Flowcharting

Chapter Objectives

- An understanding of the reasons for the review of program specifications
- An understanding of the flowchart as a program design tool
- A knowledge of the three control structures found in structured programming
- A knowledge of structured design
- An introduction to egoless programming and structured walkthroughs
- An understanding of the logic required to solve seven problems commonly found in business applications programming

---

Chapter Overview

The purpose of this chapter is to introduce the program development cycle with emphasis on the basic concepts and techniques of program design. Included is an explanation of early design methodologies, the purpose and use of flowcharting, and an introduction to structured programming and structured design. A series of common design problems is then illustrated using structured flowcharts. These flowcharts include applications involving basic input/output operations; counters, accumulators, and printing final totals; basic comparing; comparing — record codes; searching a table; control breaks; and merging two files. The chapter concludes with an explanation of the use of decision tables.

The program development cycle consists of five basic steps: 1) Review of program specifications; 2) Program design; 3) Program coding; 4) Program testing; 5) Program documentation. A program is defined as a series of instructions which directs the computer to perform a sequence of tasks that produces the desired output. To execute a computer program, it must be loaded into main computer storage as a series of machine language instructions. Although instructions to be executed must be in machine language, the programmer who writes the program uses a source language. Regardless of the source language, statements fall into six major categories: 1) Statements to define files and records; 2) Statements to define other data; 3) Statements which move data in storage; 4) Statements which cause arithmetic operations to occur; 5) Statements which compare two values; 6) Statements which cause data to be read into main computer storage.

The first step in the program development is a review of the system and program specifications. It is the programmer's responsibility to directly implement the procedures defined by the systems analyst. After the specifications have been reviewed, the next phase is to design the structure and logic of the program. To provide a means of expressing the logic which would lead to the solution of a problem, flowcharts have been used for many years. The difficulty with flowcharting is that programmers apply their own set of rules to the development of the logic of a program and there is little scientific basis for the design of the program.

Structured programming evolved in the mid-1960's as a technique to provide a more scientific basis for program design. With structured programming, three basic control structures can be used to express any logic within a program. These control structures are: 1) Sequence; 2) If-Then-Else; 3) Do While.

An alternative to flowcharting which has been developed and may be used to express program logic is pseudocode. Pseudocode uses English-like statements to express program logic without the use of special symbols.

In the late 1960's, Stevens, Myers, and Constantine described a design methodology called structured design which resulted in a program consisting of many small portions of code called modules, each of which performs one given task within the program. One widely used structured design methodology employs IPO Charts to define the output, input, and major processing tasks necessary to accomplish a given task. These major processing tasks are then analyzed to determine if they appear to be lengthy or complex. If so, these tasks are broken down and another IPO Chart created. The logic for each of the resulting modules can then be developed using either pseudocode or flowcharts. Other design methodologies — the Jackson and the Warnier — are based upon the structure of the data which is to be processed.

The concept of egoless programming and structured walkthroughs is credited to Dr. Gerald Weinberg. When egoless programming is practiced, individuals view a program not as an extension of themselves, but rather as a product which should be examined to make it better. A structured walkthrough is an organized review of a program by other programmers.

It is important to understand the logic required to perform common design problems. Each of the design problems illustrated in the textbook makes use of the three basic control structures used in structured programming, and each design should be carefully reviewed.

In some applications, there can be a number of conditions which may occur within a program and a decision table can be used to help clarify the actions which must be taken under certain conditions within the program. Decision tables can be useful to systems analysts when they document the program specifications.

Chapter 11

Key Terms

Accumulating Final Totals The process in which values are accumulated as records are processed.
ANSI American National Standards Institute.
Comparing, Logical Operations The ability of the computer to compare data and perform alternative actions based upon the results of the comparison.
Computer Program A series of instructions which directs the computer to perform a sequence of tasks that produce a desired output.
Constantine, Larry Early leader in the development of structured design concepts.
Control Break The change that occurs when a record is read in which the control field is different from the control field in the previous record.
Decision Tables Graphical representations of logical decisions that must be made concerning conditions that can occur within a program.
Do While A basic control structure used in structured programming to implement a loop.
Egoless Programming Programming attitude based upon the concept that a program is not one's personal possession but open to all to view.
Flowchart Symbols Standard symbols used to flowchart programming logic.
Flowcharting The process of graphically depicting the detailed steps in the solution of a problem.
Hierarchy Chart A chart used in structured design to show the relationship of modules within a program.
If-Then-Else A basic control structure used with structured programming that implements conditional statements.
Input/Output Operations A basic data processing function that requires the reading of data and producing some output from the data read.
IPO Chart Input/processing/output chart used in structured design to assist in designing the structure of a program.
Jackson, Michael The developer of a program design theory in which design is based upon the structure of the data to be processed.
Instructions, Computer The unique numbers, letters of the alphabet, or special characters that, when interpreted by the computer's circuitry, cause a particular operation to be performed.
Loop The repeating of a sequence of instructions.
Merging Files The process of combining two or more files into a single file.
Myers, Glenford Early leader in the area of structured design.
Pseudocode A method used to express the logic required in the solution of a problem using English-like phrases.
Searching The process in which records are examined to locate a specific record in a file or table.
Sequence Control Structure A basic control structure used with structured programming.

Key Terms

Structured Design A method of designing programs in which a large program is decomposed into small modules, each of which performs a given function.

Structured Programming A method of programming in which three basic control structures are used to develop programs.

Structured Walkthroughs The process of reviewing program design and program coding with other programmers.

Subroutine A group of instructions which are used a number of times in a program and can be called as needed.

Warnier Design Methodology A method of program design based upon the structure of the data to be processed.

Weinberg, Dr. Gerald Author of "The Psychology of Computer Programming" and advocate of egoless programming and structured walkthroughs.

NAME_____   DATE_____

Chapter 11

Project 1
Program design — Input/output operations

Instructions: Draw a flowchart illustrating the design of a program that will prepare a stock summary report.

Input   Input consists of a series of records that contain the name of the company and the high and low price of the stock for that company for the day. The input data is shown below.

COMPANY NAME	HIGH	LOW
Microte	15	12
Printer Products	29	28
Storage Media	55	49
Technical Systems	89	87
END OF FILE		

Output   Output is a daily stock summary report containing the name of the company and the high and low price for the stock for the day. The format of the report is illustrated below.

```
            STOCK  SUMMARY  REPORT

   COMPANY  NAME            HIGH      LOW

   MICROTE                   15       12
   PRINTER PRODUCTS          29       28
   STORAGE MEDIA             55       49
   TECHNICAL SYSTEMS         89       87
```

Chapter 11

Project 2
Program design — Input/output operations

Instructions: Draw a flowchart illustrating the design of a program that will prepare a list of the executives of a company.

Input Input consists of a series of records that contain the names of the officers of a company, their titles, department, and sex. The input data is shown below.

NAME	TITLE	DEPARTMENT	SEX
J. A. ADAMS	VICE-PRESIDENT	ACCOUNTING	MALE
B. L. LANE	VICE-PRESIDENT	MARKETING	FEMALE
T. U. TOWNS	VICE-PRESIDENT	PRODUCTION	MALE
W. L. WINNS	DIRECTOR	INFORMATION SYSTEMS	FEMALE
END OF FILE			

Output Output consists of a list of company officers, their titles, and the department to which they are assigned. The format of the report is illustrated below.

```
              COMPANY OFFICERS

   J. A. ADAMS              VICE-PRESIDENT
                            ACCOUNTING
                            MALE
   B. L. LANE               VICE-PRESIDENT
                            MARKETING
                            FEMALE
   T. U. TOWNS              VICE-PRESIDENT
                            PRODUCTION
                            MALE
   W. L. WINNS              DIRECTOR
                            INFORMATION SYSTEMS
                            FEMALE
```

Chapter 11

Project 3
Program design — Counters, accumulators, and printing final totals

Instructions: Draw a flowchart illustrating the design of a program that will prepare a daily hotel charge report.

Input Input consists of a series of records that contain a room number, the customer name, the cost of the room, and the cost of meals charged to the room. The input data is shown below.

ROOM NUMBER	CUSTOMER NAME	ROOM CHARGE	MEAL CHARGES
101	A. L. OLDEN	25.00	5.00
102	B. A. JONES	27.50	7.50
105	C. G. SMITH	30.00	7.50
109	D. L. MEARS	25.00	5.00
END OF FILE			

Output Output is a hotel charge report which will contain the room number, customer name, room charge, meal charges, and total charges. After all records have been processed, the total number of rooms rented, the total room charges, total meal charges, and a final total of all charges are to be printed.

```
                    HOTEL CHARGE REPORT

   ROOM       CUSTOMER        ROOM       MEAL        TOTAL
  NUMBER        NAME         CHARGE     CHARGES     CHARGES

   101       A. L. OLDEN     25.00       5.00        30.00
   102       B. A. JONES     27.50       7.50        35.00
   105       C. G. SMITH     30.00       7.50        37.50
   109       D. L. MEARS     25.00       5.00        30.00

 TOTAL ROOMS RENTED 04
 TOTAL ROOM CHARGES $107.50
 TOTAL MEAL CHARGES $25.00
 TOTAL CHARGES $132.50
```

Chapter 11

Project 4
Program design — Counters, accumulators, and printing final totals

Instructions: Draw a flowchart illustrating the design of a program that will prepare a report of real estate sales and commissions.

Input Input consists of a series of records that contain the address, city, and selling price of houses that have been sold during the month. The input data is shown below.

ADDRESS	CITY	SELLING PRICE	COMMISSION %
111 PINE AVENUE	LONGVIEW	90,000.00	6%
115 RIVER ROAD	FREMONT	80,000.00	6%
808 LANE DRIVE	LONGVIEW	95,000.00	6%
922 LAKE STREET	RIVERDALE	100,000.00	6%
END OF FILE			

Output Output is to consist of a real estate sales and commissions report which will contain the address, city, selling price, and commission paid for each of the houses. After all records have been processed, the total number of houses sold, the total selling prices of all houses, the average price of all houses sold, and the total commissions are to be printed. The format of the output report is illustrated below.

```
                REAL ESTATE SALES REPORT

     ADDRESS            CITY         SELLING PRICE    COMMISSION

 111 PINE AVENUE     LONGVIEW          90,000.00      $5,400.00
 115 RIVER ROAD      FREMONT           80,000.00      $4,800.00
 808 LANE DRIVE      LONGVIEW          95,000.00      $5,700.00
 922 LAKE STREET     RIVERDALE        100,000.00      $6,000.00

 TOTAL HOUSES SOLD 04
 TOTAL SALES $365,000.00
 AVERAGE SELLING PRICE $91,250.00
 TOTAL COMMISSIONS $21,900.00
```

NAME_____ DATE_____

Chapter 11

Project 5
Program design — Comparing

Instructions: Draw a flowchart illustrating the design of a program that will prepare a monthly report for a Legal Clinic.

Input Input consists of a series of records that contain the name of the client, the name of the attorney, and the hours worked by the attorney on the case. The input data is shown below.

CLIENT	ATTORNEY	HOURS
J. C. HIGGINS	ANTONIO	10
C. R. RANDALL	KELLY	20
T. T. TAYLOR	CERILI	21
C. M. SARLS	LUIGI	25
END OF FILE		

Output Output is a monthly legal clinic report that lists the client's name, the attorney, the hours worked by the attorney on the case, and the fee. The fee charged by the attorney is based upon the hours worked. The first 20 hours are charged at the rate of $50.00 per hour. Hours in excess of 20 are charged at the rate of $40.00 per hour. The format of the report is illustrated below. After all records have been processed, the final totals illustrated below are to be printed.

```
      CLIENT            ATTORNEY      HOURS         FEE

J. C. HIGGINS          ANTONIO         10          500.00
C. R. RANDALL          KELLY           20        1,000.00
T. T. TAYLOR           CERILI          21        1,040.00
C. M. SARLS            LUIGI           25        1,200.00

TOTAL CLIENTS 04
TOTAL HOURS BILLED 76
TOTAL HOURS BILLED AT $50.00 PER HOUR 70
TOTAL HOURS BILLED AT $40.00 PER HOUR 06
TOTAL FEES $3,740.00
```

Chapter 11

Project 6
Program design — Comparing

Instructions: Draw a flowchart illustrating the design of a program that will prepare a monthly credit card billing report.

Input Input consists of a series of records that contain the name of the person who has purchased on credit, their previous balance, purchases, and payments. The input data is shown below.

NAME	PREVIOUS BALANCE	PURCHASES	PAYMENTS
A. B. BRONSON	500.00	125.00	50.00
C. L. DAVIS	105.00	25.00	30.00
R. C. ISSAC	450.00	100.00	50.00
END OF FILE			

Output Output is a credit card billing report that lists the name, the previous balance, the purchases, the payments, the amount subject to a finance charge, the interest, and the new balance. The amount subject to a finance charge is obtained by adding the purchases to the previous balance and subtracting the payments.

If the amount subject to a finance charge is $250.00 or more, interest must be calculated by multiplying the amount by 1%. If the amount subject to a finance charge is less than $250.00, interest is calculated by multiplying the amount by 1.5%. The new balance is obtained by adding the interest to the amount subject to a finance charge. After all records have been processed, the total customers and the total of the new balances are to be printed. The format of the output is illustrated below.

NAME	PREVIOUS BALANCE	PURCHASES	PAYMENTS	SUBJECT TO FINANCE CHARGE	INTEREST	NEW BALANCE
A. B. BRONSON	500.00	125.00	50.00	575.00	5.75	580.75
C. L. DAVIS	105.00	25.00	30.00	100.00	1.50	101.50
R. C. ISSAC	450.00	100.00	50.00	500.00	5.00	505.00

TOTAL CUSTOMERS 03
TOTAL NEW BALANCE $1,187.25

Chapter 11

Project 7
Program design — Multiple comparisons — use of record codes

Instructions: Draw a flowchart illustrating the design of a program that will prepare a contract labor report for heavy equipment operators.

Input Input consists of a series of records that contain the name of the employee, the job being performed, the hours worked per day, and a code. Journeyman employees have a code of J, apprentices a code of A, and casual labor a code of C. All records have been edited and have a valid code.

HEAVY EQUIPMENT OPERATORS			
NAME	JOB	HOURS	CODE
BRUCE JATER	GRADING	6	J
SHARL LOVE	FILL	4	A
RAY LETT	FILL	4	C
OSCAR YARDS	GRADING	3	J
END OF FILE			

Output Output is to consist of a contract labor report that contains the employee name, job performed, hours worked, job code, and pay. Journeyman employees receive $12.00 per hour. Apprentices receive $10.00 per hour, and casual labor receives $8.00 per hour. After all records have been processed, the total number of journeymen, the total number of apprentices, and the total number of casual employees are to be printed as well as the total pay. The format of the report is illustrated below.

```
                    CONTRACT LABOR
      NAME           JOB        HOURS    CODE      PAY

   BRUCE JATER     GRADING        6        J      $72.00
   SHARL LOVE      FILL           4        A       40.00
   RAY LETT        FILL           4        C       32.00
   OSCAR YARDS     GRADING        3        J       36.00

   TOTAL EMPLOYEES 04
   TOTAL JOURNEYMEN 02
   TOTAL APPRENTICES 01
   TOTAL CASUAL 01
   TOTAL PAY $180.00
```

11.11

Chapter 11

Project 8
Program design — Multiple comparisons — use of record codes

Instructions: Draw a flowchart illustrating the design of a program that will prepare an automobile liability insurance estimate for customers.

Input Input consists of a series of records that contain the name of the customer, the amount of liability coverage (which is fixed at $100,000.00), the age of the customer, and a risk code. A code of 1 indicates a high risk driver with recent moving violations. A code of 2 indicates a low risk driver with no recent moving violations. If a record does not contain a code of 1 or a code of 2, the input record is in error and an error message is to be printed on the report. The format of the input is illustrated below.

NAME	LIABILITY COVERAGE	AGE	RISK CODE
T. L. ELDON	100,000.00	42	1
D. C. FOX	100,000.00	18	2
L. R. GUMM	100,000.00	26	2
M. M. MATT	100,000.00	23	1
C. R. NUMIS	100,000.00	21	
END OF FILE			

Output Output is to consist of insurance estimates for $100,000.00 liability insurance. The report is to contain the customer's name, age, risk code, a message identifying the customer as a high insurance risk or a low insurance risk, and the cost of the insurance coverage. If the customer is less than 25 years of age and has a risk code of 1 (high risk), the cost of insurance is $280.00. If the customer is 25 years of age or more and has a risk code of 1 (high risk), the cost of insurance is $250.00. If the customer is 25 years of age or more and has a risk code of 2 (low risk), the cost of insurance is $200.00. If the customer is less than 25 years of age and has a risk code of 2 (low risk), the cost of insurance is $225.00. If there is no risk code in the input record, the message "RISK CODE NOT SPECIFIED" should appear on the report. After all records have been processed, the total number of customers, the total number of low risk drivers, the total number of high risk drivers, and the total number of unknown risk types should be printed. The format of the report is illustrated below.

```
                    INSURANCE REPORT

    NAME          AGE    RISK    RISK         INSURANCE
                         CODE    TYPE         COST

   T. L. ELDON    42      1      HIGH RISK     250.00
   D. C. FOX      18      2      LOW RISK      225.00
   L. R. GUMM     26      2      LOW RISK      200.00
   M. M. MATT     23      1      HIGH RISK     280.00
   C. R. NUMIS    21             RISK CODE NOT SPECIFIED

   TOTAL CUSTOMER 05
   TOTAL LOW RISK 02
   TOTAL HIGH RISK 02
   TOTAL UNIDENTIFIED RISK TYPE 01
```

Chapter 11

Project 9
Program design — Searching a table

Instructions: Draw a flowchart illustrating the design of a program that will prepare a daily income report for a television repair facility.

Input Input consists of a series of records that contain the customer's name, a repair code, and the cost of parts for the repair which was performed. In addition to the input records, a table is required to produce the report. The table contains the repair code, the repair type, and a standard labor charge. The format of the input record and the table are illustrated below.

INPUT RECORD

NAME	REPAIR CODE	PARTS
BARNES	03	16.50
LANG	09	14.00
LILLY	07	12.00
MATTES	08	41.00

TABLE

REPAIR CODE	REPAIR TYPE	STANDARD LABOR
01	AMPLIFIER	10.95
03	ANTENNA	24.50
07	HIGH VOLTAGE TUBE	59.95
09	RECTIFIER	25.95
15	TUNER	95.75

Output Output is to consist of a daily income report from television repairs. The report is to contain the customer's name, the repair code, the repair type, the standard labor charge, the cost of parts, and the total cost of the repair (labor charge plus parts). The repair type and the standard labor charge are to be extracted from the table based upon the repair type code found in the input record. If the repair code in the input record is not found in the table, the message "INVALID REPAIR CODE" should be printed and no charges should be printed or added into the final totals. The customer, however, should be counted in the final total. After all records have been processed, final totals of customers, parts, labor, and total income are to be printed. The format of the output is illustrated below.

```
                        TELEVISION REPAIR

  NAME        REPAIR       REPAIR              LABOR      PARTS      TOTAL
              CODE         TYPE                CHARGE     CHARGE     CHARGE

  BARNES      03           ANTENNA             24.50      16.50      41.00
  LANG        09           RECTIFIER           25.95      14.00      39.95
  LILLY       07           HIGH VOLTAGE TUBE   59.95      12.00      71.95
  MATTES      08           INVALID REPAIR CODE

  TOTAL CUSTOMERS 04
  TOTAL LABOR CHARGES $110.40
  TOTAL PARTS CHARGES $42.50
  TOTAL INCOME $152.90
```

NAME_____ DATE_____

Chapter 11

Project 10
Program design — Searching a table

Instructions: Draw a flowchart illustrating the design of a program that will prepare a paramedic report of services rendered.

Input Input consists of a series of records that contain the paramedic unit number, the time the service was rendered, a code indicating the problem, and a code indicating the service rendered. In addition to the input record, two tables are required to produce the report. The first table contains the problem code and related problem, and the second table contains the service code and the service given. The input and two tables are illustrated below. All input data has been previously edited and the codes in the input records are all valid.

INPUT

UNIT	TIME	PROBLEM CODE	SERVICE CODE
10	8:00 A.M.	05	01
12	8:30 A.M.	04	03
10	9:15 A.M.	02	09

TABLE1

PROBLEM CODE	PROBLEM
01	FAINTING
02	FRACTURE
03	HEART ATTACK
04	GENERAL ILLNESS
05	LACERATION
06	SHOCK

TABLE2

SERVICE CODE	SERVICE
01	BANDAGE
03	GENERAL FIRST AID
05	ICE PACK
07	HOT PACK
08	NON PRESCRIPTION DRUGS
09	SPLINT

Output Output is to consist of a report that lists the unit, time, problem, and service rendered. After all records have been processed, the total number of calls are to be printed.

```
                        PARAMEDIC REPORT
  UNIT        TIME            PROBLEM              SERVICE

  10       8:00 A.M.       LACERATION           BANDAGE
  12       8:30 A.M.       GENERAL ILLNESS      GENERAL FIRST AID
  10       9:15 A.M.       FRACTURE             SPLINT

  TOTAL CALLS 03
```

11.14

Chapter 11

Project 11
Program design — Control breaks

Instructions: Draw a flowchart illustrating the design of a program that will prepare a semester grade report.

Input Input consists of a series of records that contain the student identification number, student name, class taken, units for the class, grade assigned, and grade points. The format of the input record is illustrated below.

STUDENT NUMBER	STUDENT NAME	CLASSES	UNITS	GRADE	GRADE POINTS
10019	LOTT	INTRO TO BUSINESS	3	C	6
10019	LOTT	ENGLISH I	2	B	6
10019	LOTT	BIOLOGY	4	A	16
22359	MANN	COMPUTER SCIENCE	4	A	16
22359	MANN	HISTORY	3	C	6

Output Output is to consist of a semester grade report that contains the student number, student name, class, units, grade, and grade points for each class. When there is a change in student number, a control break occurs and the grade point average for the student (total grade points divided by total units) and the total units should be printed. After all records have been processed, the total number of students should be printed. The format of the output report is illustrated below.

```
STUDENT      STUDENT           CLASSES              UNITS    GRADE   GRADE POINTS
NUMBER       NAME

10019        LOTT              INTRO TO BUSINESS      3        C          6
10019        LOTT              ENGLISH I              2        B          6
10019        LOTT              BIOLOGY                4        A         16

GRADE POINT AVERAGE 3.11           TOTAL UNITS        9

22359        MANN              COMPUTER SCIENCE       4        A         16
22359        MANN              HISTORY                3        C          6

GRADE POINT AVERAGE 3.14           TOTAL UNITS        7
                  .
                  .
                  .
TOTAL STUDENTS 350
```

Chapter 11

Project 12
Program design — Control breaks

Instructions: Draw a flowchart illustrating the design of a program that will prepare a daily police report.

Input

Input consists of a series of records that contain a police officer's badge number, a ticket number, a violation code, and the amount of the ticket. A table is also required to produce the required output. The table contains a violation code and the violation description. The format of the input and table are illustrated below. All input data has been previously edited, and all records contain valid violation numbers.

INPUT

BADGE NO.	TICKET NUMBER	VIOLATION NUMBER	FINE
10	1034	03	25.00
10	1035	01	5.00
10	1036	09	150.00

TABLE

VIOLATION NUMBER	DESCRIPTION
01	ILLEGAL PARKING
03	ILLEGAL U TURN
05	ILLEGAL LEFT TURN
09	RECKLESS DRIVING
10	SPEEDING
15	EQUIPMENT VIOLATION

Output

Output is to consist of a daily police report containing the badge number, the ticket number, the violation number, the violation description, and the fine. When there is a change in badge number, a control break occurs and the total number of tickets written by a particular police officer, as identified by the badge number, is to be printed. After all records have been processed, the total number of tickets for the day and the total amount of fines are to be printed.

```
                        DAILY POLICE REPORT
    BADGE     TICKET      VIOLATION       VIOLATION           FINE
    NO.       NUMBER      NUMBER          DESCRIPTION

    10        1034        03              ILLEGAL U TURN      25.00
    10        1035        01              ILLEGAL PARKING      5.00
    10        1036        09              RECKLESS DRIVING   125.00

          TOTAL TICKETS 03                TOTAL FINES      $155.00
                    .
                    .
                    .
   TOTAL TICKETS 50
   TOTAL FINES $1,500.00
```

11.16

Chapter 11

Project 13
Program design — Merging

Instructions: Draw a flowchart illustrating the design of a program that will merge two files of records together to create one file.

Input Input consists of a series of records for all tenured professors containing a teacher number, teacher name, and the division in which the individual teaches. A similar file exists for all nontenured professors. Both files are stored on magnetic tape. The formats of the input records are illustrated below.

TENURED PROFESSORS		
NUMBER	NAME	DIVISION
20010	SUE BATES	COMPUTER SCIENCE
30555	BOB CARR	ENGLISH

NONTENURED PROFESSORS		
NUMBER	NAME	DIVISION
10099	LINDA APPLE	BUSINESS
43911	TOM DOOLEY	HISTORY

Output Output is to consist of a magnetic tape file containing both the tenured and nontenured professors. As the records are merged, an output report should be printed listing all of the professors. After all records have been processed, the total number of records processed and the total number of tenured and nontenured professors should be printed. The format of the printed report is illustrated below.

```
NUMBER        NAME              DIVISION

10099         LINDA APPLE       BUSINESS
20010         SUE BATES         COMPUTER SCIENCE
30555         BOB CARR          ENGLISH
43911         TOM DOOLEY        HISTORY
                 .

TOTAL RECORDS PROCESSED 200
TOTAL TENURED PROFESSORS 105
TOTAL NONTENURED PROFESSORS 95
```

NAME_____   DATE_____

Chapter 11

Project 14

Decision tables

Instructions: Draw a decision table to graphically illustrate the tuition charges at a college for resident and non-resident students taking above and below 15 units of graduate or undergraduate courses. The narrative below summarizes the various conditions and charges.

Residents, 15 units or more of undergraduate courses are charged $500.00
Residents, less than 15 units of undergraduate courses are charged $450.00
Residents, 15 units or more of graduate courses are charged $750.00
Residents, less than 15 units of graduate courses are charged $500.00
Nonresidents, 15 units or more of undergraduate courses are charged $1,000.00
Nonresidents, less than 15 units of undergraduate courses are charged $750.00
Nonresidents, 15 units or more of graduate work are charged $1,500.00
Nonresidents, less than 15 units of graduate work are charged $1,000.00

Fill in the decision table below.

		1	2	3	4	5	6	7	8
CONDITIONS									
ACTIONS									

NAME_____ DATE_____

Chapter 11

Project 15
Testing your knowledge — Key Terms

Instructions: Fill in the blanks with the appropriate term from the list of terms on the right side of the page.

E 1. A _flowchart_ is used to graphically represent the steps in the solution of a problem.

A 2. ANSI stands for _____.

C,F,K 3. The three basic control structures used with structured programming are _____, _____, and _____.

J 4. _Pseudocode_ is used to express logic for a program using English-like statements.

N 5. A series of computer instructions which accomplishes a given task and can be called by various portions of a program is called a _subroutine_.

L 6. _Struc design_ is the methodology in which a program is broken down into small portions of code called modules.

G 7. The _IPO_ Chart is used in structured design methodology to define the output, input, and major processing tasks for a given problem.

H, P 8. The _Jackson_ and the _Warnier_ design methodologies are based upon the data which is to be processed.

D 9. When _egoless_ programming is practiced, the individual views a program not as a personal extension but as a product which should be examined.

M 10. An organized review of a program by other programmers is called a _struc walkthru_.

C 11. The control structure to implement a loop is called the _Do While_.

F 12. The control structure to implement a comparing operation is the _If-Then-Else_.

O 13. To reference the elements within a table, a _subscript_ is used.

I 14. _Merging_ is the process in which two or more files are combined into one file.

B 15. A _decision table_ is a graphical representation of the logical decisions that must be made concerning certain conditions which can occur within a program.

A. American National Standards Institute
B. Decision table
C. Do While
D. Egoless
E. Flowchart
F. If-Then-Else
G. IPO
H. Jackson
I. Merging
J. Pseudocode
K. Sequence
L. Structured design
M. Structured walkthrough
N. Subroutine
O. Subscript
P. Warnier

11.19

NAME_____   DATE_____

Chapter 11

Project 16
Testing your knowledge — Definitions

Instructions: Briefly define or explain each of the following terms:

1. Decision table

2. Egoless programming

3. Flowchart

4. Pseudocode

5. Structured design

6. Structured programming

7. Structured walkthrough

8. Subroutine

NAME_____   DATE_____

Chapter 11

Project 17
Testing your knowledge — True/False Questions

Instructions: Circle the T if the question is true and F if the question is false for each of the true/false questions below and on the following page.

(T) F 1. The program development cycle consists of a review of program specifications, program design, program coding, program testing, and program documentation.

(T) F 2. A program is defined as a series of instructions which directs the computer to perform a sequence of tasks that produces a desired output.

(T) F 3. To execute a computer program, the program must be loaded into storage as a series of machine language instructions.

T **(F)** 4. The programmer must write instructions to the computer system in machine language.

(T) F 5. Instructions are available to the computer programmer to define data, operate on data, and read and write data.

T **(F)** 6. The program specifications given to the programmer by the systems analyst may be changed at the programmer's discretion.

T **(F)** 7. The least important phase of the program development cycle is program design, as a design is constantly modified.

(T) F 8. To provide a means of expressing the logic which would lead to the solution of a problem, flowcharts are commonly used.

T **(F)** 9. There is little standardization in flowcharting, as nearly all companies use their own set of graphics.

T **(F)** 10. The value in flowcharting is that it provides for a scientific approach to problem solving.

T **(F)** 11. With structured programming, two basic control structures are used to express the logic of any problem.

(T) F 12. The If-Then-Else control structure is used to implement comparing operations.

(T) F 13. The Do While control structure is used to implement looping operations.

T **(F)** 14. An important concept in structured programming is that there is only one entry point but multiple exit points in any given control structure.

(T) F 15. Pseudocode may be used as an alternative to flowcharting as a means of expressing program logic.

T **(F)** 16. Pseudocode uses English-like statements to define the structure of a program.

T **(F)** 17. A subroutine is one of the basic control structures used with structured programming.

11.21

Testing your knowledge — True/False Questions

F 18. Subroutines can only be used with structured design.

T 19. With structured design methodology, a program is designed in such a way that the program will consist of many small portions of code, called modules, that accomplish a given task.

F 20. The IPO Chart, when used as a design tool, is used to express the logic of a program.

F 21. The Warnier and Jackson design methodologies were first used by von Neumann prior to the developing of flowcharting standards.

T 22. When egoless programming is practiced, the individual views a program as a product which should be examined to make it better.

F 23. Structured walkthroughs are a review technique used to train beginning programmers.

T 24. An end-of-file indicator must be placed at the end of sequential input files to indicate there is no more data to be processed.

F 25. The logic for a basic input/output operation where records are read and printed makes use of the sequence control structure to repeat a series of operations.

F 26. There can only be a single comparing operation in a program.

T 27. In some business applications, data is stored in the form of a table, and the table is accessed during the processing of the input records.

F 28. A limitation of the use of data in a table in a program is that the data cannot be used in arithmetic calculations.

T 29. A subscript is a field containing a value used to reference an item in a table.

T 30. A control break occurs when data in a control field changes from that found in the previous record.

F 31. In the logic of control break reporting, the record that caused the control break to occur is never printed when a control break occurs.

T 32. Merging is the process in which two or more files are combined into one file.

F 33. In a merging operation, only one of the files must be in some predetermined sequence.

T 34. A decision table is a graphical representation of the logical decisions that must be made concerning conditions which can occur within a program.

F 35. A decision table is often used in place of a flowchart or IPO Chart to assist in the design of the structure of a program.

NAME_____   DATE_____

Chapter 11

Project 18

Testing your knowledge — Multiple-Choice Questions

Instructions: Circle the correct response to the multiple choice questions below and on the following page.

1. The program development cycle consists of:

    A. Program coding, testing, and implementation.
    B. Program design, coding, and testing.
    C. Review of program specifications, program design, testing, and implementation.
    D. Review of program specifications, program design, program coding, testing, and documentation. *(circled)*

2. After reviewing the program specifications:

    A. It is the programmer's responsibility to directly implement the procedures as defined by the systems analyst. *(circled)*
    B. It is the systems analyst's responsibility to design the program.
    C. Changes in procedures or design format are the responsibility of the programmer.
    D. Changes should never be made by either the analyst or the programmer.

3. One of the earliest design tools used to express the logic of a program is the:

    A. Flowchart. *(circled)*
    B. IPO Chart.
    C. Pseudocode Chart.
    D. Hierarchy Chart.

4. Disadvantages of the use of the flowchart as a design tool include:

    A. Programmers apply their own set of rules to the development of logic.
    B. There is little scientific basis on which to develop logic.
    C. Programmers are not aware of the overall design until the flowchart is completed.
    D. All of the above. *(circled)*

5. The method of programming that uses three control structures to form highly structured units of code that are easily read and, therefore, easily maintained is called:

    A. von Neumann charts.
    B. Flowcharts.
    C. Structured programming. *(circled)*
    D. Jackson and Warnier programming.

6. The three control structures used with structured programming are:

    A. Input, processing, and output.
    B. List, compare, and loop.
    C. Sequence, If-Then-Else, and Do While. *(circled)*
    D. Sequence, If-Then-Else, and loop.

7. The control structure that is used to control looping is:

    A. Do While. *(circled)*
    B. Sequence.
    C. Repeat.
    D. If-Then-Else.

11.23

Testing your knowledge — Multiple-Choice Questions

8. An important concept associated with structured programming is that:

    A. There is but one entry point and multiple exit points in all control structures.
    B. There is but one entry point and one exit point in all control structures.
    C. There are multiple entry points and multiple exit points in all control structures.
    D. There are multiple entry points and one exit point in all control structures.

9. Pseudocode is used:

    A. As an alternative to flowcharting to express the logic for a program.
    B. To express the logic for a program using English-like statements.
    C. To decompose a program into small units of code called modules.
    D. For both A and B.

10. A set of instructions that may be called from several points within a program is called a:

    A. Subroutine.
    B. Pseudocode.
    C. Decision table.
    D. SORT routine.

11. With structured design methodology,:

    A. The programmer begins by defining the precise sequence in which steps are to occur.
    B. The structure of the program is defined after determining the individual steps to solve the problem.
    C. The program is decomposed into small modules which perform a particular function.
    D. The detailed steps in a program never need to be defined.

12. In structured design, the IPO Chart is used to:

    A. Specify the individual steps in the solution of a problem.
    B. Specify the output, input, and major processing tasks required in a program.
    C. Specify the logical decisions that are made in a program.
    D. Document the instructions in a program.

13. An organized review of a program by other programmers is called:

    A. System evaluation.
    B. Program evaluation.
    C. Egoless programming.
    D. A structured walkthrough.

14. In a program design problem in which basic input/output operations are performed, the program execution is normally terminated:

    A. When there are no more records to be read, and a blank record is encountered within the input.
    B. When a given number of records have been processed.
    C. When an end-of-file indicator is encountered at the end of the records to be processed.
    D. After looping a given number of times as determined by the Do While control structure.

15. A decision table is used:

    A. Within a program to define comparing operations.
    B. Within the IPO Chart to define comparing operations.
    C. By the computer operator to determine which operations to perform.
    D. As a graphical representation of the logical decisions that must be made concerning certain conditions which can occur within a program.

Chapter 11

Project 19
Developing Communication Skills

Instructions: Prepare an oral or written report on one or more of the following subjects.

1. Prepare a research report on the historical development of structured programming.

2. One of the major problems in the data processing industry is programmer productivity. Prepare a research report on methods of improving programming productivity.

3. Several authorities have documented a number of major problems that have plagued the software industry. Prepare a research report on problems existing in the software industry.

4. Prepare a report summarizing the contents of the book, The Psychology of Computer Programming, by Dr. Gerald Weinberg.

5. Prepare a research report on the methods of conducting structured walkthroughs. Include in the report the advantages and disadvantages of walkthroughs.

6. Prepare a report on the Jackson and Warnier design methodologies.

7. Prepare a book review of the book by Glenford Myers entitled, Reliable Software Through Composite Design.

8. Contact, by phone, five companies in your community that have data processing installations to determine if they are using structured design or structured programming methodologies.

9. A number of articles have appeared in data processing periodicals during the past five years documenting the use of structured programming in the data processing community. Review these articles and prepare a report on the use and success of structured programming in industry.

Chapter 11
Answers to selected projects

Chapter 11, Project 15, Testing your knowledge — Key Terms

1. E	4. J	7. G	10. M	13. O
2. A	5. N	8. H, P	11. C	14. I
3. C, F, K	6. L	9. D	12. F	15. B

Chapter 11, Project 17, Testing your knowledge — True/False Questions

1. T	8. T	15. T	22. T	29. T
2. T	9. F	16. F	23. F	30. T
3. T	10. F	17. F	24. T	31. F
4. F	11. F	18. F	25. F	32. T
5. T	12. T	19. T	26. F	33. F
6. F	13. T	20. F	27. T	34. T
7. F	14. F	21. F	28. F	35. F

Chapter 11, Project 18, Testing your knowledge — Multiple Choice Questions

1. D	4. D	7. A	10. A	13. D
2. A	5. C	8. B	11. C	14. C
3. A	6. C	9. D	12. B	15. D

Chapter 12
Programming Languages — Coding and Testing Programs

Chapter Objectives

- A familiarization with the seven most widely used programming languages: Assembler Language, FORTRAN, COBOL, PL/I, RPG, BASIC, and Pascal
- An understanding of compilers and interpreters
- An introduction to program testing procedures
- An understanding of the role of program documentation
- An understanding of the role and use of operating systems

Chapter Overview

Writing a program is accomplished by a series of steps called the program development cycle which consists of the following: 1) Review the system and program specifications; 2) Design the program; 3) Code the program; 4) Test the program; 5) Document the program. There are many programming languages available to the programmer when coding the program. These languages include Assembler Language, FORTRAN, COBOL, PL/I, RPG, BASIC, and Pascal.

Assembler languages use symbolic notation to represent machine language instructions and are closely related to the internal architecture of the computer system on which they are used. They are called low-level languages. An assembler language statement consists of a label which serves to identify or reference an instruction, an operation code which is a symbolic notation which specifies a particular operation to be performed, and an operand which represents a register or the location in storage where the data to be processed is located. The principal advantage of assembler language is that programs are very efficient in terms of execution time and main storage usage. Disadvantages include little compatibility between different languages for different machines, and assembler language programs normally require a larger number of statements to accomplish a given task than do some other available languages. Assembler languages are often more difficult to write, read, and maintain than other languages.

A high-level language is one in which the program statements are not closely related to the internal characteristics of the computer. One statement in a high-level language will develop a number of machine language instructions. FORTRAN is a high-level language developed by IBM in 1957 to be used by scientists, engineers, and mathematicians. The language is noted for its ability to express mathematical expressions and equations easily. FORTRAN was the first programming language that was standardized through the auspices of the American Standards Association. The advantage of FORTRAN is the easy expression of complex mathematical calculations through the use of arithmetic operators. The primary disadvantages are that FORTRAN does not have the versatility of an assembler language in manipulating records, individual characters, or bits within a byte; and it has limited file processing capabilities.

COBOL is one of the most widely used business programming languages. COBOL was released in 1960; one of the stated objects was that the language was to be machine-independent, was to be written in English-like form, and was to be self-documenting. A formal structure must be used in coding a COBOL program, which is divided into an Identification Division, Environment Division, Data Division, and Procedure Division. The advantages of COBOL are machine independence, file handling capabilities, and relative ease in writing programs. Disadvantages include the fact that a COBOL program which translates COBOL statements is usually large and requires large main storage. Some also feel COBOL is excessively wordy.

PL/I is a language designed to be useful in a wide variety of areas and was released in 1966. The strongest characteristic of PL/I is its breadth and detail. It is a good language for structured programming, but has never achieved the widespread use originally anticipated by IBM.

RPG was originally developed by IBM in the late 1960's for small scale computer users to allow reports to be easily generated. To write a program in RPG, a series of forms is filled out with the specifications in predetermined columns. Enhancements to the language have led to RPG II and, more recently, RPG III. The principal advantage of RPG is the ability to generate routine business reports quickly and easily. Because of the fixed logic used in RPG programming, problems which do not fit into the fixed logic can be difficult to program.

BASIC was developed at Dartmouth College in 1965 for use in an academic environment, and has become widely used in timesharing environments and with many small business-oriented computer systems. The primary advantage of BASIC is its ease of use.

Pascal was one of the first major programming languages developed after the concept of structured programming and is finding increased use.

Coding a program is a very exact skill and involves the actual writing of the statements on a coding form. After the program has been coded, it should be subjected to a walkthrough by other members of the staff.

After the program has been coded, it must be translated into machine language prior to execution. A compiler is a program that translates source program statements into machine language instructions and produces an object program. An object program is the entire program expressed as machine language instructions. It is the object program which is loaded into main computer storage for execution.

An interpreter is a program stored in main computer storage which will read a source program one statement at a time and cause the execution of that statement. Interpreters are commonly found on microcomputers.

Regardless of the programming language used, it is important to produce a program which is easy to read and understand.

After the program has been coded, it must be tested. The development of test data is an important responsibility of a programmer. Test data should be designed to find errors in the program. Stub testing is used with structured programming to test modules one at a time. Using this approach, it can be assured that portions of a program are operational before the entire program is completed.

Documentation of a program is a vital part of any program which is written. Documentation should include an abstract and general description of the program, record layouts, a system flowchart, a detailed description of the processing, the structure of the program, the logic within each module, a listing of the source program, a listing of the test data, a console run form, and a user guide.

A collection of programs that allows a computer system to supervise its own operations is called an operating system. An operating system is composed of a control program, processing programs, and data management programs. The processing programs consist of language translators and service programs which perform many of the common types of functions which must be accomplished. The data management programs are used to control the organization and access of data used by programs.

One problem which programmers have encountered is that the programs written require more main computer storage than is available on the computer system. To overcome this problem, virtual storage is used. When virtual storage is used, segments of a program which are not immediately required for processing are not stored in main computer storage but are stored on a direct access device and are called into main computer storage when needed.

Chapter 12

Key Terms

ANSI American National Standards Institute

Applications Packages Prewritten programs for common applications.

Assembler Language A symbolic programming language that uses symbols and abbreviations to represent the function to be performed.

BASIC A programming language developed at Dartmouth University for use in academic computing, but now widely used on personal computers and small business systems.

COBOL Common Business Oriented Language: One of the most widely used business programming languages.

Coding The process of writing instructions for a computer.

Compiler A program that interprets computer statements written in a symbolic form and converts the statements to machine language instructions.

Computer Program A series of instructions which directs the computer to perform a sequence of tasks that produces a desired output.

Control Programs Programs that are a part of an operating system that provide for automatic control of computer resources.

Data Management Programs Programs supplied as a part of a system's software that handle such operations as the blocking and deblocking of records, accessing files, etc.

Documentation, Program The detailed recording of the facts about a program through supporting materials and within the program itself.

FORTRAN A high-level language designed for scientists, mathematicians, and engineers.

High-level programming language A programming language far removed from the internal characteristics of the machine.

Interpreter A program that reads source statements and immediately causes the statements to be executed one at a time.

Job Control Language (JCL) A language that serves as a link between the operating system and the application programs to define jobs being processed, programs to be executed, and provide for job-to-job transition.

Kemeny, Dr. John J. Early advocate of the use of computers in education; President of Dartmouth College; developed the BASIC language.

Libraries, System Areas on direct-access auxiliary storage that are used to store load modules, object programs, or subroutines, and source statements.

Linkage Editor Programs that are a part of the operating system that are used to transform object programs into load modules.

Low-level Programming Languages Programming languages which are closely related to a particular machine.

Machine Language Instructions A series of numbers, letters, and other bit configurations which can be interpreted by the electronic circuitry of a computer, causing operations to be executed.

Macro A statement specified in an assembler language that generates a number of machine language instructions.

Object Program The machine language instructions resulting from a compilation of source statements.

Operand That portion of a computer instruction that commonly indicates the address of data to be processed.

Operation Code That portion of a computer instruction which indicates the operations to be performed.

Operating System A collection of programs that allows a computer system to supervise its own operations.

Pascal A programming language designed to make it easy to write programs using using structured techniques.

PL/I A programming language developed by IBM for use as a general-purpose language in both business and scientific applications.

Processing Programs Those programs that are a part of the operating system which perform commonly required functions; they include the language translator and the service programs.

Program Development Cycle The well-defined sequence of steps in writing a program that includes review of specifications, design, code, test, and document.

Programming Languages The software supplied as a part of the computer system that provides a means of instructing the computer to perform operations.

Programming, Machine-Language The writing of instructions for a computer by means of numbers, letters of the alphabet, and special characters that can be understood by the electronic circuitry.

Programming, Symbolic Programming using simple words or abbreviations to express the operations to be performed.

RPG Report program generator: a programming language designed to provide an easy method of generating routine business reports.

Software Programs written for computer systems.

Software, Application Computer programs written for computer systems to solve a particular type of business or mathematical problem.

Software, System Programs written to aid in the operation of a computer system.

Software Industry The group of companies that specialize in writing system or application software.

Stub Testing The process of testing a program one module at a time.

Supervisor A program that is part of the operating system that controls and schedules the resources of a computer system.

Test Data Data created to test the reliability of a program.

Testing, Program The process of checking to assure that a program produces reliable and accurate results.

Utilities, System Programs that are a part of an operating system that are used to perform frequently used applications such as file-to-file conversion and sort-merge operations.

Virtual Storage A storage method in which portions of a program are stored on auxiliary storage until needed, giving the illusion of unlimited main storage.

Chapter 12
Project 1
Identifying programming languages

Instructions: Identify each of the following programming languages and briefly explain their use or application in industry.

1.
```
READAGIN  GET   CARDFLE                      READ A CARD                          PAY00180
          MVI   PRNTOUT,X'40'                CLEAR REPORT AREA                    PAY00190
          MVC   PRNTOUT+1(131),PRNTOUT                                             PAY00200
          MVC   NAMEPRT,NAMECD               MOVE NAME TO PRINT AREA              PAY00210
          MVC   NUMBPRT,NUMBCD               MOVE EMPLOYEE NUMBER TO PRINT        PAY00220
          MVC   HOURSPRT,HOURSCD             MOVE HOURS TO PRINT AREA             PAY00230
          MVC   RATEPRT,RATECD               MOVE RATE TO PRINT AREA              PAY00240
          PACK  RATEWORK(4),RATECD(3)        PACK PAY RATE INTO WORK AREA         PAY00250
```

Language: _____

Use: _____

2.
```
     1 READ(1,200)NUMBER,SCOST,CCOST,REQ
       IF(NUMBER-999)2,3,3
     2 EOQ=SQRT(2.0*(REQ*SCOST)/CCOST)
       IEOQ=EOQ
       IREQ=REQ
       WRITE(3,300)NUMBER,IREQ,SCOST,CCOST,IEOQ
       GO TO 1
```

Language: _____

Use: _____

3.
```
010010       MULTIPLY LOAN-AMOUNT-INPUT BY INTEREST-RATE-CONSTANT GIVING    SUBLIST
010020           INTEREST-AMOUNT-WORK ROUNDED.                              SUBLIST
010030       MOVE INTEREST-AMOUNT-WORK TO INTEREST-AMOUNT-REPORT.           SUBLIST
010040       ADD LOAN-AMOUNT-INPUT, INTEREST-AMOUNT-WORK GIVING             SUBLIST
010050           TOTAL-AMOUNT-WORK.                                         SUBLIST
```

Language: _____

Use: _____

4.
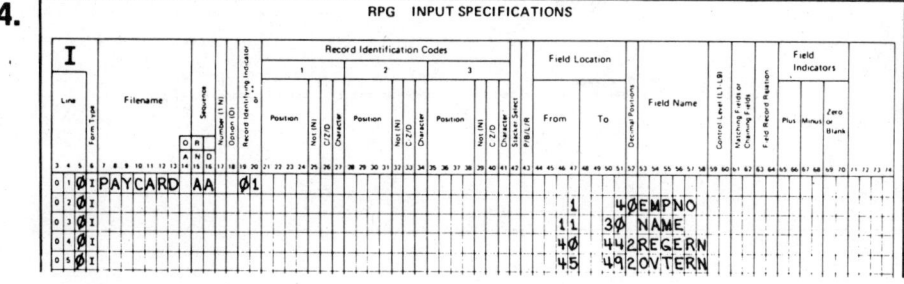

Language: _____

Use: _____

12.5

NAME_____ DATE_____

Chapter 12

Project 2
Compiling a program

Instructions: Explain each of the steps in compiling a program as illustrated in the diagram below.

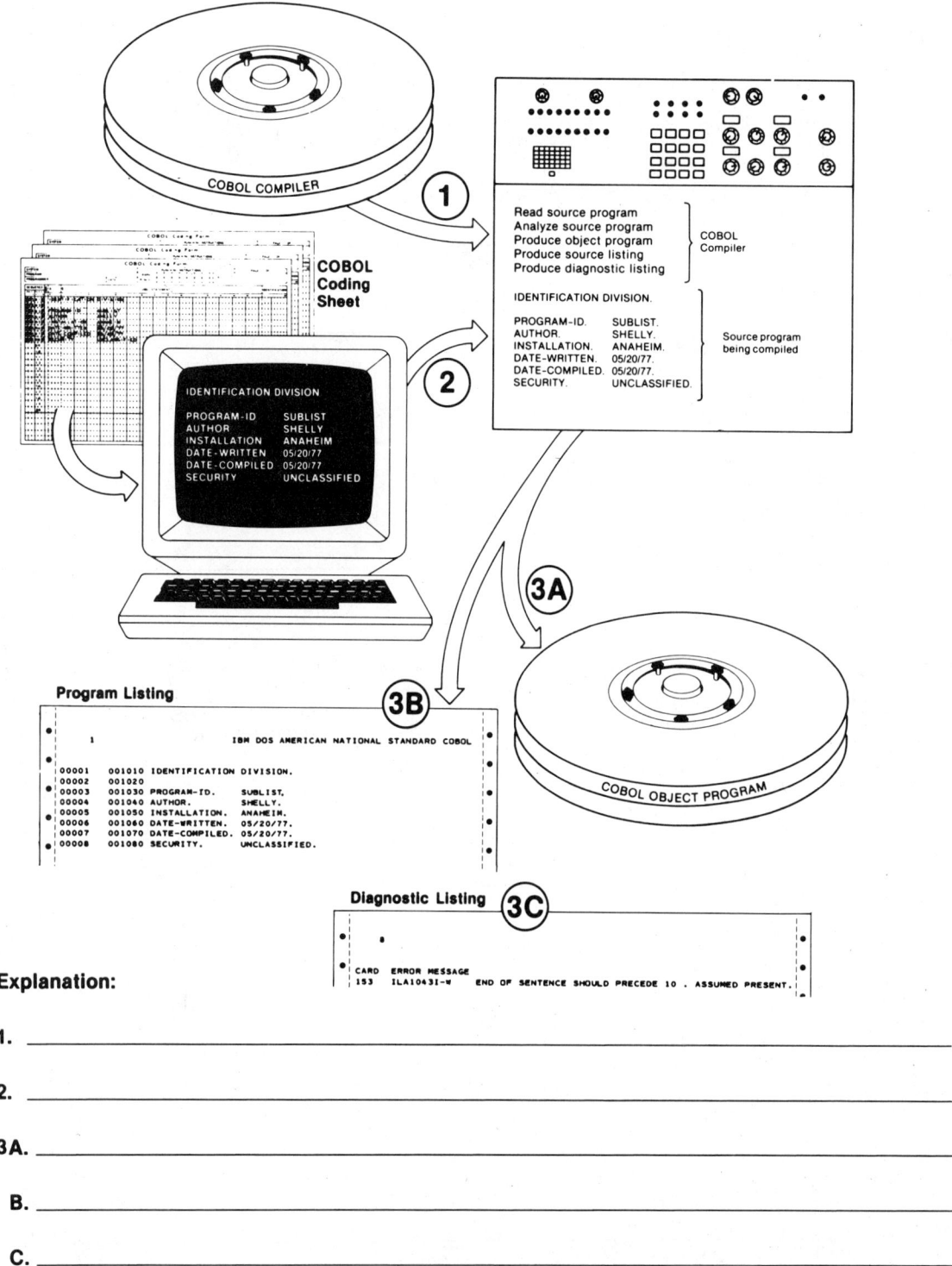

Explanation:

1. _____

2. _____

3A. _____

  B. _____

  C. _____

NAME_____   DATE_____

Chapter 12
Project 3
Testing your knowledge — Key Terms

Instructions: Fill in the blanks with the appropriate term from the list of terms on the right side of the page.

A 1. The programming language that is closely related to machine language and the internal architecture of a computer system is called an _____.

I 2. Assembler languages are _____ programming languages.

N 3. That portion of an assembler language statement which specifies the operation to be performed is called an _____.

J 4. A _____ is an assembler language statement that will generate a series of machine language instructions.

F 5. _____ is a high-level programming language useful in scientific, engineering, and mathematics.

C 6. One of the most widely used business programming languages is _____.

Q 7. The _____ division of a COBOL program contains the instructions which are executed.

P 8. _____ was developed as a general purpose language by IBM incorporating some of the characteristics of both FORTRAN and COBOL.

R 9. A programming language designed for small scale business systems to allow reports to be generated easily is _____.

B 10. _____ is a programming language developed at Dartmouth College and is now widely used with microcomputers.

O 11. The first major programming language developed after structured programming concepts evolved was _____.

D 12. A _____ is a program that translates source program statements into machine language instructions.

K 13. An _____ contains the machine language instructions which are developed after a source program is compiled.

H 14. An _____ is a program which will read a source program a statement at a time and cause execution of that statement.

M 15. An _____ is a collection of programs that allows a computer system to supervise its own operations.

A. Assembler language
B. BASIC
C. COBOL
D. Compiler
E. Data
F. FORTRAN
G. High-level
H. Interpreter
I. Low-level
J. Macro
K. Object program
L. Operand
M. Operating system
N. Operation code
O. Pascal
P. PL/I
Q. Procedure
R. RPG
S. Source program

NAME_____ DATE_____

Chapter 12

Project 4
Testing your knowledge — Definitions

Instructions: Briefly define or explain each of the following terms:

1. Assembler language

2. COBOL

3. Compiler

4. FORTRAN

5. High-level programming language

6. Object program

7. Operating system

8. RPG

NAME_____ DATE_____

Chapter 12

Project 5
Testing your knowledge — True/False Questions

Instructions: Circle the T if the question is true and F if the question is false for each of the true/false questions below and on the following page.

(T) F   1. Assembler language closely resembles the internal architecture of the computer system.

T **(F)**   2. A macro is an assembler language statement that generates a single machine language instruction from that statement.

(T) F   3. An operation code is a symbolic notation which specifies the particular operation to be performed, such as add, move, and so on.

(T) F   4. An operand is that portion of an assembler language statement that specifies the register or storage location where the data to be processed is located.

T **(F)**   5. An advantage of assembler language is that the same instructions are executable on all computer systems.

T **(F)**   6. FORTRAN was developed by a group of manufacturers and users as an all-purpose language for mathematical-oriented applications.

(T) F   7. A series of arithmetic operators such as the plus sign and minus sign are used in FORTRAN to express the calculations to be performed.

T **(F)**   8. A programming language in which the program statements are not closely related to the internal characteristics of the computer is called a low-level programming language.

T **(F)**   9. FORTRAN can be used effectively for business applications because of its strong file handling capabilities.

T **(F)**   10. An advantage of FORTRAN is that the language can easily manipulate records, individual characters, and even bits within a byte in the same manner that assembler languages can.

(T) F   11. COBOL stands for Common Business Oriented Language.

T **(F)**   12. COBOL is primarily limited in use to IBM computer systems.

T **(F)**   13. A limitation of COBOL is that a program written for one computer cannot be executed on another computer system without extensive modification.

(T) F   14. COBOL uses verbs such as ADD and SUBTRACT in sentences to cause operations to be performed.

T **(F)**   15. Although a COBOL program is divided into four divisions, there is no formal structure to the language.

T **(F)**   16. The Identification Division of a COBOL program is used to specify the name of the computer system being used.

Testing your knowledge — True/False Questions

T (F) 17. The Data Division of a COBOL program is used to specify the executable instructions.

(T) F 18. The COBOL translator program which translates a COBOL source program into machine language is usually quite large; therefore, COBOL is usually not found on computer systems that do not have large amounts of main storage.

(T) F 19. PL/I was designed to be useful in a wide variety of application areas and incorporated some of the features of both FORTRAN and COBOL.

(T) F 20. An RPG program is written by filling out a series of specification forms which define the input, output, and processing that is to occur.

T (F) 21. RPG is primarily used on very large scale business systems to generate routine reports.

T (F) 22. BASIC is used almost exclusively in a timesharing environment.

(T) F 23. BASIC is noted for its ease of use.

(T) F 24. Pascal is a programming language that contains features which make it easy to implement the control structures utilized in structured programming.

(T) F 25. A compiler is a program that translates source program statements into machine language instructions.

(T) F 26. The object program that is generated from a compiler consists of a series of machine language instructions that are to be executed on the computer.

T (F) 27. An interpreter and a compiler operate in exactly the same manner when used to translate source statements into machine language instructions.

T (F) 28. The essential characteristic of a quality program is that the program should be as brief as possible.

(T) F 29. The development of test data is an important task of any programmer.

T (F) 30. An operating system is composed of three elements — a control program, processing programs, and data management programs.

(T) F 31. The supervisor portion of an operating system is loaded into main computer storage when the operation of the computer system is begun.

T (F) 32. In any one operating system, there is only one language translator that is a part of that operating system.

(T) F 33. The linkage editor programs are used to transform the object programs generated from the language translators into load modules which are ready for execution.

(T) F 34. Operating systems normally contain libraries stored in an area on a direct access device that contain load modules, object programs or subroutines, and source statements.

(T) F 35. When virtual storage is used, segments of a program which are not immediately required for processing are not stored in main computer storage but are stored on a direct access device and are called into main computer storage when needed.

12.10

NAME_____ DATE_____

Chapter 12

Project 6

Testing your knowledge — Multiple-Choice Questions

Instructions: Circle the correct response to the multiple choice questions below and on the following page.

1. Which of the following is a low-level programming language which uses symbolic notation to represent machine language instructions?

    A. Assembler language.
    B. FORTRAN.
    C. COBOL.
    D. Pascal.

2. An assembler language statement that will generate a series of machine language instructions is called:

    A. An operator.
    B. An operand.
    C. An operation code.
    D. A macro.

3. A programming language developed by IBM for mathematical applications is called:

    A. Assembler language.
    B. FORTRAN.
    C. COBOL.
    D. BASIC.

4. The primary disadvantage of FORTRAN is that:

    A. It is difficult to express complex mathematical calculations easily.
    B. It cannot readily manipulate individual characters or bits in a byte.
    C. It has limited file processing capabilities.
    D. Both B and C.

5. One of the most widely used business programming languages is:

    A. Machine language.
    B. FORTRAN.
    C. COBOL.
    D. Pascal.

6. COBOL was developed by:

    A. IBM.
    B. Dartmouth College.
    C. Blaise Pascal.
    D. A group of computer users and manufacturers.

7. Which of the following divisions of a COBOL program is used to specify the steps which are to take place in the solution of a problem?

    A. Identification Division.
    B. Data Division.
    C. Environment Division.
    D. Procedure Division.

12.11

Testing your knowledge — Multiple-Choice Questions

8. Which of the following best describes COBOL as a programming language?

    A. Programs are written in English-like statements.
    B. The language is very concise.
    C. The language has limited file handling capabilities.
    D. Both A and B.

9. The language which was designed to be useful in a wide variety of applications and combines some of the characteristics of both COBOL and FORTRAN is:

    A. BASIC.
    B. Pascal.
    C. PL/I.
    D. RPG.

10. RPG is a programming language designed for:

    A. Small scale computer systems for generating business reports.
    B. Large scale computer systems for generating business reports.
    C. Timesharing operations.
    D. Academic environments.

11. A programming language widely used on personal computers and small business computer systems is:

    A. FORTRAN.
    B. COBOL.
    C. BASIC.
    D. PL/I.

12. The disadvantage of application packages sold by software vendors for particular applications is that:

    A. The systems frequently do not meet the existing requirements of a company.
    B. The programs are written in a nonstandard programming language.
    C. The systems are only available for large scale computer systems.
    D. The systems are only written in RPG.

13. The program that translates a source program into machine language instructions is called:

    A. An object program.
    B. An application program.
    C. A macro.
    D. A compiler.

14. An operating system consists of:

    A. Macros, operation codes, and operands.
    B. Supervisor and application programs.
    C. Control programs, processing programs, and virtual storage.
    D. Control programs, processing programs, and data management programs.

15. When using virtual storage, the process of calling a portion of a program into storage is called:

    A. Compiling.
    B. Interpreting.
    C. Paging.
    D. Linkage editing.

Chapter 12
Project 7
Developing Communication Skills

Instructions: Prepare an oral or written report on one or more of the following subjects.

1. Contact the data processing manager of a local computer installation and obtain a printout of a "typical" program in that installation. What language was used? Bring the printout to class. How many statements are in the program?

2. Prepare a research report on the current use of the various programming languages in industry.

3. Research advertisements in current microcomputer periodicals to determine the types of programming languages available for use on the various microcomputer systems.

4. Prepare a report on the development of programming languages between the years of 1950 and 1960.

5. Prepare a research report on the historical development of the COBOL programming language.

6. Prepare a research report on the historical development of FORTRAN as a programming language.

7. In the late 1960's, PL/I was stated to be the language of the future by IBM. Prepare a report documenting the reasons why PL/I has never been widely implemented in industry.

8. Contact five computer installations to determine the type of programming languages used in each installation. Share your findings with the class.

9. Analyze the classified advertisements in the local newspaper. List the number of job openings for various types of programmers and the programming language knowledge requested.

10. The Bureau of Labor Statistics publishes job openings and projections for the future. Prepare a report on the future of programming as a profession.

Chapter 12
Answers to selected projects

Chapter 12, Project 3, Testing your knowledge — Key Terms

1. A	4. J	7. Q	10. B	13. K
2. I	5. F	8. P	11. O	14. H
3. N	6. C	9. R	12. D	15. M

Chapter 12, Project 5, Testing your knowledge — True/False Questions

1. T	8. F	15. F	22. F	29. T
2. F	9. F	16. F	23. T	30. T
3. T	10. F	17. F	24. T	31. T
4. T	11. T	18. T	25. T	32. F
5. F	12. F	19. T	26. T	33. T
6. F	13. F	20. T	27. F	34. T
7. T	14. T	21. F	28. F	35. T

Chapter 12, Project 6, Testing your knowledge — Multiple Choice Questions

1. A	4. D	7. D	10. A	13. D
2. D	5. C	8. A	11. C	14. D
3. B	6. D	9. C	12. A	15. C

Chapter 13
The Future of Computers in Society

Chapter Objectives

- To provide an insight into problems faced by the data processing profession in the years ahead
- To develop an awareness of some of the ethical considerations confronting those in data processing
- To point out some of the problems facing society with the utilization of data banks and electronic funds transfer systems
- To develop an awareness of the potential threat posed to freedom and privacy by computer systems

Chapter Overview

There is little doubt that the computer is an integral part of the world's activities. Some have begun to question, however, whether the computer will ultimately contribute to the quality of life for the next generation. One of the most significant effects of the advances in computer technology has been the great decrease in the cost of computer hardware and the increase in the number of computer systems in use. Although computer hardware has progressed amazingly during the past forty years, the ability to program these machines has not changed radically. In addition, the industry continues to be plagued by unreliable software.

In many areas of life where public safety and welfare are considerations, society has seen fit to authorize governmental agencies to license personnel prior to allowing them to practice their professions. Some have suggested that data processing personnel should be licensed.

As an occupational area progresses to a professional level, ethics often become a consideration of the profession. In data processing, ethical behavior and computer crime are new areas of concern.

The computer will have a significant influence on the way in which society functions in the future. One of the pressing issues facing the industry is that modern computer systems have made it technically possible to store large volumes of data about citizens in our society that can be readily accessed. Some feel these "data banks" offer a great potential for the loss of privacy and threaten our basic freedoms.

Several years ago, there was much discussion about the future cashless society. Today, under the term of Electronics Funds Transfer, this concept is being implemented. Some authorities also feel this concept offers threats to our freedom because, conceivably, EFT could provide governmental agencies with a complete record of every facet of a person's life.

The data processing industry and society face a challenging and exciting future.

Chapter 13

Key Terms

Crime, Computer The use of a computer system to steal, embezzle, or maliciously access or destroy data or files used with computer systems.

Data Banks A collection of data which is stored on auxiliary storage devices.

Electronic Funds Transfer A method of receiving and paying for goods and services by which funds are transferred from one account to another electronically under control of one or more computer systems.

Social Issues Those issues relative to the use of computers and its impact upon how people live.

Society, Computers in The use of computers in all aspects of daily living.

Project 1
Developing Communication Skills

Instructions: Prepare an oral or written report on one or more of the following subjects.

1. Prepare a report for or against the licensing of professional data processing personnel such as computer programmers and systems analysts.

2. Several authorities have stated "computer fraud has the potential of destroying our largest corporations." Prepare an in-depth report on computer crime and computer fraud and its threat to business enterprises.

3. Research current periodicals and prepare a report on recent computer crimes.

4. Some authorities have stated that Electronic Funds Transfer systems pose one of the greatest threats to our basic freedoms that mankind has ever encountered. Prepare an in-depth report on "the computer and its threat to a free society."

5. Computerized data banks are becoming increasingly prevalent in both business and government. Prepare a report on the use of data banks and their impact on society.

6. Some have predicted that by 1985, home computers will be as common as home television sets. Prepare a report on the use and impact of the home computer on our lives.

7. Prepare a research report on artificial intelligence.

8. Industrial robots that are computer controlled are now being used in industry. Prepare a report on the use and application of industrial robots in business.

9. Describe the world in which we will live in the year 2025. What part will computers play in our lives?

APPENDIX A
Programming in Basic

Introduction

The textbook provided an introduction to many of the statements used in the BASIC language which will allow the programmer to solve a wide variety of problems. This appendix is designed to introduce additional BASIC statements and functions which provide even greater flexibility and power in programming specialized problems.

String functions

There are many types of applications in which it is desirable to have the ability to manipulate alphabetic or alphanumeric data. To provide this ability, a number of specialized string functions are provided with many BASIC interpreters. The following paragraphs explain some of the widely used string functions.

LEN function

The LEN function is used to determine the length of a string by counting the number of characters in a string constant or string variable. To utilize the LEN function, a string constant or string variable must be enclosed in parentheses following the characters LEN. Upon execution of the statement containing the LEN function, the length of the string may be stored for future reference and may be printed as required. The following example illustrates the use of the LEN function in determining the length of a string constant.

```
100 PRINT LEN("UNITED STATES")

13
```

In this example, the string constant "United States" is contained within parentheses within the LEN function. Upon execution of the Print Statement, the number of characters in the words "United States" is displayed as 13.

Appendix A

An example of the coding in which a name is entered into storage utilizing an Input Statement, and the length of the name is determined and printed through the use of the LEN function is illustrated below.

```
100 INPUT "ENTER NAME"; A$
110 LET C = LEN(A$)
120 PRINT C; "CHARACTERS ARE IN "; A$


ENTER NAME? DAVIS
 5 CHARACTERS ARE IN DAVIS
```

In the example above, through the use of the Input Statement, a series of string characters may be entered. Note the use of the string constant "ENTER NAME" in the Input Statement. This programming technique is used to identify the type of data to be entered when the program is executed. In the example, the name Davis has been entered. The length of the name that has been entered is stored in the area referenced by the variable name C through the use of the Let Statement and the related LEN function in statement 110. The value contained in C is then printed together with an identifying message. When the program is executed, it is indicated that there are five characters in the name Davis.

LEFT$ function

The LEFT$ function is used to make available a specified number of characters from a string starting with the leftmost position. A string variable or string constant is specified within parentheses followed by the number of characters to be returned. The following example illustrates the use of the LEFT$ function to print the first 18 characters of a string constant contained within a Print Statement.

```
100 PRINT LEFT$("COMPUTER EDUCATION AND RESEARCH", 18)

COMPUTER EDUCATION
```

The statements above, when executed, caused the words COMPUTER EDUCATION (the first 18 characters of the string constant specified in the LEFT$ function) to be printed.

Appendix A

A more complex example in which a variable name is specified in the LEFT$ function is illustrated below. In this example, the first three characters from the word INCORPORATED are to be extracted and printed.

```
100 LET A$ = "INCORPORATED"
110 LET B$ = LEFT$(A$,3)
120 PRINT B$; " IS THE ABBREVIATION FOR "; A$

INC IS THE ABBREVIATION FOR INCORPORATED
```

On line 110 above, the entry LEFT$(A$,3) specifies that the first three characters referenced by A$ (which contains the word INCORPORATED) are to be stored in the area referenced by B$. The printing of B$ by the statement on line 120 causes the characters INC to be printed along with an identifying message.

RIGHT$ function

The RIGHT$ function is used to make available a specified number of characters from a string starting with the rightmost position. A string variable or string constant is specified within parentheses followed by the number of characters to be returned. The following coding illustrates the use of the RIGHT$ function. In the example, the year employed, the last four characters of the string constant "DATE EMPLOYED — JUNE 1,1980" are to be extracted from the string and printed.

```
100 LET D$ = "DATE EMPLOYED - JUNE 1, 1980"
110 LET Y$ = RIGHT$(D$,4)
120 PRINT "YEAR EMPLOYED "; Y$

YEAR EMPLOYED 1980
```

In the example above, the four rightmost positions of the value stored at D$ are returned to Y$ by the statement on line 110. The entry RIGHT$(D$,4) specifies that the four rightmost positions of the data referenced by D$ are to be returned to the variable referenced by Y$ in the Let Statement. Y$ (which will contain 1980) is then printed by statement 120.

In the example below, the RIGHT$ function is specified within the Print Statement. Thus, it can be seen that the programmer has great versatility in the use of string functions within a program.

```
100 LET D$ = "DATE EMPLOYED, JUNE 1, 1980"
110 PRINT "YEAR EMPLOYED "; RIGHT$(D$,4)

YEAR EMPLOYED 1980
```

Appendix A

MID$ function

The MID$ function is used to make available a given number of characters from the middle of a string. Contained within parentheses following MID$ are: a string constant or string variable; the starting position of the characters to be retrieved; and the number of characters to be retrieved. The following example illustrates the use of the MID$ function to retrieve the first three digits of a zip code from a 16 character string variable called A$.

```
100 LET A$ = "ZIP CODE - 90808"
110 LET Z$ = MID$(A$,12,3)
120 PRINT Z$
                    STRING     STARTING    NUMBER OF
908                 VARIABLE   POSITION    CHARACTERS
```

Line 110 contains the statement to retrieve the first three digits of the zip code. The MID$ function specifies that for the string variable called A$, starting at the 12th position, three characters are to be retrieved and stored in Z$. Statement 120 then prints Z$ which now contains 908, that is, the first three characters of the zip code. As with other string functions, string constants may be specified in parentheses, and the MID$ function may be specified within a Print Statement.

STR$ function

In some applications, it may be necessary to change numeric data into string data so that the data may be manipulated using the string functions that are available. The STR$ function is used to convert a numeric value into a string. The following example illustrates the operation in which a six-digit employee number, defined as numeric data and stored in the area referenced by D, is converted to string data, and the last three characters representing the department in which the employee works is printed.

```
100 LET D = 100425
110 LET D$ = STR$(D)
120 PRINT "DEPARTMENT NUMBER IS "; RIGHT$(D$,3)


DEPARTMENT NUMBER IS 425
```

In the example above, on line 110 the variable D is specified in parentheses following the STR$ function. The effect of this statement is to store the numeric value referenced by D in the area referenced by D$. The data may now be processed as string data. Line 120 causes the string variable D$ to be printed as specified by the RIGHT$ function. Thus, the digits 425 are printed. The use of this technique allows numeric data to be manipulated using any of the string functions. Data which is defined as numeric cannot be used with the string functions.

Appendix A

VAL function

The VAL function may be used to change numbers in a string into numeric values that may be used in calculations or otherwise processed as numeric values. When using the VAL function, the string variable referenced is specified in parentheses following the VAL. The following illustrates an example in which the last three numbers in a string representing a part number are extracted from the string, converted to numeric values that can be used in a calculation and then used in a Print Statement as a part of a calculation.

```
100 LET A$ = "A24225"
110 LET B$ = RIGHT$(A$,3)
120 LET P = VAL(B$)
130 PRINT P * 2

450
```

In the example, the part number is A24225 and is stored in A$. The statement on line 110 takes the rightmost three characters in the string and stores the characters in B$. The statement on line 120 using the VAL function stores the three character string referenced by B$ in P. The three digits can now be processed as numeric values and used in a calculation. The Print Statement on line 130 multiplies the numeric value in P (which will contain 225) by two. The resulting answer is 450.

Additional functions

In addition to the string functions previously discussed, there are several additional functions which are valuable in a number of different application areas. These are the INTEGER function and the RANDOM function. These functions are explained in the following paragraphs.

INT function

The integer function may be used to round off a number to its whole number (integer) value. For example, if the number 122.25 is in storage and it is desired to print the number as 122, the INT function can be used. The following example illustrates the use of the INT function.

```
100 LET A = 122.25
110 PRINT INT(A)

122
```

In the example, it can be seen that the number 122.25 is assigned to the variable A in statement 100. Statement 110 prints the integer value of A by specifying the variable name in parentheses after the INT entry in the Print Statement. The output produced is the number 122.

Appendix A

RND function

An extremely valuable function for simulations and other types of problems is the RND function. This function serves to generate random numbers. The routine below will generate a random number between 0 and 1.

```
100 FOR I = 1 TO 12
110 PRINT RND(0),
120 NEXT I


 .855779        .152638        .323745        .549884
 .270409        .531957        .831231        .408174
 .49952         .198488        .518523        .0743985
```

The For/Next Statement is used to control the printing of 12 random numbers between 0 and 1. The random numbers are generated by the entry RND (0) in the Print Statement

In most applications where random numbers are needed, there will be a need to generate a range of numbers. For example, to simulate the roll of a dice in which the numbers from 1 to 6 would appear, the following routine may be used.

```
100 FOR I = 1 TO 12
110 PRINT INT(6*RND(0) + 1),
120 NEXT I


 6              5              2              2
 1              2              3              2
 6              4              2              3
```

To generate random numbers from 1 to 6, the integer value of 6 times the random number plus 1 is used. Utilizing this basic formula, random numbers within any given range can be generated by changing the value 6 to the top range of the numbers to be generated.

Appendix A

Controlling the format of the printed report

The BASIC programming language was initially designed to allow users to interact with the computer as simply and as easily as possible; and originally, there was very little control over the output produced. As the language became more widely used, additional statements were incorporated into the language to provide added capabilities in controlling the output, such as suppressing leading zeros in a field, printing fields with a dollar sign, comma, and decimal point if required, and other similar functions.

Print Using Statement

One of the statements used to control the format of data printed on an output report is the Print Using Statement. When using the Print Using Statement, a number of special characters are placed within the statement to control the format of the output. The # symbol is one of the most important symbols used. Within the Print Using Statement, a # symbol is recorded for each numeric character to be printed. When used in this manner, zeros to the left of a number will not print, and the field will be aligned in a columnar fashion based upon the rightmost digit. An example of the output from a Print Statement and a Print Using Statement is illustrated below.

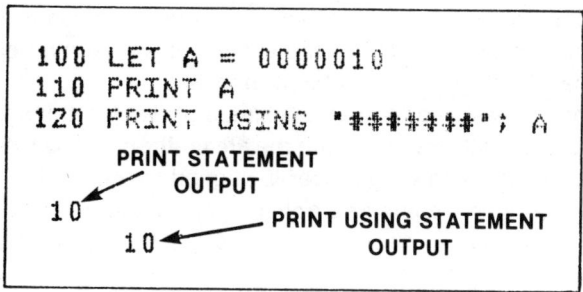

In the example above, when the value 0000010 is printed using a Print Statement, the leading zeros are not printed, and the field is moved to the left.

The statement on line 120 illustrates the use of the Print Using Statement. Following the words PRINT USING, the programmer uses the # symbols contained within quotation marks to specify the format of the output that is to occur. Note that there is a # symbol for each digit in the numeric field. The "#######" is followed by a semicolon and the variable name of the field being printed. The output resulting from the Print Using Statement causes the value 0000010 to be printed as 10. The leading zeros are suppressed, and the number is aligned to the right.

Appendix A

To control the printing of a dollar sign, comma, and a decimal point in a numeric field representing dollars and cents, a dollar sign, comma, and decimal point are used in conjunction with the # symbol to provide a "mask" for the data that is to be printed. To control the printing of a floating dollar sign (a dollar sign which will appear to the left of and adjacent to the first significant digit), two dollar signs are used within the mask. The following coding illustrates the use of the Print Using Statement to print an Item Number, a Sales Amount, and the Cost Amount. The Sales Amount is to be printed with a fixed dollar sign, comma, and decimal point; and the Cost Amount is to be printed with a floating dollar sign, comma, and decimal point.

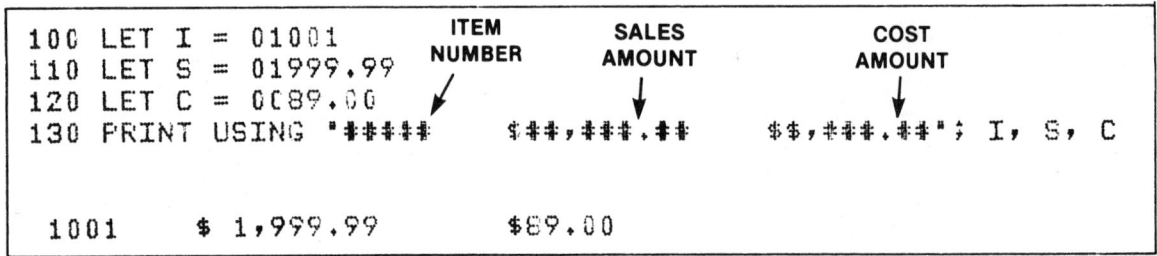

Line 130 above contains the Print Using Statement to control the output line that is to be printed. Note that there are three masks (one for each field), and the masks are contained within a single set of quotation marks. The space between the masks provides for the spacing between the fields. Following the mask is a semicolon and the variable names of the fields to be printed.

The Item Number field has a mask that contains a series of five # symbols, one symbol for each of the digits. When executed, the number 01002 contained in the area referenced by the variable name I is printed as 1002. The leading zero is suppressed, and the number is aligned to the right.

The mask for the Sales Amount field contains a dollar sign, comma, and decimal point in addition to the # symbol for each digit. Thus, the Sales Amount defined as 01999.99 is printed as $1,999.99. Note the fixed position of the dollar sign.

To obtain a floating dollar sign, two dollar signs are used in the mask as illustrated by the third mask in the Print Using Statement on line 130. The second dollar sign is used in place of a # symbol to represent the first digit. When the Print Using Statement is executed, the Cost Amount field defined as 0089.00 is printed as $89.00. The dollar sign has been floated and placed adjacent to the first significant character — the 8.

It is important to always utilize the proper number of # symbols for each of the fields being edited; otherwise, incorrect output may result.

There are numerous other capabilities within the Print Using Statements. For additional information, consult the language specifications manual for the system being used.

NAME_____ DATE_____

Appendix A

Project 1
Supplementary programming assignments

Instructions: The following is a series of programming assignments that are designed to stimulate your interest in both systems design and computer programming. The specifications are very general. The design of the output is left to the discretion of the student. Be sure to use good programming techniques to produce a program that is well documented and easy to understand, modify, and maintain!

1. Write a program for a word processing application which will permit the operator to enter an individual's title (Mr. or Ms.) and name and street address and generate the following real estate sales letter. Information should be inserted in the letter in the spaces indicated. Spacing should be exactly as specified in the example below.

> Dear __(title and last name)__ :
>
>   Have you ever considered selling the _____(last name)_____ residence? Your home located at _____(street address)_____ is in an area of future industrial development.
>
>   _____(title and last name)_____ , our company is prepared to offer you a premium price for your home.
>
>   Sincerely,
>
>   American Real Estate

2. Write a program that will generate a computer user identification utilizing the first three characters of the last name and the middle two characters of the social security number. Output should consist of the name, social security number, and identification number. Test data is illustrated below.

ARNOLD	551-52-8871
BARBER	309-33-221
MAYBEE	452-83-9709

3. Write a computer assisted instruction program that will randomly display a series of addition problems such as 4 + 3 = ? and provide for the answering of the problems by the student. Be creative in your design.

4. Write a program that will display a 10 question true/false examination on BASIC programming and will indicate after each response if the question has been answered correctly. After the test has been completed, the total number of correct answers on the first response should be displayed.

Supplementary Programming Assignments

5. Write a program that will simulate the tossing of a coin. Indicate each toss by printing the word HEADS or TAILS.

6. Write a program that will allow the computer to randomly select a number between 1 and 100 and provide for the terminal operator to guess as to the number selected. If the guess is too high or too low, a message should be printed, with the provision for another number to be selected. The total "guesses" should be printed when the correct number is determined.

7. Write a program that will permit an inquiry into a file. The file contains credit information and includes a consumer identification number, name, and credit status indicated as either satisfactory or unsatisfactory.

8. An individual decides to jog a mile the first day, two miles the second day, doubling the mileage each day for 10 days. Write a program that will print out the miles to be run for each of the 10 days.

9. An individual bets $1.00 on the first game, $2.00 on the second game, and doubles the amount of the bet each time a game is played. Print out the amount of money bet on each game and the total losses after each game. Assume there are 15 straight losses.

10. Write a program that will sort a series of records in alphabetical order. The records contain the names of employees in a company.

11. Write a program that will print out the hourly pay, weekly pay, and yearly pay beginning at 3.00 per hour and increasing to 10.00 per hour in increments of .25 cents per hour. Example, 3.00, 3.25, 3.50, 3.75, etc. The format of the report should be: HOURLY PAY   WEEKLY PAY   YEARLY PAY.

12. Write a program that will search a file containing the names and batting averages of nine players on a baseball team and will print out the player with the lowest batting average and will also print out the player with the highest batting average.

NAME_____   DATE_____

Appendix B

Project 1
Interpreting the 80 Column Card

Instructions: Analyze the punching in the 80 column card in this project and interpret the card in the space provided.

Employee Number _____

Name _____

Department _____

Sales Amount _____

NAME_____   DATE_____

Appendix B

Project 2
Interpreting the 80 Column Card

Instructions: Analyze the punching in the 80 column card in this project and interpret the card in the space provided.

[80-column punch card with fields: EMP NO (cols 1–5), NAME (cols 6–29), DEPT (cols 30–33), SALES AMT (cols 34–39), GLOBE NO. 1 STANDARD FORM 5081]

Employee Number _____

Name _____

Department _____

Sales Amount _____

B.2

NAME_____ DATE_____

Appendix C

Project 1
Converting binary numbers to decimal

Instructions: For each of the binary numbers given below, write the decimal equivalent in the space provided.

	BINARY		DECIMAL
1.	0001	1.	_____
2.	1001	2.	_____
3.	0101	3.	_____
4.	0010	4.	_____
5.	1000	5.	_____
6.	0011	6.	_____
7.	0111	7.	_____
8.	0110	8.	_____
9.	0100	9.	_____
10.	10001	10.	_____
11.	100000	11.	_____
12.	101000	12.	_____
13.	1000000	13.	_____
14.	1000001	14.	_____
15.	1111111	15.	_____

Appendix C

Project 2
Converting hexadecimal numbers to decimal

Instructions: For each of the hexadecimal numbers given below, write the decimal equivalent in the space provided.

HEXADECIMAL	DECIMAL
1. 5	1. _____
2. B	2. _____
3. E	3. _____
4. F	4. _____
5. 10	5. _____
6. 11	6. _____
7. 15	7. _____
8. 17	8. _____
9. 19	9. _____
10. 1A	10. _____
11. 1B	11. _____
12. 1C	12. _____
13. 1D	13. _____
14. 20	14. _____
15. 2F	15. _____
16. 30	16. _____

NAME_____ DATE_____

Appendix C

Project 3
Hexadecimal addition and subtraction

___

Instructions: Add the following hexadecimal numbers and record the answer in the space provided.

```
   8        3        9        7        6        8
 + 4      + 7      + 6      + 6      + 5      + 6
 ___      ___      ___      ___      ___      ___


   A        F        D        E        B        F
 + 6      + A      + 6      + 3      + C      + B
 ___      ___      ___      ___      ___      ___


  11       10       2E       2E       1A       1C
 +11      +1A      +11      +12      +2A      +2D
 ___      ___      ___      ___      ___      ___
```

Instructions: Subtract the following hexadecimal numbers and record the answer in the space provided.

```
   B        F        A        C        D        E
 - 4      - 1      - 1      - 2      - 3      - 2
 ___      ___      ___      ___      ___      ___


   F        D        B        E        D        F
 - D      - C      - A      - A      - A      - D
 ___      ___      ___      ___      ___      ___


  10       12       14       20       25       22
 - F      - B      - C      - A      - D      - E
 ___      ___      ___      ___      ___      ___
```

Appendix C

Project 4
Converting octal numbers to decimal

Instructions: For each of the octal numbers given below, write the decimal equivalent in the space provided.

OCTAL	DECIMAL
1. 1	1. _____
2. 2	2. _____
3. 3	3. _____
4. 4	4. _____
5. 5	5. _____
6. 6	6. _____
7. 7	7. _____
8. 10	8. _____
9. 11	9. _____
10. 12	10. _____
11. 13	11. _____
12. 14	12. _____
13. 15	13. _____
14. 16	14. _____
15. 30	15. _____

Appendix C

Project 5
Adding and subtracting in octal

Instructions: Add the following octal numbers and record the answer in the space provided.

```
   2        5        6        7        6       275
  +2       +2       +2       +2       +4      +234
```

Instructions: Subtract the following octal numbers and record the answer in the space provided.

```
   7       16       15       16       20       624
  -3      -06      -06      -07      -17      -275
```

NAME_____ DATE_____

Appendix C

Project 6
Converting ASCII characters to octal

Instructions: Complete the chart below by recording the octal value for each of the ASCII characters illustrated.

ASCII Character	Meaning	ASCII Bit Pattern							Octal Value
0	Zero	0	1	1	0	0	0	0	_____
1	One	0	1	1	0	0	0	1	_____
2	Two	0	1	1	0	0	1	0	_____
3	Three	0	1	1	0	0	1	1	_____
4	Four	0	1	1	0	1	0	0	_____
5	Five	0	1	1	0	1	0	1	_____
6	Six	0	1	1	0	1	1	0	_____
7	Seven	0	1	1	0	1	1	1	_____
8	Eight	0	1	1	1	0	0	0	_____
9	Nine	0	1	1	1	0	0	1	_____